So Many Worlds

Invention, Management,
Philosophy, and Risk
in the Life of Leroy Hill

So Many Worlds

Invention, Management, Philosophy, and Risk in the Life of Leroy Hill

Craig Miner

Texas Tech University Press

© 1997 Craig Miner

This book was set in Cheltenham and Geometric 231 printed on acid-free paper that meets the guidelines for permanence and durability of the Committee on Production Guidelines for Book longevity of the Council on Library Resources. ∞

Design by Rob Neatherlin

Printed in the United States of America

Library of Congress Cataloging-in-Publication Data
Miner, H. Craig.
    So many worlds : invention, management, philosophy, and risk in the
life of Leroy Hill / Craig Miner.
        p.   cm.
    Includes bibliographical references and index.
    ISBN 0-89672-380-1 (alk. paper)
    1. Hill, Leroy, 1894-1981. 2. Aeronautical engineers—United
States—Biography. 3. Businessmen—United States—biography. I. Title.
TL540.H446M56   1997
629.13'0092
[B]—DC21   97-11191
            CIP

97 98 99 00 01 02 03 04 05 / 9 8 7 6 5 4 3 2 1

Texas Tech University Press
Box 41037
Lubbock, Texas 79409-1037 USA
800-832-4042
ttup@ttu.edu

For my family: Suzi, Hal, Wilson

Contents

Preface

*L*eroy Hill's life was unusual in many ways, not the least in its variety, but also because he was clearly a mechanical genius. He went from being the most clever teenage inventor in Berkeley, California, to the president of Air Associates, a major aircraft supply firm in the 1930s. Through his life he was involved, mostly as owner, manager, and product developer, with more than sixty business firms. He became, after age fifty, an outstanding spokesman for and contributor to conservative political causes. But even the ordinary parts of his life were of extraordinary interest, thanks partly to the reflective habits of a man who carefully kept records of nearly everything that happened to him.

William Dean Howells, the great proponent of realism in fiction, said that if literature was to teach through substitute experience, the experience presented must be total, authentic, and in a context familiar to readers. Too often in biography mostly the public figure emerges—the guarded, somewhat designed, and artificial persona. That cannot be the case with Hill if the Hill archives are used properly. He censored and edited nothing. He preserved not only all his business correspondence, but letters to and from his daughters and even his traffic tickets, budget books, and auto repair bills. He kept a diary during most of his life. The whole man emerges in all his connections and attributes. For this reason, direct quotations from his papers appear largely just as they were written.

His alphabetical letter files are a treasure. Some of them, such as the one labeled "Girls," may be skirted lightly in a general biography. Others could be books on their own. There is the lifelong correspondence with the gifted but flawed and lonely Alice Blue, who probably fell in love with Hill in 1918 and remained deeply attached to him into the 1970s. There are rich exchanges with Libertarian theorist Leonard Read of the Foundation for Economic Education. There is a series of letters exchanged with his first wife, married as a teenager and fallen from Hill's grace and high-toned circle into near poverty. Hill's files of letters exchanged with people like his close friend Ray Acre or Harold Crow, or Victor Lougheed, the "black sheep" of the famous aviation family, show the development of Hill's thinking, his method of dealing with problems, his visions and hopes, and the stakes for which he played.

For a man of action, Leroy Hill was especially self-aware and organized. He saw his personal history as a tool for learning and decision-making while he was active. And it may serve the same purpose now for others able, by the light of his illuminated life, to experience again past events on Hill's horizon as though they were new and present, for the joy and pain and wisdom in them.

For the archival resource, now housed in the Special Collections Department at Ablah Library, Wichita State University, I thank Leroy Hill. For the opportunity to write this biography and much help in doing so, I thank Ellen Hill. I acknowledge the Department of History at Wichita State University for continuing to believe in research. Thanks to Susan Hess for help with photographs. And, as always, through lo these many years, thanks to my immediate family for their steady support.

So many worlds, so much to do, So little done, such things to be

—cover of Hill's 1918 diary, quoting Tennyson

So Many Worlds

Invention, Management,
Philosophy, and Risk
in the Life of Leroy Hill

Leroy Hill: Boy Engineer

*E*ntrepreneurs, writes management guru Peter Drucker, are *rerum novarum cupidus* ("eager for new things").[1] That was true of Frank Leroy Hill almost from the beginning.

His cradle behavior is not certain—only that he opened his eyes first in Port Huron, Michigan, at 7:00 a.m. on July 16, 1894, in the midst of a family where rapid change and relatively high risk were the normal state of affairs.[2]

In the Kodak photograph pasted in his son's boyhood diary, Frank L. Hill, Sr., whom Leroy called "Papa," stares out from his oak roll-top desk with piecing eyes and a confident, assured expression. He had a large thick mustache, neatly combed and cropped hair, a strong, square jaw, and an orderly Progressive Era professional appearance. There is a message of no nonsense about him and great physical presence.[3] As a commentator once said of a portrait of J. P. Morgan, his eyes recalled the headlights of an onrushing locomotive. He looks much like his own son Leroy in photos taken in the 1940s. There is the same jaw, the mustache (though not quite so full), and the determined look.

The senior Mr. Hill, born in 1854 in Kingston, New York, had shouldered much of the responsibility for himself since his father died when he was a boy. He was brought up by his grandfather, Sam Hill (the family got a laugh every time they heard the expression "What the Sam Hill?" or "It rained like Sam Hill") and never went to college. While Frank Hill always seemed to be employed, he did not stay in one place or one job long. He was once a traveling salesman and had worked as a reporter for a Chicago newspaper. When son Leroy was an infant, his dad moved often. The family went to Salt Lake City in 1895 where

Mr. Hill was an officer in a gold mining enterprise and had a share in a drugstore. Shortly they returned to Port Huron, Michigan, then removed to St. Joseph, Michigan, Sioux City, Iowa, and Rogers Park, a northern suburb of Chicago—all before 1900.[4]

The settings were residential, domestic, and pleasant enough. Rogers Park, for example, was scenic, with most of the houses set back from the swampy lakefront along elevated Ridge Avenue—yet pretty much the village it had been since its founding in 1878. Although annexed to Chicago in 1893, Rogers Park's boom and change from rural/idyllic to cosmopolitan/metropolitan came only with the completion of the Northwestern Elevated line to Howard Street in 1908 and the beginning of high-density construction. When the Hills were there, birch forests could still be seen from rows of Victorian homes and two-story, owner-occupied shops, and the proximity to Northwestern University meant that morality vis-à-vis a liquor ban was strictly enforced.[5] However, it seemed the Hills lived on the fringes of this middle-class life. Their circumstances—the fact that they lived with an aunt and uncle in Iowa and with Mrs. Hill's friends the Cosbys in Rogers Park—suggest strained finances. There would have been some concern whether Father Hill could strike the right balance between restlessness and security. It was doubtless a relief therefore when Hill in about 1902 got a job as sales manager of the Manitowoc Aluminum Novelty Company in Manitowoc, Wisconsin. It was standard employment in a standard organization. But the family could finally afford a "nice house" of their own.

Mr. Hill's restless and enterprising personality, however, did not remain restricted long. When in 1906 the San Francisco earthquake provided an entrepreneurial opening in California to develop new real estate ventures, Hill quit his management position with the Wisconsin manufacturer to move again. The aluminum company went on to prosper, but Hill, in his fifties at the time of the California move, felt it was not too late to take on one more new challenge.

Leroy's mother Nellie (née Potter) met her future husband on an excursion steamer plying Lake Michigan between Chicago and St.

Joseph, Michigan. She was by every test a competent and generous woman. When Frank, Sr., went to California alone to try to find housing amid the ruins, Nellie closed up the family's affairs and organized the three-day train trip west with a twelve- and six-year-old and all the household possessions. Leroy was no darling with whom to deal, but his mother never quenched his adventurous spirit by anything more than the most fundamental of cautions. Very often an enterprise with his friends would be carried out "with the reluctant permission of our mothers."[6]

Families are training grounds—"little commonwealths," one historian has it—for the transmission of the habits of the culture through daily illustration. Conflicts are normal, and in those conflicts comes socialization, the development of character, a gaining of competence for the child in various domains, a balancing of dependence and autonomy, a mediation of internal and external discipline. These come through patterns of living, from getting up and bedtime to how much time to study and how much to spend with friends. More than ever in the early twentieth century, with its extended period of childhood dependence, its limited family size, closer sibling spacing, emphasis on the role of experts and expertise in everything from politics to toilet training, optimistic belief that the world could be changed through better home life, and its new psychologies, social theories, and pediatric maxims, there was pressure on mothers and a "reconstruction of childhood and adolescence in primarily middle-class terms."[7]

It was Nellie Hill who enforced financial responsibility and taught the basics of personal economics, such as that sixty cents earned from shoveling snow could not be spent on lumber for a homemade scow until the boy had paid for rubbers to replace the ones he had lost.[8] Leroy was required to help her with the cooking, keep to a strict bedtime, and go to Sunday school. She indulged him in his youthful enthusiasm for setting up experiments (sometimes noisy and dangerous) and expanding his household "shop," but partly because her son learned how to fix all manner of things around the house—even in one case to hand-build "Mission" furniture for the living room—and was willing to do so whenever needed. She paid for these jobs but kept a strict accounting of any damage he did to offset those fees. It was a regular little business, filled with duty and character.[9]

As is often the case with women married to restless and opportunistic men, Mrs. Hill was a kind of anchor in the regular family storms. Perhaps it came in part from being the third of nine children in her own family and having to handle those inevitable crises. Her personality, while cheery, had been touched by tragedy. The couple's first child, Helen, born in 1892, had died of typhoid in Salt Lake City in October 1896. Leroy had no memory of Helen, but one of his earliest recollections was of his mother grieving for the lost daughter in their house at Port Huron. Isabella, a younger sister, was born in 1900. She was to Leroy for some years mostly an "unavoidable annoyance," but he came to appreciate her when he became more interested in girls in general.[10]

Self-made men of this era, of whom Hill was an exemplar, often did not consider themselves self-made, but cited their mothers as a major life influence. They grew "as the twig was bent," went the common late-Victorian social assumption among entrepreneurs, and the habits of character, instilled at hearth and home by Mother, were their major strength in gaining wealth and reputation. Training for honor by Mother had the inevitable by-product of success. "When the boy ventured into the world," wrote Irving Wyllie in *The Self-Made Man in America*, "his memories of home and mother were supposed to be a source of powerful influence on his future."[11] Her love and inspiration were of constant importance no matter what the changes in sophistication and life experience of the son. Hill's relationship with his mother throughout his life was exceptionally close and constant. Through extraordinary changes, he could still, and often did, return to her for child care or for his special cake on his birthday: she was an anchor for the self, as Hill's second wife Ellen became, in a life that had few others. Seymour Lipset and Earl Raab, in analyzing conservative politics in America at mid-twentieth century, the kind Hill became much involved in late in his life, argue that the otherwise disparate right-wing movements that Hill supported had in common a moralistic view of the world—a belief that human events are totally shaped by right beliefs and right intentions, in short by character.[12] That was an attitude, perhaps Victorian, that Leroy would have taken in with mother's milk, and it awaited only time and circumstance to emerge in his grown-up behavior. He was not moralistic in superficial ways certainly, not even religious, but at a deep level, the one that came from childhood, he was.

Certainly in the transitional period (the opening of the modern era) in which Hill grew up, the nuclear family itself, particularly as it existed in or near large and sometimes threatening cities, had become an institution more intense and defensive than ever. Sex roles were specialized, urban geography was segregated by class, and mothers, even if they were much less considerable personalities than Nellie Hill, came to have great influence in the domestic sphere in adapting children's behaviors to the perceived future world. In the late-nineteenth and early-twentieth centuries, historians have concluded, there was an imbalance of power and authority in urban suburbs, with women emerging as "the strong-willed aggressive ones" while husbands were described in contemporary accounts as "sweet" or "docile."[13] One man who grew up in this era remembered that "though my father made the family decisions and set the rules, my mother presided, subject to his occasional veto, over our daily lives. She provided the family with two important things that my father, for all his virtues, could not: a light touch and expressed affection."[14]

These men, partly because of their urban commutes and suburban homes, increasingly withdrew from social life outside the home, putting ever more pressure upon the family relationship and what encouragement or pressure wives provided. Children were perceived as having less economic value than before, but far more sentimental value, as they gave the nuclear family unit its purpose. "Family life," Richard Sennett concludes, "was terribly intense."[15]

The Hill family relationship was a good one. It included summer picnics and steamer excursions, as well as games played together in the parlor on the snowy and dark Michigan evenings, when, as Leroy the young diarist recorded, it could be "cold as time."[16] When he returned from trips, Papa always brought Isabella candy and Leroy usually some sort of mechanical toy.[17] Sometimes Mr. Hill took his boy with him on sales trips, as in 1906 when they went to Sheboygan on the train. Frank, Sr., by then in the printing business on the side, called on factories to get jobs, and Leroy bought postcards for his friends. Boy and father ate dinner at the hotel, and it made the boy in the equation proud.[18]

There was an extended family also. Young Leroy was fascinated as a five-year-old listening to pioneer stories told by his grandfather on his mother's side, Bert Potter. The old man with the long white beard told of coming down the St. Joe River in a canoe in the 1820s, settling the town of St. Joseph, Michigan, and fighting Indians.

Then there were Uncle Fred and Aunt Edna and Uncle Lauren and Aunt Harriet from exotic Honolulu. Nellie Hill's sister Harriet had worked at a ticket booth at the Columbian Exposition in Chicago in 1893. Her post was the Hawaii Building, which was in charge of an attorney from Honolulu named Lauren Thurston. The two were married, moved to Hawaii, and Thurston later hired his wife's brother Fred, first to work as a linotype operator on the *Honolulu Advertiser* and then as manager of the Honolulu Aquarium, which Thurston owned. Both Hawaii couples came to the states regularly (Fred had made over forty crossings by the 1950s), visited the Hills in California, and paid special attention to Leroy.[19]

Uncle Fred was particularly close and influential. He brought tropical fishes from the aquarium with him on the ship and spent time playing mandolin and guitar duos with the boy, who admitted that his mandolin talent did not hold a candle to Uncle Fred's genuine gift for the guitar.[20] Whenever winter blues overtook the family (as was common in the Wisconsin years), they could talk about going to Hawaii to visit the relatives. At least once, in 1910, they actually did go, an unusual experience for an American boy of that era.[21]

Leroy as a young boy could be described as an energetic omnivore. The energetic part could verge on obnoxious, more so as Leroy got older and more savvy. But already at three he was playing with older boys in the neighborhood, one of whom "took over" his tricycle. Not one to be left behind, Hill tried to ride on the back of it and was thrown off so hard his leg was broken. He remembered all his life sitting on the front porch of the Port Huron house in a red armchair with his leg in a cast, watching the parade of local volunteers marching off to the Spanish-American War in 1898.[22] Not much later he became a bit of a prankster and tough guy. After hearing a reading from Hans Brinker by the teacher at school in 1906, eleven-year-old Leroy and some friends were sliding on the ice when a resident "tried to chase us off with his big mouth. We asked him if he owned the street."[23] He was quite good at fastening pieces of paper to pen points and throwing them as missiles, even though he learned that being hit by one could "hurt like the devil."[24] When he was hospitalized at a Catholic hospital for an appendectomy, he befriended the nuns who let him ride in a wheelchair until they caught him coasting down the staircase in it and making "a terrible racket."[25]

He pole-vaulted (and set a record for twelve-year-olds), boxed, hiked, explored and hunted (especially in California's glorious open weather), and quoted schoolboy doggerel with the best of them.[26]

Leroy was fiercely loyal to his friends and always had a special one with whom he spent much time. He was regularly part of a boy's club, and usually head of it. An early one was the Sleepy Hollow Huckleberries, doubtless inspired by the obviously seminal experience of reading Twain.[27] These clubs abounded with secret ritual and medieval talk, usually direct from Sir Walter Scott.[28] Leroy was a master of slick slang, sometimes ethnic, as when he called Chinese "chinks" in California, but more often just pre-adolescent and adolescent patois of a type that, had he not been a diarist, would have long since disappeared from anyone's memory. The notebooks in which he began keeping a diary in 1906 were emblazoned with skulls and crossbones, smoking guns, bloody knives, and warnings to "Keep Out."

The house at 1010 St. Claire Street in Manitowoc had a big yard with a barn and woodlot behind. It was only a block or two from the

Manitowoc River and a "wonderful swimming hole." Of course, there was sledding and skiing in the winter. Other than regular bouts with poison ivy, Leroy enjoyed the kind of vigorous good health that enhances natural intellectual acuity. In short, for better and for worse, Leroy Hill was a boy's boy.

While he had some special opportunities to observe mechanical things, it was not so much these opportunities as his special reaction to them that counted. No doubt the Eugene Field School in Rogers Park (where he attended grades 1 and 2) and the Luling School (grade 3) in Manitowoc had something to do with Hill's early love of reading, but it cannot explain his mechanical aptitude, his creativity, or his boundless drive to understand and to apply what he came to understand immediately.

His dad was important there. Frank Hill had had his surviving children late in life, and perhaps this accounts partly for the fact that they were his true friends. He allowed much, perhaps pushed a little. Leroy had an early memory of floating on his back in the Great Salt Lake during the Utah sojourn, screaming while his father laughed. He could not at that time have been more than three years old.[29] Once Leroy rigged an electric fence to keep his rabbits in. When his father got angry at him for not attending Sunday school, Leroy noticed that Dad was resting his hand on that fence. He hit the current and said he would not shut it off until the senior Hill agreed not to punish him.[30] That they could later laugh about it showed the strength of the basic relationship.

The elder Hill was accessible to his son, and so was all the interesting paraphernalia of his business, first as a salesman and promoter, then as an executive in a manufacturing operation, and finally as a real estate promoter in the Golden State at its most golden. Leroy's early youth was a time when fathers often came home for lunch and when their workplaces had not become separated entirely from the domestic sphere.

Manitowoc was a small place when the Hills were there, and Mr. Hill rode his bicycle or walked to the office at the company. However, the Manitowoc Aluminum Novelty Company was something quite advanced for the time. It was one of the earliest fabricators of aluminum and later became part of Aluminum Company of America (ALCOA). Its products were novelties such as combs, cups, pots and pans, cigar cases, and aluminum cards with calendars and company names.[31] Leroy was enterprising enough to sell some of these products to his friends at a profit.[32] He was also deeply enthralled by the plant itself, as he was to be through his young life with settings involving heavy machinery and organized production, from construction sites to shipyards.

Leroy visited the company a few times during working hours and met Henry Vitz, its German emigrant manager. But his major joy was going there with his dad on Sundays when the machinery was quiet and the boy had the run of the place while his father sat in his office catching up on correspondence by dictating into his Edison machine, using wax cylinders. There was all manner of machinery, but predominating were punch presses driven by belts from line shafts powered by a steam engine. It was still the pre-electric, pre-plastic, coal-powered, brass- and nickel-girded industrial age, where the highly mechanical engineering innards of machinery were visible to the eye of the beholder and set up a gorgeous cacophony in operation that exercised a firm pull on the imagination of at least most males of the species. The stationery steam engine at the Manitowoc aluminum works might not have been quite as dramatic a machine in action as a steam locomotive hissing and roaring at the front of the local freight, but its connections were more complex and its purposes just as practical.

Leroy did a lot of looking and learning on those Sundays, but his interest was never purely an intellectual exercise. He was practical and he was forward. He wanted to try things and find out what would happen, and was not afraid to do so. Consequently, on one of these Sunday visits, little Leroy found himself in the boiler and engine room. Noticing that there was a head of steam in the boilers and remembering from observation how the big steam engine was started, he started it. His father, hearing the noise of all the line shafts and machinery moving, jumped out of his chair, rushed onto the plant floor, grabbed his son, admonished him over the din to turn off the engine, and, when that was done, administered a good spanking.[33]

Leroy was probably about ten at the time of the steam engine incident and already, in this epiphanal way, about his future business. Henry Ford at twelve was said to have asked remarkably sound questions of men driving a steam farm tractor, and, of course, there was Jesus with the scholars in the temple. The point is that representative activities, interests, and drives in talented people often emerge at an early age and do not change fundamentally through a career of high achievement.

Unlike Ford, however, who was primarily an inductive tinkerer, young Hill was a inveterate reader and a self-studying diarist. He subscribed to magazines from an early age. There were, for example, *St. Nicholas* and *American Boy*. The latter particularly was one of those turn-of-the-century boy's magazines that were full of projects that could be built at home. It was an age of a great deal less ready-made; a time when more tools and expertise within a family could be assumed, when the average hardware store (not to mention the specialty shops Leroy frequented while visiting his father's office in San Francisco) would be a mystery and a revelation to a modern hobbyist; and a time when the American ideal of handy self-reliance as an essential for young men was still very strong. There are innumerable boy's books of projects from that period with the stamped bright-colored covers and not one project in them that most modern boys could hope to accomplish. Peter Egan, an auto journalist racer and mechanic, parodied these books recently with only slight exaggeration in a humorous essay which chronicled his attempts to build a model of a steam-powered submarine at home from the instructions in one of these volumes (c. 1918). The list of materials was daunting: "3 ft. bar stock of flame-annealed tungsten . . . 6 gal. limpid teak reducer . . . 64-ft. brass boiler tube with sweated on Farragut reduction fittings . . . 4 × 8 sheet of 0.025 thickness ammonia-quenched zinc." The tools, Egan observed, required "everything from a turret lathe to a desk-top Bessemer converter. . . . The author seemed to imagine that the reader lived in some sort of naval surplus dump, just after the

Battle of Jutland. Even if I could have found the materials, my level of craftsmanship at that stage didn't go much beyond driving a bunch of roofing nails into a 2 × 4."[34] The Horatio Alger "boy saves millionaire's daughter" books of the nineteenth century were being replaced in the twentieth by those of the *Tom Swift: Boy Electrician* variety. These emphasized preparation and knowledge more than luck as a juvenile asset necessary for success in a modern world of higher technology.

All around Leroy were new mechanical devices for sale, drawings and patents and gadgets, business plans and corporate charters, and news of mergers and undertakings of vast extent. Everything, it seemed, was amenable to the magic of the machine, and its contribution was benign and beneficial, freeing humanity from the repetitious and noncreative through the creativity of engineers.[35]

Leroy Hill would read his *American Boy* and then carry out the tricks and projects in it with considerable discipline. He was always making something or improving something mechanical. In February 1906, he and his friend Tata improved Hill's sled for running the "shoot-the-shoots" and the "jack-rabbit slide," local runs where you could bounce ten feet high, by putting in four screws to make it stronger.[36] Shortly thereafter, after watching the blasting and steam shovel excavation on Rapids Hill, studying the operation of pumping out the dry dock at the lake with big steam pumps, and taking a tour of the ore boat *Christopher Columbus*, the two began planning to build a boat of their own for spring adventures. Leroy made drawings. They found the hull in the form of a large piece of tin near Sluthky's old secondhand store. The mast was the end of Leroy's one-dollar fishing pole. They tried the prototype on a pond on March 3, but it was still too slushy with ice. The boat project was slowed, maybe abandoned, when Frank Hill advised that it would be easier to buy one ready-made, and his son sent for a boat catalog. The relevant Manitowoc diary on the "sea trials," if any happened, was lost in the move to California.[37]

Leroy read fiction as well as scientific prose. The move to California gave him access to the Berkeley library, where he got a lending card in

June 1907; at the age of twelve he began spending many afternoons there with his friends. His fiction reading tended toward adventure. He was reading *The Fur Seal's Tooth* after his first visit to the Berkeley library and *The Last of the Mohicans*.[38] But even in fiction he had a tendency to take the inspiration seriously and try things out. In the spring of 1907, for instance, he was reading *Huckleberry Finn*, having already consumed *Tom Sawyer*. He and his best friend, Clifford Cosby, got hold of some English curve-cut tobacco. Leroy fetched his clay bubble pipe, Clifford got his, and they rode their bicycles to some trees at the corner of town where they sat down, smoked, and read. Clifford got dizzy and fell over when he tried to stand up. "I said I had enough and I emptied my pipe and put it in my pocket. Then all of a sudden up comes a whole lot of strawberry and pancakes." Hill went home, lay down to read *Huckleberry Finn* for the rest of the afternoon, and took the lesson to heart by swearing off smoking.[39]

Other boys were readers. Maybe some even kept scrapbooks, as Leroy did. Many traded for marbles; some were entrepreneurial enough to sell their bicycles or deal in small trinkets, all of which Hill did in the Manitowoc period.[40] But it is doubtful that many eleven-year-olds started diaries that continued with good regularity for seven years of adolescent trauma.

The diary as historical document has been a thing much studied and speculated upon. As a phenomenon of adolescent popular culture, characterized by locked book and romantic emotion, it has been primarily in the female sphere—a domestic activity, with overtones of "triviality, excessive sentimentality or femininity," that active boys were supposed to shun.[41] There was never a boy with more unmixed X chromosomes than Leroy Hill. Yet he kept a diary, and, though it became in the busiest years a series of reminder notations, in his adolescence it was reflective and "literary,"—recording his adventures and his reactions to them. The original diary lasted from 1906 to 1913. He kept briefer daily notes between 1918 and 1922 when he was working on engine design for several companies, and he jotted down daily impressions again from 1942 (soon after his philosophically defining experience as president of

Air Associates with a major strike) to 1967—his longest continuous diary record. He also saved an unusual number of his personal and business papers, providing context for the personality that the diary record alone could not provide.

The purpose in the early and late diaries, the letter files, the inventories, and the careful financial records, was the same, according to Hill. He wanted historical perspective, mostly to avoid illusion, particularly self-illusion, or delusion. He chided himself in his boyhood volumes for his "laziness" in not making entries during certain busy periods, but always came back to it with renewed determination.[42] While he confessed in first writing in the notebook with the Manitowoc Car Ferry ad on the outside cover, begun in the winter of 1906, that he was recording only "Part of the Doings of Leroy Hill," when he reflected on the enterprise he thought it was a good idea. "I am going to start a diary again," he wrote in the front flyleaf of the first surviving volume. "I started one three times before. The last time I kept it up for three months. This time I am going to keep it until next year."

He started right out with details. He told any reader that he was in the sixth grade at the Luling School in Manitowoc on Lake Michigan. The school was a block from his house. He had a six-year-old sister named Isabella, and in his room there were sixty-eight pictures on the wall, two single maps, and one mapbook with six maps.[43] In January 1908, writing in California after a four-month or so gap in the diary, he renewed his resolve. "I am going to start again. I might as well keep records of my life so when I am big I can look back on the days of my childhood (joke)."[44] But it was not a joke, as his application to it showed. "This diary business is pretty much trouble," he commented a few months later as he wrote in his diary, lying in bed at night with the aid of a droplight. "But as I want to keep a record of my childhood happenings, I guess I will get another book and write some more."[45] He kept up that series continuously through July 1913 and through six volumes laced with "kodaks," drawings, and dreams—an unusual record of the development of the mind and personality, while still "in short pants," of a man who was to have considerable business and engineering success.[46]

The diary emerged in the Renaissance with the revival of classical learning and of the idea that individual freedom on conscience mattered. The diary and the essay ran in parallel, the subject being the writer (as in Montaigne's famous musings) and the purpose an impulse "to observe life and to contemplate the meaning of one's own observations."[47] Diary writing reflected a basic self-confidence that the writer's experience was somehow remarkable. It was a safe place where new roles and ideas could be tried out, and it could serve a commonplace book of collected thoughts, a record of spiritual development for a Puritan conscience looking for evidence of election, a chronicle, a confessional, or a psychological self-repair kit. Many were all these from time to time.

The words "diary" or "journal" themselves suggested in their Latin roots the discipline that was so associated with them—the dailiness and the obligation that Hill punished himself about and that caused many late-Victorian parents to think it wise to encourage their children to keep diaries. Hill's comments about his purpose of historical perspective—to look back upon himself and his origins in later life and to analyze scientifically the instrument as well as its works—was only a less elegant version of Francis Bacon's statement early in the seventeenth century that "It is . . . an use well received in enterprises memorable . . . to keep Dyeries of that which passeth continually."[48] Or as J. M. Barrie, author of the story about a boy who never grew up, put it: "The life of every man is a diary in which he means to write one story, and writes another, and his humblest hour is when he compares the volume as it is with what he vowed to make it."[49] The habit of reflection was a useful one, and Hill was not afraid of the truths that knowing himself might reveal. There can be 20,000 days in a life with luck, and one can write down a million things. "I've learned," writes one diarist, "that nothing never happens."[50]

Diary writing in Hill's case was not unrelated to the sense of self that made him a successful entrepreneur. He expected change and transience and thrived on analyzing it and adjusting to it. Young male diarists of the early-twentieth century, wrote Harvey Graff, went about, through their diaries and their reading, anticipating alternatives in their imagination and "comparing and building from contrasting observations from various points across the life course" in a world removed from the social experience of their elders. Their diaries "provide direct (although not unmediated) access both to the experience of growing up and the tasks of expressing and creating meaning out of it . . . personal testimony captures the rich diversity of human experience in growing up as well as the unevenness, contradictions, conflicts, and consequences of the epochal transformations of the early life course in this period. These sources also heighten awareness of their creators as active agents in their own and their society's history." Seemingly relatively idle, ranging the city with his peers, reading and writing, a middle-class youth like Hill established a "third world" suited just to him and "better than school and more helpful than home." It provided a "life path" which, along with Mother's influence on good habits, allowed the boy becoming man to thrive on new things and flux.[51]

All of this is germane to Hill as a future entrepreneur. Karen Burke LeFevre in *Invention as a Social Act* has noted that creative people were thought to have a "daimonion," such as Socrates and Emerson talked of. *Ne te quaesiveris extra* ("Do not search outside yourself") was the motto. Really, however, there is considerable socialization involved in invention and a kind of internal dialogue with an imagined other that "supplies premises or structures of belief guiding the inventor"—not to mention the institutions and trends in the outside world that American inventors and enterprisers at least since Edison have held as applied targets in the backs of their minds.[52] Thomas Kuhn's famous concept of "paradigm communities" as social structures disciplining the emergence of the new is another way of describing the social influences on consciousness that may come through the family, peers, and reflection at an early age. The self of an adolescent diarist, wrote Gayle Davis, "is continuously forged" in an interplay among the diarist, the social environment, and the standards of propriety as perceived.[53] It is a kind of spiritual base camp from which the adventurer fares and to which he returns every night to inventory his resources.

Thomas Cochran, one of the pioneers in business history seen from a biographical as well as an institutional point of view, explains the distinctive behavior of entrepreneurs as a combination of external and internal forces. Most important are the personality of the individual, which Cochran stresses is the product of childhood and school experiences, the expectations of "defining groups" that hold the keys to one's success, and the dynamics of the specific business in which the entrepreneur is engaged. Cochran emphasizes the importance of the "copybook maxims" that were drilled into boys like Frank Leroy Hill—ideals of devotion, discipline, and efficiency; of abhorrence of debt and waste, respect for private property, acceptance of competition, as well as the businesslike virtues of hard-headed practicality and application.[54] We appreciate the importance of these qualities all the more in a late-twentieth-century world where Americans are far from being able to take them any more for granted than they can sound education or honesty.

Entrepreneurs by definition are people who take responsibility and undertake risk for a living. They are those who, according to Joseph Schumpeter's analysis, are "creative" in introducing new techniques in product, organization, production, or market to forge some combination that never existed before. They are not only comfortable with change, but see it as normal and can deal with it effectively. And, to summarize many analysts, they are people who thrive on opportunity, are able to make decisions under conditions of uncertainty, and crave real feedback from these decisions.[55]

Leroy Hill's early background suited him almost perfectly for such a career. In his family change was constant, values were strong, and the world was viewed, in the best "progressive" mode, as changing for the better in ways that one had only to discover how to participate in. Management consultant Tom Peters, looking toward the twenty-first century, has identified the requisite skill for the future as the ability to "thrive on chaos."[56] It was not so different in 1900.

California

In 1906 a watershed arrived in young Leroy's life with his father's decision to move to California. The date was no accident. April 1906 was the time of the great San Francisco earthquake and fire—the most tremendous natural disaster of many years and at the same time the greatest opportunity imaginable for contractors and salesmen, like Mr. Hill, who might be able to switch from selling novelties to selling lots and new homes in the rebuilt metropolis.

The fire that followed the earthquake lasted seventy-four hours, burned 4.7 square miles, and destroyed 28,000 buildings. Losses were estimated at $500 million, but $229 million of it was insured and the citizens of San Francisco were both immeasurably fond of the site and its clime and optimistic about the speed and quality of the rebuild. The elegant Daniel Burnham plan for a "City Beautiful" on the Bay, which the earthquake would have provided a unique opportunity to implement, was ignored. Instead the old "Instant City" pattern of rapid but decentralized development, driven by thousand of private decisions by real estate buyers and sellers, prevailed.[1]

There was no question for the residents that San Francisco would be rebuilt. Local man Lawrence Harris expressed it in a poem called "The Damndest Finest Ruins." The sentiment was that "the fools" who said it would take a million years to get it done should help get to work. "On my soul, I would rather bore a hole / And live right in the ashes than even move to Oakland's mole." The poet said he'd rather be a brick among San Francisco's magnificent ruins than own the proudest building in any other city.[2]

San Francisco was an entrepreneurial city of great vitality and varied industry. Since the founding excitement of the gold rush, it had grown in a rush: 56,000 people in 1860, 150,000 in 1870, and 300,000 in 1890. Its people, accustomed to "living with chance and change," had largely dispensed with formal governmental regulation and focused on profit and the promotion of their own brand of urban magic. The banalities of "culture for the moment" did not seem to phase the boosters in their "determined pursuit of the useful."[3] "It's an odd place," wrote one resident, "unlike any other place in creation, and so it should be; for it is not created in the ordinary way, but hatched like chickens by artificial heat."[4] The Hills with their pragmatic no-nonsense activism, their great metabolic and constitutional energy, and a hint of the romantic in ultimate visions fit right in.

The elder Hill had kept in touch with his Chicago friend Hogan Cosby, who had moved to California in 1904 and whose family was living in a tent in Golden Gate Park when Cosby began writing Hill of the opportunities he saw in the problems of the earthquake and fire that had destroyed their house. The senior Hill could not wait to get out there to redevelop the rubble too.

Economic promise was there, and there was a good chance that, like the German fleet—powerful because it was new—and paralleling the rise of Chicago from its 1871 fire, San Francisco would emerge stronger than ever. The "slot" in which the cable for the cable cars ran divided the city into industrial and cultural districts. North of it were the theaters, hotels, and shopping districts, and south were, in Jack London's words, "the factories, slums, laundries, machineshops, boiler works and the abodes of the working class," all of which kept everything going.

Hill arrived at the beginning of another great boom. The population of San Francisco in 1900 was 342,000. In 1910 it was to be 416,912; in 1920, 506,676; and in 1930, 634,394. All that while, until the Depression changed things for him, the senior Mr. Hill ran a successful real estate business and gave his son a model to observe the rewards that risk and willingness to change location, job, and mode of doing business could bring.

The Hill family was able to watch the "clamor of a commercial city" expand. The assessed valuation of the city went from $413 million in 1900 to $820 million in 1920; by 1911 its bank clearings nearly equaled those of Los Angeles, Portland, Seattle, Tacoma, Oakland, and San Diego combined. According to its Chamber of Commerce, "San Francisco bears the same relation to the Pacific Coast that New York does to the nation." While the size and importance of the city's industrial plant declined relatively in the years immediately following 1906, major industries, like shipbuilding, thrived and spawned large numbers of small-scale manufacturing concerns—foundries, machine shops, and engine makers of the type that would fascinate a boy with an inventive bent—to supply them. San Francisco became more than ever a world-class financial center, a place where investment capital was available to the promoters of new businesses and where business advice, financial and legal, was particularly available. In fact, the crisis of the earthquake and fire created a "wonderful fraternalism" among area business people. Said William F. Humphrey, president of the Tidewater Oil Company: "Old rivalries were forgotten; old jealousies disappeared, and even bitter enmities of long standing were wiped out. Everyone was in the same boat, so we forgot all else and pulled as a team."[5] San Francisco was an earnest city, hardly a bread-and-circuses mecca for sun-seeking tourists, but the climate was lovely, and just beyond its suburban reaches were still ranges of undeveloped hills filled with ranches and wildlife.

Leroy recalled nearly seventy years later that the move to California was nothing automatic or easy. His dad had a secure job, and Henry Vitz, the manager, did not want Hill to quit the Aluminum Novelty Company. Housing was scarce in San Francisco (the family lived in a "makeshift apartment" on Belton Street at first), and the new real estate office at 10 East Street (later Embarcadero) was "started on a shoe-string, and I don't think it prospered, although they [Hill and Cosby] seemed to eke out a living."[6] There was no question, however, that the family would move. It happened that, for Leroy especially, the chance to rejoin his young friend from Chicago days, Clifford Cosby, in the metropolitan phoenix on the Pacific, where, in contrast to Michigan, it seemed summers were eternal and activity unceasing, was an opportunity from which he was equipped to take the full measure.

Leroy entered the Lincoln School in Berkeley. About one year later, when their son was thirteen, the family moved to a flat at 2119½ Russell Street in Berkeley that was owned by a Chinese man named Tape. If the situation followed the pattern, Tape was probably living and doing business without his family, as did about 90 percent of the Chinese population in the San Francisco area at the turn of the century. Somewhat unusual was his residence outside Chinatown and his ownership of rental housing. Chinese were much represented in laundry work, textile milling, and boot and shoe making. Then, as now, they were imaginative and ambitious, often supplementing their income with truck farming, fishing, or peddling, with their wares suspended from wicker baskets on a long pole. So this Chinese man, whose full name Hill never bothered to give, and his Berkeley rental enterprise was perhaps not so atypical as might first appear.[7] Leroy climbed to the top of Tape's windmill next door and snapped an aerial picture of the place to paste in his diary.[8]

North Berkeley was still at that time semi-rural and innocent of zoning. The university was the raison d'être of Berkeley certainly. It was the reason the former site of the Rancho San Antonio of the Peralta family was named in 1868 for George Berkeley, the eighteenth-century Irish philosopher. It was the reason that intellect was superimposed on gorgeous nature there. Residents could hear famous speakers and plays at the 7,000-seat Hearst Greek Theatre, constructed in 1903, and decorum was so elevated that when a professor appeared on the campus without a hat about 1912, it was speculated that he must be a socialist.[9] There was a balance of business and the academic, of nature and nurture.

The moment of the Hill family's arrival was one of dramatic local change, not so much in the fundamentals of the place as in its scope and pace. In 1876 Berkeley had a population of 948. In 1905 it was 23,378 and in 1907, 38,117. The intervening event was, of course, the earth-quake, which devastated San Francisco but, though destroying library books in a San Francisco bindery and restricting the university's tax base, did no damage in Berkeley beyond toppling a few chimneys. There was considerable emigration and new settlement, therefore, eastward on the perception that Berkeley was safer, and it became in 1906 a much more active and less cloistered place. The Key Route streetcar and interurban system had departures every thirty-eight minutes from Berkeley to San Francisco in 1906, and in the same year paving of Berkeley's streets began. The University of California went from a student population of a little over 2,000 in 1900 to nearly 7,000 shortly after Leroy Hill's graduation from its College of Engineering in 1917.[10]

The new bustle and the old charm were both reflected in young Leroy's adventurous youth. Adjoining the Hill homestead on one side was the Alpine Wood & Supply Company, reflecting the major impor-tance of the lumber trade and paper manufacturing to the redeveloping area.[11] Behind the house was a yard large enough for the curious teenager's ever-expanding shop, his pets, and his impressive radio tower. Clifford and Leroy explored the hilly terrain of the town on their "wheels" (bicycles), while groups of young friends regularly hiked into the "wilds" of the nearby back country for extended and adventurous hunting and camping trips. Every morning Frank Sr. got on the Key Route electric interurban at Berkeley and rode it to the end of the pier, where he boarded the ferry boat: there was neither a Golden Gate Bridge nor a Bay Bridge.[12]

All this town exploring was most stimulating. California, especially then, was a dream for Americans, and especially for midwesterners like Hill. And, like Daisy's voice in *The Great Gatsby*, it was a dream that could scarcely be overdreamed. It was, in imagination at least, the "American Mediterranean" with a good mix too of Oriental and Hispanic imagery and garden aesthetics.

In the early twentieth century the question was how to maintain the magic amid its own popularity and the enormous influx of population and money. The Panama-Pacific International Exposition, held in San Francisco in 1915, symbolized more "might have beens" than the practical realities of the "lost simplicities" of nineteenth-century America. But amid its architectural fantasies were many industrial exhibits: the machinery display was dominated by diesel engines and heavy equipment. "The persistent California quest," Kevin Starr has written in *Americans and the California Dream,* was "how to maintain both vigor and refinement, a sense of fresh beginnings and fertile possibilities, as well as a sense of order, design, historicity." It was a question of how to balance indulgence and restraint. Most would say indulgence had the upper hand.[13]

The historian Henry May remembered Berkeley in the second decade of the twentieth century as a place where "the East existed only in school geography books or very occasional and baffling group reminiscence. Snow was an exciting legend . . . . Winter meant greenness. In summer, of course, the hills smelled of dry grass in the afternoon sun before the white fog rolled in through the Golden Gate." Excursions to San Francisco were "festive outings" from this natural fastness.[14]

Dorothy Riber Joralmon, an artist and writer, and, to be sure, a different personality from the ornery, mechanical Leroy Hill, also grew up in Berkeley in those decades and wrote a sensitive memoir about it. She attended Miss Head's School for Young Ladies, where "young ladies did not chew gum" and where Leroy later sent his daughter. "Memory is a Californian," she wrote. "It can always see plum trees in bloom . . . spring, youth." Berkeley between 1900 and 1917 was a small community of "shingled houses, velvet brown. Geraniums spilling over gardens—scarlet, vermillion. The squawk of blue jays cutting the air like rusty scissors. A rag-bottle-sacks man ringing his bell. A horse-drawn watering cart wetting down the dust. An occasional motor car passing." Below the town was San Francisco Bay with its "ferry boats wreathed in white sea gulls." From it came the trade winds smelling of "waves, wet sand and salt." Above rose "barren hills where streams were edged by dark laurels. The call of quail and the scent of wild currant floated from the canyons," and no one locked his doors at night. Joralman remembered that sex hygiene classes started in the school about 1912; spooning became necking and girls began smoking. Yet residents of Berkeley seldom spent the outrageous twenty-five cents it took to ride the ferry to San Francisco, and instead often walked to the east—to Muir Woods or the caves on the slopes of Grizzly Peak or along Canyon Road where children followed Thornton Wilder on hikes, imitating Indians. Rooms were still filled more with bird song than with radio, streets more with pedestrians than with cars—but all was in flux.[15]

The new mechanical intrusions in Berkeley bothered Leroy Hill not in the least. Typical of young Hill, but unusual for the average boy, was his home workshop on Russell Street and his various engineering and mechanical arts projects. Not satisfied with reading, he was an indefatigable experimenter. Clifford Cosby had a "pretty good steam engine" early in 1908, and Leroy hoped to acquire a secondhand dynamo motor, which would power four-candle-power lamps and run a sewing machine. He was building a pair of stilts to strap on his legs. He made a telegraph instrument in the early months of 1908 and built himself a tool cabinet.[16]

He described his home shop: "I have quite a few tools and get more when ever the money rolls along. It isn't very big. It was supposed to be a coal shed but papa said I could use it for a shop if I could build a smaller coal shed, which I did. I cut a window and the Chink that owns this house put an electric light in it." One of his first shop projects was an induction coil for a wireless, constructed for $2.90 from plans in *American Boy*. Hill also made a "little shocking machine," and delighted to have his friends grab hold of the bar on a bet that they would not be able to let go. He then threw the switch and watched them beg for mercy. Other early constructions were a clockwork boat, an electric motor, and a wire-coil rheostat. The latter was mostly to vary the current on his shocker according to how much of a lesson he wanted to teach a smart-alecky friend. Leroy himself was so fascinated with the shocker that he admitted that "my arms are stiff from taking shocks."[17]

Dec. 13, 1911. Wednesday. Well, lots of things have happened. Last summer I went up to the Russian river for a week. I have been going to school right along. In shop I am makeing the patterns for a gas engine I am makeing and in Mechanical Drawing I am makeing the drawings for it. It is a 3 cylinder 25 H.P. gasoline engine.

I have made my shop twice as large and have put a shingle

The child inventor shows off his shop plan in the California diary.

By the time he entered high school in the fall of 1908 at the age of fourteen, the creations had become more complex. Leroy planned an aerial trolley (a kind of monorail on a wire) run by electricity from a gravity battery. In the spring of 1909 he started on a wireless and a telegraph sounder and began drawings for an antenna pole in the backyard. He got a Eucalyptus tree from the Alpine company next door for his radio tower.[18] A visit to San Francisco yielded supplies for an "electrolithic detector" and a condenser. These included 18-inch square brass rod and a piece of square brass tubing for the sliding contact on the tuning coil, one pound of sheet tin foil for condensers, and some sheet spring brass. While in the city he also picked up a copy of *Popular Electricity* to check on the soundness of his radio experiments.[19] By September 1909, he was getting "awful plain" reception while sitting on a three-legged wireless bench of his own design and construction, but he mentioned that "I owe a lot of money."[20]

In 1910, he piped his shop for gas and installed a single burner. He used a $1/20$ hp motor to run a grinder (sharpening neighbors' knives for a fee), a buffer, and an emery wheel with belts.[21] As he got older, he bought a motorcycle and did all the overhaul and repairs on it. He learned to overhaul cars too, an activity he would delight in throughout his life, especially in periods of business stress when the well-understood hands-on activity was a palliative. He rigged the electric transformers for the arc lighting system used in the school plays. He designed an electric fly trap, which did not work.[22] As his first aviation enterprise, he considered building a dirigible balloon in partnership with a friend named Chester MacElroy, whom Hill claimed had built an automobile on his own. Another friend had a toy cigar-shaped gas balloon, which Leroy modified by taking the paper basket off, building an aluminum one for it, and creating a rubber-band motor with propeller. "It worked class," Hill wrote. However, when the boys tried to refill the balloon, it blew up.[23]

Doubtless Hill's most impressive project in this era was carried out mostly in the shop of the high school, where Leroy got only average grades in the basic subjects but excelled in the mechanical arts. Encouraged by a teacher named Charles Evans, Leroy began on the ambitious project to design and build a cabin cruiser. Since he knew he could not finance such a thing, the first step was to lay out and build a three-cylinder 25 hp gasoline marine engine. He reasoned that he could sell castings from the patterns, once he had built them, to raise money for the next steps.[24]

"Needless to say," Hill wrote years later, "the project was beyond me." However, so impressive was the effort that the patterns remained on display for many years at the Berkeley Trade School. The design was a perfectly workable one, and Hill built the engine and installed it in a motorboat later.[25] It was the origin for him of a lifelong interest in engine design and construction, which he applied successfully both to marine and aviation engines.

The coterie of teenage boys that gathered every Sunday morning in these years at Hill's shop on Russell Street to read his latest issues of *Machinery* or *Scientific American*, to listen to the wireless, to get a shock, to electrocute cats, and to talk about their designs was a training ground, and Leroy was the prophet of a future for them in an engineering age.[26]

There were accidents, of course. In May 1908, Leroy was trying to mix wax and turpentine by melting the wax. The mixture caught fire. He tried to blow it out and it singed his hair and eyebrows. The boys working in the shop dropped it on the floor; it spilt and the floor started burning until it could be beaten out with coats.[27] On another occasion, a friend visiting Leroy's room with a shotgun let it go off with a loaded shell and blew a hole in the ceiling—"Papa didn't like the accident with the gun a little bit."[28] Quite a few house fuses were blown by experiments, though Leroy generally fixed them before anyone noticed. The family reaction when he "set off powder by electricity," as he did several times, is not known.[29]

A more serious danger were the tall transmission poles, which several boys had and which were erected and guy-wired by the group of them. Leroy's was about 68 feet high, and he confessed later it "caused Mother much worry."[30] In March 1911, Clifford Cosby died. He had fallen off a wireless pole he was helping another boy erect. After a week in the hospital he seemed to recover, only to suffer a burst appendix and die on the operating table. "It hit me pretty hard," Hill wrote, "because I've known Clifford longer than I can remember . . . . He was my best friend."[31]

Cosby's death, while perhaps not directly a result of the boy's dangerous activities, highlighted the patience of Frank and Nellie Hill in giving Leroy the freedom he needed in many areas without entirely abandoning their parental responsibilities. The young friends, for instance, did a great deal of hiking and camping, which included hunting with loaded guns. Usually these trips were to Orinda and Wildcat Canyon—now built-up suburban communities, but then rather remote and separated from the town by farming country. Leroy in his recollections makes light of any risk in this, recalling that in 1907 when he and Clifford went by way of the narrow-gauge railway to Muir Woods for one of their early camping trips, they felt "far away from civilization when much to our disgust, our mothers appeared to say good morning to see if their little boys were safe."[32]

However, there was risk. In February 1908, amid California's wonderful open weather, Leroy and his friend Elwood Schurein—carrying a frying pan, a lard pail with four potatoes, some coffee, four eggs wrapped in rags, some bacon, and some coffee—took their .22 caliber rifles via streetcar and along a telegraph line into the Berkeley hills. They shot a wood rat and a woodpecker (they tried to roast the bird on a stick) and created a fine camp, a "Bird's Eye View" of which Leroy included in his diary. The only problem was the prevalence of and Leroy's sensitivity to poison oak. The next morning he recorded that he had it on his face, arms, and penis and was miserable. Two days later, he wrote that he could hardly see and itched "like the deuce." The next month he went out again, and, despite taking a bath of carbolic acid, got poison oak again. It was nearly a week this time before he could get out of bed and get dressed, and he swore never to go camping again. By summer, however, he was writing that he was "shooting stuff all day."[33]

A trip with friend Will Turpin in October 1909 created a more serious concern. Hill had gotten a 16-gauge shotgun the previous Christmas, so he and his friends did a good deal of bird hunting.[34] As Leroy described this trip's main incident in his diary:

> I haven't been writing all this time for a good reason. Well, Sunday Oct. 2, Bill and I went quail hunting. He got one. About 6 o'clock as it was beginning to get dark, we had started to go home another way, we were in a clump of brush looking for quail. Bill went in first and I went in by a path about 30 ft. below him. Pretty soon Bill saw me move and took me for a quail and took a shot at me. I got it right in the neck, shoulders and head (Bill's a good shot). I didn't know I was *shot* for a couple of seconds. I felt all numb and my ears rung. I fell over and yelled loud as I could and Bill came running down to me and he washed some of the blood off and tied his shirt around my neck and helped me walk up to the road (about 100 yards up) and leaned me up against a fence post and took off his shoes and ran to the nearest ranch which was Kern's over in Wildcat Cañon (this was where the road goes around the hill from Orinda Valley into Wildcat Cañon). Pretty soon my neck began to stiffen up and I got up and started to walk.[35]

Mr. Kern took Leroy in a buggy to Roosevelt Hospital in Berkeley where the doctors found about 200 holes in him. The next day the boy's head was shaved, and a team of doctors dug out as much of the no. 7 shot as they could and swathed his neck and head in a bandage. "For years afterward," Hill wrote in his memoirs, "an occasional no. 7 shot developed a sore and would pop out unexpectedly much to the amusement of witnesses. There are dozens of them still under my skin and X-rays show them up distinctly." The impact was in the head and shoulders. Had it not been an old-fashioned smooth-bore shotgun, which scattered the charge, the career of Leroy Hill could have ended right on that California hillside.[36]

Still, on the good days, hunting and trapping and camping were glorious fun for Hill. He took his diary and pen with him, and recorded both the friendliness of farmers along the way, who gave the boys eggs and milk for nothing, or their occasional ire. "We urinated in Mr. Stone's grainery [sic] bin," he wrote on one trip, and Mr. Stone advised them never to come back. He carved his name that day in the door panel of a country school, cut the rope on a flag pole, shot a frog, looked around the small towns, and camped in a wheat field with pancakes for supper and fresh straw for a mattress. "We went right down the main street in Haywards with our tin pans clanging behind us."[37] Those were perfect outings—as Leroy might have said, "a peach without a stone."[38]

As a teenager, Leroy's increasing physical vigor, combined with the natural intellectual curiosity and adventurous spirit he had long demonstrated, made him a true connoisseur of experience—a trait he would retain all his life. He often went to extremes. After Thanksgiving dinner once he wrote: "I am still alive. I ate so much I couldn't hardly walk. We had oysters, celery, cranberry sauce, stuffing and gravy, mashed potatoes and gravey [sic], Turkey, Squash, pie."[39] Nellie Hill loved to cook, and especially for Leroy. In the late 1930s, when he was far away in New York and both mother and son were going through a difficult period, she wrote him describing meals in detail, thinking that everything would be okay if she could just have him there and feed him right as she used to do.[40] He lifted weights, boxed, sometimes got involved in informal street fights, and by June 1912, at his graduation from high school, weighed a solid 169 pounds, could stand on his hands a little, and had drawn a design for an original fan motor. A friend of his, by contrast, he recorded, weighed only 107 pounds and had hardly any talents out of the ordinary.[41]

As before, he was most observant and seemed to learn from every experience. In May 1908, when the fleet was in, Leroy went on board the *U.S.S. Louisiana.* He worked all the big guns "and got way down where I wasn't allowed to go." He met a sailor who showed him his ditty bag and gave him a badge and some postcards from South America. He even got an onion from the cook. Just a few days earlier, he and some friends had watched the trial of a large airship 450 feet long. Its bag burst when it was high in the sky and the whole thing fell, injuring a great many people seriously. Hill got a piece of the gas bag as a souvenir, made a careful drawing of the layout of the ship, and even recorded the financial details: it had cost $90,000 and was a total loss.[42] In the spring of 1912, he inspected a tunnel on the Oakland-Antioch railroad by climbing up an air shaft. At the same time, he examined a quarry and a rock crusher run by three 350 hp gas engines. There was a half-mile conveyor belt to carry the crushed rock to the railroad, and part of Leroy's inspection there was to ride the belt "some."[43]

Henry May described street life for boys similarly. Clodfights, he said, "were perfectly friendly, carried out from forts, with santuraries [sic] and agreed rules of war." But soon enough the vacant lots filled with houses in a conglomeration of styles. May's own house, he said, was a sanctuary— "safe, a little boring, beloved when I was away and thought about it, but for the most part simply taken for granted."[44]

Travel, like street life, was a sensual high. The Hills did not do much of it, but they did go to Hawaii in the summer of 1910. Leroy didn't keep up on his diary while in Honolulu and chastised himself for that later, saying he was too lazy. But he did write a few entries on the ship back home about the chorus girls on the ship, goat shooting in the mountains, and "swimming like a fish" in the ocean.[45]

Leroy went over with his cousin Bob Thurston, who was coming home from Yale aboard the S.S. *Lurline.* Leroy was sixteen, and it was quite an adventure to be on his own with a twenty-two-year-old. His mother, father, and sister followed two weeks later, and the whole family stayed at the Thurston house in Nwnanu Valley. There were horses in the stables, lots of land, a stream flowing in back of the house, a natural swimming pool, a glass-enclosed conservatory, and mango, papaya, and guava trees in the yard. There were no automobiles on the island at the time, and the sense of tropical isolation was enhanced by Chinese and native servants at their beck and call. Uncle Fred took Leroy to the aquarium and showed him the ropes of feeding the fishes and of catching new specimens or buying them from the natives. Leroy swam in the "shark tank" at the aquarium (minus the sharks) and was regaled by Uncle Fred's stories of how he swam with the sharks and was never bothered by them at all. Uncle Lorrin Thurston had a weekend cottage near the top of Mount Tantalus and remote from the city. While the others went up by carriage, Bob and Leroy arrived by packhorse, slid downhill on tihi leaves, and were once marooned on the mountain for several days by torrential rains, when they had to live on poi available from the natives. Bob was given a 20-foot catboat built by a native boat builder as a present. It had a one-cylinder auxiliary engine, but Bob mostly relied on the sail. He took Leroy sailing around the inner harbor and even down the coast to Pearl Harbor. Once, while racing the sampan of a Japanese fisherman, the boys overturned and had to be rescued by tugboat by the construction crew just beginning the naval base at Pearl Harbor. Leroy took the little engine all apart the next day, cleaned it, and got it running again. The family rode the narrow-gauge railroads, they camped on the beach, and they walked barefoot. Isabella and her parents returned to the mainland after about a month, but Leroy stayed longer and returned with Bob on his way back to Yale. The boy's imagination worked full time on all this. Many years later, he remembered it as "a thrilling experience."[46]

His joie de vivre continued to express itself too in naughtiness and pranks. He had pets in pens in his backyard, particularly rabbits and guinea pigs, and seemed to dote on them—recording day after day, for instance, that his rabbits were still alive. But on other occasions he exhibited a cruel streak toward animals. Cats, maybe because they went after his rabbits, were particular enemies. There was the aforementioned cat electrocution on the "shocker," for which he trapped the victim. Another time he killed a cat, which was "monkeying" with his rabbits, with his rifle after missing it several times with an axe. As a high school senior he took the junk from the foundry and jammed it into some other boys' closet, tied their overalls in knots, and wet them and smeared them with jam. He then poured hydrogen sulfide over everything and locked the door.[47] During his sophomore year, he got into such a serious argument with the shop teacher, Charles Evans, that Evans had him arrested. He had the experience then of being photographed and fingerprinted in the local police department.[48] One assumes, too, that the talk could get rough at the private lunches Leroy joined in at school, where a group of boys made coffee and used the gas plate from the machine shop to heat soup and beans that Harry Horgan got wholesale from his father's grocery. "I guess you can say," he wrote later, "that I was a forerunner of the modern rioting delinquent."[49]

Hill took no interest in girls for quite some time, being involved as he was with so many other passions, but when he did notice them, the opposite sex became a major preoccupation. He later claimed that the chorus girls on the ship back from Hawaii in 1910, when he was sixteen, were the origin of it. He flirted seriously with one of the girls in what he described as a "burlesque company" until cousin Bob "took me aside and told me I was making a fool of myself and I became normal again."[50] Actually, as early as 1909, there is in his diary an indication of more than casual interest in the "pretty nice sister" of his friend Harry Hogan. That year too there was Aloyse Furlong, whose speaking to Leroy in the library rated a diary entry. "Foolishly called up Aloyes this morning," he recorded on May 15, "and got slammed but I didn't tell her who I was."[51] Early in 1912 he described in his diary a girl named Ruth Berry: "She sure is speedy. She teaches a Sunday School class, but she don't look a bit like that. . . . I like her an awful lot . . . . I can't help it, she's got my goat (also several other fellows')." Two months later it was a girl named "Cutey," who Hill said was "speed," not "fruit." He sat and "queened" with her for a time.[52]

As in everything else, Hill was doubtless precocious in romance and sexual interest, but he was also living in the middle of a genuine revolution in sexual mores and at the cusp of the emergence of "dating" as the modern age knows it. While in an earlier era women largely controlled heavily supervised courtship contacts, about the time of World War I "dating" replaced "calling" and, as one author put it, the locus went from the Front Porch to the Back Seat.[53] The joke was that when a boy arrived at a house, his girl "had her hat on"; that is, she expected to be taken out—out of her traditional home environment and into the stimulating, anonymous, commercial city of dance halls, movies, drinking, jazz, and petting.[54] There was in the early twentieth century a great desire for freedom, expressing itself in the "flaming youth" identity. As was so evident in Scott Fitzgerald's 1920 best-seller, *This Side of Paradise*, a major defining element for homogenized, rebellious youth was the college experience.

Hill participated as deeply in those Jazz Age/flapper customs at the University of California as Fitzgerald did at Princeton, but already at an earlier age he was experimenting with his sense of self to some degree through experimenting with girls. Sexuality and romance were no longer anchored to tradition: they were open to individual joy and pain. Freudian theory, of course, led to a popular view that repression was bad for you, and women with bobbed hair and cigarettes—"hard-boiled virgins," Fitzgerald called them—suggested they were subject to the same passions and vices as men.[55] There seemed to be a "pleasure basis of living," where consumerism and material goods filled all voids, life was "relentlessly heterosexual," and Father's money was used to keep up with fads and ensure popularity.[56] Adolescents were fawned upon though their idealism, and moodiness had little immediate value. They were "vulnerable, awkward, incapacitated by the process of maturation, but simultaneously the object of almost rhapsodic praise, the very bud and promise of the race." Maybe, too, as Jane Addams thought was the case when she wrote *The Spirit of Youth and the City Streets*, "a dull and dehumanizing industrial regime drove young people to seek both excitement and pathetic forms of self-expression in recreation."[57] It was a time of an "enlarged range of casual social intercourse," enhanced by the telephone and by a claim to family spending. "The dance halls dazzled and featured lively jazz, the surroundings and the music (sometimes aided by liquor) encouraged the easy and spontaneous contact between unacquainted or slightly acquainted members of the opposite sex. The music was sensual, offering a rhythm in which two bodies moved smoothly to that music together." Movies were "morally innovative." Girls with bobbed hair, flattened breasts, and short skirts created "a well-poised tension between the informal boyish companion and the purposefully erotic vamp."[58]

It was Hill's nature that he should play the game as newly defined for all it was worth. From puberty forward, Hill's relationships with women were meteoric and unconventional. In the process, he courted some extraordinary ones, always with style, and evolved in his own understanding and feeling through the maturing of his love and loves until he brought about a total transformation of himself. And he recorded each stage.

In the spring of 1912 came Irene Van Buskirk, who represented some sort of sexual/romantic watershed for Hill. In his memoirs he recalls that he went steady with Irene that summer of 1912 and "as she was my first love, I shall never forget her." In May he notes in his diary that he went to the canyon with her. "It's the first time I ever had my arms around a girl, and Irene is some girl too." Leroy was seventeen at that time and Irene was fourteen. "I used to think that Ruth Barry was a pretty girl, but Irene is a million times prettier than Ruth Barry."[59]

Other than that summer being the beginning, coincidentally or not, of Leroy's taking cold baths when awakening in the morning, the exclusivity of the affair was not long-lasting. By September he was taking a girl named Nanette to the Orpheum. "She's some peach but I don't seem to get next to her very well."[60] However, even the next year, when Hill was a freshman at the University of California at Berkeley, the "sparking" was more hot than heavy. On his sister Isabella's thirteenth birthday, Leroy toured the Berkeley campus with Irene "and we walked around thro' dark, unlighted paths on the campus for over an hour and stood on bridges and etc., etc., etc. You see I can't put everything in here because the wrong people might see it. Anyway I never forget things like that."[61] It does seem that at college Hill advanced quickly in the *ars amoris*, and there is no question that his slow start with women was a function of the times more than his constitution or inclinations.

In California Leroy continued to do household jobs for specific pay from his mother. He washed windows, beat rugs, and oiled floors, as well as built and fixed things. But he also branched out some in his pursuit of employment and income for his experiments. His first outside job was a newspaper route, which went on for several months in the spring of 1908, though there is evidence that Leroy got into several considerable arguments with his boss.[62] In June 1909, he got a job with Alpine Wood & Supply carrying firewood from the curb where their truck dumped it to the customer's backyard or basement. Often the dump point was at the end of the road, and he had to start by throwing the wood down the hill.[63] He was paid fifty cents a cord for stacking the wood in people's homes, but it could be a difficult job, especially when the houses were on the hill side of the street and he had to carry the wood by the armful up a flight of stairs to get it into the basement. It could take as much as three or four hours to deliver a cord of wood that way. Leroy also delivered 100-pound coal sacks which were sold by Alpine, as well as filling them on a scale for one cent a sack. "Carrying in wood and wrassling 100# sacks of coal did more for my physical development than the iron dumbbells, the punching bags and the fist fights," he remembered. During the Christmas season of 1908 he added to his income by taking orders for Christmas trees for the Alpine Company, which had 1,500 of them in inventory that year.[64]

While Leroy learned from these jobs, no doubt as important to his developing sense of salesmanship was observing his dad making real estate deals. Frank Sr. was in these years specializing in country lands, especially lots on Half Moon Bay south of San Francisco, which a projected electric railway south to Santa Cruz promised to make accessible. Hill would take prospects by rail from San Francisco to San Mateo and then hire a four-horse, twelve-passenger carriage and drive them over the mountains through the redwoods to Half Moon Bay. One memorable Sunday in particular he included Nellie, Isabella, and Leroy on a trip. "It was great fun. We waded in the ocean and listened to Dad's sales talk. We enjoyed a lovely lunch which was brought along for the prospects and got back home in the late evening." The older and wiser Leroy added in his notes that "I doubt if Dad ever sold enough land to make his effort worthwhile."[65]

But that was written from the post-Depression perspective. In the 1930s, the elder Hill's real estate business fell apart, and his son's later memories of him were filled with furtive requests for money to pay the father's debts and eventually of a rather pitiful old man damaged by several strokes. Beyond that time barrier, however, back in the golden years when California was a paradise for development, the talks and the trips with Dad had to have been exciting to his son. Certainly, it was a family environment when business of the most risky sort was the accepted norm. Enterprise was a natural part of every day, and Leroy absorbed that lifestyle right along with his breakfast oatmeal. The importance of that deep and unconscious psychology transmitted by family tradition is hard to overemphasize.

To the family's credit, too, was Leroy's basic humanistic balance. It would have been easy for him to have become a man with a total technical orientation, and therefore one unsuited to the top management positions he later occupied. But while the basic course was a trade one, his high school also required Latin and literature, and the general culture of the university town was something Leroy utilized through its libraries. His mother added a good deal to that. In 1907, much to his dismay, she took Leroy to dancing school. Even though he rebelled at the bottom of the stairs going up to the second-floor dance studio to the point that Nellie Hill had to drag him up by one ear, she did manage to expose him to at least one dance lesson.[66]

More willingly, Leroy was always involved in music as a boy. He began mandolin lessons in Manitowoc in 1906 and maintained a disciplined regimen of practice, no doubt with some prodding. His best friend of the early California days, Clifford Cosby, played the violin, and the two sometimes practiced together. And of course there were the sessions with Uncle Fred from Hawaii and his guitar. In 1912, after a visit from Fred on the occasion of Frank Sr.'s fifty-seventh birthday, Leroy took up the guitar and admitted to practicing five hours one day. About that time Leroy did some ensemble playing. The group included first violin, first and second mandolin, and, as Leroy put it, "another Chinaman kid played the guitar."[67]

Certainly all this provided a veneer of civilization, as one might expect of a dweller in a sophisticated metropolitan area. Leroy recorded once after a meal with his parents at a San Francisco restaurant: "I had Tenderloine of Sole a La Tartar." The footnote to this note read: "A Kind of Fish and a cup of Custard."[68] But it didn't extend all the way through. Leroy's diary records a great deal of skipping of church, despite his mother's best efforts. "Then ma called me in to go to Sunday School," he wrote in November 1908. "I started but I didn't get there as I stopped at Arthur Patterson's and boxed and did stunts on his wheel with him and his brother."[69] Leroy Hill as a high school senior was well spoken, relatively well educated, and very intelligent, but he couldn't exactly be called genteel. He was sure of himself, and when crossed he would become argumentative, if not violent. In his senior year, for instance, he was thrown out of shop class for cussing, one of many similar incidents.[70]

Still, Hill was not such an individualist as to be unable to make the compromises necessary ultimately to succeed in an organization without becoming a patsy to it. In December 1912, he graduated from high school and marched across the stage to get his sheepskin. He wrote in his diary: "Hoo-ray, I'm educated."[71] He knew perfectly well, however, that he was not. Immediately upon graduation, he began the search for a serious job, and after two years of the kinds of jobs a high school graduate could get, he enrolled at the University of California at Berkeley to pursue an engineering degree.

Neither college nor a particular kind of work was automatic: it is certain that Hill's parents' direct influence over his major decisions ended about 1912. But as a pragmatist, as a reader, and as a thinker, he had a sophisticated sense not only of himself and his possibilities, but of the nature of the world in which his talents would have to be applied, complete with the rules other people made. Rebellious as he seemed, he did not even have the usual teenage falling out with his parents; he lived at his family home, partly to save money in the early businesses he owned, even after returning from his World War I service and into the 1920s. His relationship with his mother particularly remained so close that he later sent his daughter by a failed marriage to live with her, and the two corresponded regularly and warmly well into the 1940s. Still, when Hill's full-time work career began in earnest in 1913, he moved, spiritually at least, out of his home, took up a good part of his own support, and began his unique, single journey through life.

Work and War

For Christmas in 1912 Leroy Hill got a set of books, the *American Cyclopedia of Applied Electricity*, from his father, a shark's-tooth watch charm from his mother, and $5.25 from his aunt and uncle. His present to his mother was an instantaneous heater for the bathroom, which her son promptly installed.[1] The new high school graduate was making twenty-five cents an hour doing drafting for the Cosby-Winter Company, officed right next door to his father in San Francisco, but he was looking hard for something better. He had also decided that the type of jobs he could get with a high school education would not be satisfactory in the long run. Therefore, in January 1913, he got the entry information from the University of California at Berkeley and resolved to start degree work there the next fall.[2]

The Bay Area was filled with the type of jobs Leroy would like to have had, not so much for the salary as for the experience. He applied to local railroads and to the Great Western Power Company office in Oakland, but his best prospect was the Hall-Scott gas engine works. Uncle Lorrin had contacts there, since Hall-Scott had made a couple of engines for his Helo Railway in Hawaii.[3] While Hall-Scott was a relatively small company and closely held by one family, it was in the forefront of engine design and building at the time. Many of the pioneering aircraft being built by Curtiss and several individual builders at this time were powered by the Hall-Scott V-8 engine, a remarkably light unit for its 60 hp output.[4] Uncle Lorrin and Aunt Hattie happened to be in the country that January of 1913, and before they sailed for Honolulu on the *Siberia*, Thurston took young Leroy to call on his acquaintances at Hall-Scott and with other companies.[5]

Leroy visited with E. J. (Al) Hall of the Hall-Scott company, whom he called "the creative brains of the outfit," and spent an entire morning looking over the shops and examining the drawings. However, there were no openings at that time, and he was advised to come back in a month.[6] Hill was persistent, and by January 29, 1913, he was being allowed to come to work at Hall-Scott to draw. His recall of it later was that Hall told him, "Well, I'll have to give you a job to get rid of you." His first drawing was a transmission case for a gasoline railroad motor car, and he started right in on it without even knowing what his pay was to be.[7]

It turned out that the pay was $12 a week, which Hill thought was fine as there was a chance for advancements and raises. At first, he was just the blueprint boy and general flunky, though he had promoted his abilities as a designer so much that his boss jokingly introduced him to the chief draftsman as "a young man who is going to show you how to design engines." Blueprints were made by putting the paper and tracing in a wood frame with a glass front, exposing it to sunlight, then washing and developing the paper in a chemical tank. Hill got to carry the heavy frame indoors and back out again, a tiresome job for which his wood-carrying days at Alpine Supply had prepared him.[8]

There was a high-tech atmosphere about the place. Early in February someone brought in a Stutz racer (the company for a time took a try at building auto racing engines) and always there was the aura of advanced aviation about. Leroy saved virtually all his paycheck and splurged on a big box of valentine candy for his girlfriend Irene, whom he called "Kirk."[9]

Hill apparently did well at Hall-Scott, as he was rapidly given more responsibility. In the early months of 1913, he made an assembly of a generator drive and fan bracket, designed some brackets and pulleys, and worked on details of a new 100 hp areo engine. By late spring he was working outside the drafting room enough to hurt his finger on the pneumatic riveting hammer, and he was doing assembly work on the erecting platforms where rail cars were built. He began riding home with

The approach to the University library, University of California at Berkeley.

the boss, Al Hall, and within months became his regular assistant, at a raise to $100 a month in salary.[10]

"I considered it a great privilege to work at the Hall-Scott Motor Car Company," Hill wrote later, "and was keenly interested in everything that went on." That included talking to a pattern maker named Ritchie, who had read lots on psychic phenomena and philosophy. He recommended books to Leroy, who picked up *Looking Backward* by Bellamy and *The Evolution of the Soul* by Hudson on his recommendation. The salary was first rate, even though Leroy's mother began charging him $20 a month board to live at home. Hill rode to work on a four-cylinder Pierce motorcycle he had bought for $100.[11]

However promising an immediate business career looked, however, college came first. Hall tried to talk Leroy out of college, but the young man told him his long-term interest lay there and he could work part-time even while in school.[12] In June he quit his job at Hall-Scott in order to devote his time completely to a summer school session on the Berkeley campus to prepare to enter regular degree work that fall. He had $50 saved, $15 of which he devoted to tuition for two courses—"Dutch" (German) and "Trig" (Trigonometry). His German class met at 9:00 a.m. and 2:00 p.m., and the math class at 10:00. Much of the rest of the time was spent in the library. Hill had $7 in bets with his friends that with this preparation he could pass the entry exams and matriculate as a regular student at the college.[13]

The university was filled with class and fraternity traditions, many of which had more than a tinge of rowdiness. There were "orgies," song-and-drink fests, elaborate "funerals," and parodies, all involving lots of roughhousing and hazing practices that had to be throttled by official decree. Still, "general hell-raising and mayhem in connection with inter-class warfare occurred only a few times a year," the rest being available for classes. The president, Benjamin Ide Wheeler, who had been a professor of philology and Greek at Cornell, set a high academic tone and communicated his ideas at a university meeting held every other Friday morning. Time was allowed there for student discussion, and there was even student involvement in the program. Wheeler announced that students should feel free to sing or yell and to enjoy themselves within the limits of good order. Still, he said, "You are called upon to be the children of the University, and I am called to preach the Gospel." Included in this gospel was the admonition to "beware of the men who advise you to be a little practical when they mean for you to be a little bad" and the precept that "an educated man will not be swayed by clamour or cowed by gossip and rumor. Human herds sometimes stampede like cattle, but one chief reason why we are taking pains to educate men is to eliminate the stampede."[14]

Of course, for Hill college was partly girls. "Kirk" seems to have faded in favor of someone called "Mae Belle," who looked up the hard words in the German book while Leroy read Washington Irving's *Alhambra*.[15] He played poker, ate at Bud's, drank root beer, and ate chocolate. While studying at the library that June, Leroy saw "a little sandy haired queen," but though he wrote her a note on the shade of a table lamp, she would pay no attention to him. He called her a "peachy little blondy" but said she was "awfully proper & I can't get even a glance out of her." Finally he walked right up and talked to her but noted, in one of the last entries in his diary before he abandoned it for five years, that "she isn't so classy close up." He took Mae Belle to the picture show that night.[16]

Hill did well in his classes that summer, and even better in the fall. The engineering course he took required instruction in mechanical design, machine shop practice, and pattern making. When Hill brought samples of drawings he had done and patterns he had made at Hall-Scott, the instructor made him his assistant. "It was obvious to me," Hill wrote, "that I knew more about design than he did." Since things went so smoothly at school, he began working again part time at Hall-Scott and joined a fraternity, Alpha Sigma Phi. His fraternity brothers introduced him to drinking, though there was no liquor allowed on the campus proper, and subjected him to some rough hazing, which he in turn participated in as an upperclassman. His fraternity also pressured him to go out for athletics—football and crew—though he did not like these sports much and never lettered. It is not so unusual that little remains to document Hill's college years, except that there is so much for the rest of his life. His habit of recording and saving everything apparently suffered a slight hiatus during his collegiate term.

He did make two fast friends early in his college years, friendships that were to last a lifetime. Harold Crow was a fellow engineering student much interested in automobiles and engines. Crow had the special distinction of having worked for a time at the Mercer Automobile Company in New Jersey when the Mercer Runabout was the most exciting sports car on the road. Through his life, Hill tended to have one close and fast male friend. It had been Clifford Cosby in his early teens, for instance, and in the 1920s and 1930s it would be Harold Crow. The other lifelong friend made in college was a woman—Alice Clemo. Alice was a shy girl who was a fine pianist and would later gain some regional fame under the stage name Alice Blue. Hill was close also to Scotchie Campbell and Gordon "Willy" Wells. These two lived in San

Diego and had a motorboat on which Leroy was invited to explore the bay before there was a naval base and when the city was very small. There was an auto-racing course on Point Loma where the young men watched races between cars with narrow tires and enormous displacement engines.[17]

Hill was participating in the engineering honor fraternity, Pi Beta Phi, and working on his senior thesis, leading to his graduation with a B.S. in engineering in June 1917, when in April the United States entered World War I. He had no hesitation about enlisting immediately. His interest was in naval aviation, but he had to enlist as a regular seaman with an application pending for officer training in aviation. To be accepted for officer training, one had to pass a physical, including an eye test. Leroy did fine, but his friend Scotchie Campbell could not read the eye chart. He asked for a second chance, and Leroy copied the letters for Scotchie to memorize. When it came to the actual test, however, Scotchie was asked to read them backward and so he spent the war as "an ordinary gob."[18]

Naively Hill expected to go off to the front in an airplane immediately. No such thing happened. He reasoned that since he and Campbell had enlisted the first day after war was declared, their papers must have gotten on the bottom of the stack. His only immediate communication from the navy was that he was forbidden to leave the Twelfth Naval District in California. Meanwhile, he was put in charge of creating and teaching a course in aircraft engine instruction as part of an army air corps ground school (the U.S. School of Military Aeronautics) held at the university. Hall-Scott engines and various other American and European aircraft engines were provided to him. He wrote courses of instruction and set up stands to demonstrate and work on the engines outdoors. In addition to engines, the ground school course included meteorology, aerodynamics, and military drill. One of Hill's students in the engine section was a very young Jimmy Doolittle.

Al Hall, with whom Hill had worked at Hall-Scott, was called to Washington in the early months of the U.S. involvement in the war to design the new twelve-cylinder Liberty engine for aircraft. Shortly he was

Leroy Hill about 1917.

made the officer in charge of all American aircraft production. Upon returning to Berkeley from his engine design assignment, Hall looked up Hill and gave him a good tongue-lashing for enlisting in the regular navy. Hall wanted Hill on his staff and would now have to go through the naval bureaucracy to get him. Meanwhile he started using him immediately anyway. Just as Hill got his engine course at the university going, Hall employed him to lay out a four-cylinder engine to put in training planes, using the cylinders and some other parts from the Liberty. Hill worked on it day and night for about a week, and Hall took the design to Washington hoping to land a big training-plane engine order for Hall-Scott.[19]

Hall definitely wanted Hill to come to work for him full time on war aircraft design. However, Hill did not do so immediately. As was so often the case in his life, his first instinct was to go into business for himself and to be the boss of something he personally owned. Doubtless he would like to have owned Hall-Scott, but it was too large for him. Instead he focused on the J. L. Hicks Gas Engine Company, located in two buildings on Howard Street in San Francisco.

J. L. Hicks had founded the company in 1860 and now faced a classic situation in a family business. His two sons Frank and Robert were at odds, and the family itself was, according to Hill, in a "continual squabble."[20] While Frank was a college graduate and good design engineer, Robert was "utterly incompetent." Rather than oversee a struggle between them, the old man was willing to sell Leroy Hill a three-quarter interest in the company, retaining one-quarter for the time being for himself, on the understanding that Frank would continue to be employed. An agreement was drawn up between Hicks and Hill in September 1917—in effect, an option—and Hill went to work to raise the money to buy the company.

Hill did his own due diligence on this deal and thought the prospects were tremendous. The Hicks company made mainly marine gas engines used for fishing boats in the Bay Area. There were seven models, ranging from 6 hp to 60 hp—all of the heavy-duty distillate-burning type. The company had a tremendous following among fisherman in the area based on quality differentiation and sold its entire modest output easily. The elder Hicks was satisfied with the level of business and did not want to go to the bother of installing more modern manufacturing equipment or management systems, but Hill definitely thought the market was there for a great expansion.

No regular drawings were used in the shop—the memory of Frank Hicks was the whole thing. No books were kept (making it difficult for Hill to come up with financial statements to show investors), prices were determined by guess, inquiries and even orders often went unanswered, no costs were figured, and no catalog or price list had ever been issued. There was no advertising to speak of, and practically all the business came "from unsolicited and voluntary orders due to the merits of the engine." Still, Hill estimated profits from the previous year to have been about $9,650 or 25 percent.

Hill's prospectus to potential investors emphasized his own experience with Hall-Scott and said that his connection with the Hicks company "will give it the benefit of the most up-to-date scientific information concerning the theory and practice of the construction of gas engines, combined with practical knowledge of the latest efficiency methods of buying, accounting and shop management." He thought he could provide greater output and profit by changing from individual construction (Hicks was producing only about fifty engines a year) to "multiple construction of a standardized character" of several engines of a similar design. He would market the engines aggressively on the Pacific Coast and in the fisheries of British Columbia, Alaska, Japan, and the Pacific Islands.[21] He promised to his relatives, whom he asked to sell stock, that he would get four times the previous year's production the first year he was there without any new equipment.[22]

It was quite a claim for a recent high school graduate, but Leroy Hill was perfectly comfortable with it. He resigned his job at the University of California in October 1917 because, as he put it, "an opportunity to enter into business has presented itself to me which I feel bound to grasp."[23]

He put Uncle Fred Potter in Honolulu to work on commission trying to sell $15,000 in stock in a company created to take up the Hicks option. Potter did not get much of a welcome among the friends he visited (not untypical for new ventures) and wrote his nephew increasingly discouraging letters. "I am devoting all my spare time to the new concern," he wrote from Hawaii late in October, "and I hope to meet with some success soon. One man objected to the large percentage of capital represented by good-will and leasehold; another found fault because it seemed to be a one-man affair and what if you sold out there would be nothing to it, etc., etc., ad libitum ad nauseum. I have been turned down by fourteen prospects to date, but I am just getting started."[24] By November, however, Uncle Fred had given up trying. He had talked to the current and former heads of the Honolulu Iron Works, who gave a negative evaluation. Though Leroy pointed out they might be prejudiced since they were then using the Standard brand engine, Uncle Fred did not think so. One of these men, he said, "gave me quite a lengthy dissertation of the vicissitudes of a machine shop, citing instances of his own knowledge where they had risen and fallen . . . . He said it was one of the most uncertain games on earth; that one year a shop would make a lot of money and the next year lose it all, etc." He advised Leroy not to waste the money to come to Hawaii himself and said he was sorry to hear that the young man had resigned from his university post: "Never let go with one hand till you have a good sure grip with the other."[25]

All that wisdom from his elders phased Hill not a bit, though the lack of capital slowed him down. He wrote that he "didn't feel a bit discouraged" by his uncle's letters. "According to your friend," he told him, "a small shop will make a greater per cent of profit than a large one. This is true only when it is attempted to apply small shop methods to large sized shops and that is just what has been done on this coast wherever a gas engine company has expanded." E. J. Hall had invested in his company, Hill said, "and no one knows more about the gas engine business than he does." There was always naval aviation, Hill said, but he wanted to give the business enterprise a go first.[26]

The Hicks deal did not work because young Leroy could not raise the money. The company was purchased by D. C. Demarest, with whom Hill kept in contact for some time. Demarest had been a subscriber to Hill's company and was himself the head of the Angels Iron Works, a company with considerable shipbuilding business into which the Hicks company was later merged.

In 1918, when his war service was finished, Hill proposed to the new owner that he manage the Hicks shop on somewhat the same lines he had proposed when offering to buy it. Through the war he kept in contact with Frank Hicks about the details of the operation and knew exactly what he would do with it. He would (1) establish a definite organization; (2) put into effect a simple shop system, including keeping accurate costs on all manufactured products, planning work in advance "to get a maximum of working hours out of each machine and man," creating a store system, and creating a drawing and part-numbering system; and (3) "produce more engines at least cost than ever before produced in that shop." This, he said, "does not mean a large outlay of money, printing innumerable forms, moving the machinery and disruption of the shop in general, but a smooth steady improvement by the application of known methods and principles and a little common sense."[27] It was not, however, to be. Hill never was formally associated with the Hicks company. Much of his character as an entrepreneur, however, was revealed in that initial acquisition attempt.

The Hicks acquisition failure turned Hill's attention by default back to the war and the military. To be sure, he seemed an ideal candidate for military service. One letter of recommendation for him to the navy noted that "besides being a splendid specimen of virile young American manhood, [he] is particularly fitted to serve in some executive or official capacity by reason of his professional training and experience . . . . His personal integrity and habits have never been questioned, and in every way he has impressed me as being an exceptional young man."[28] However, Hill himself liked the service less and less after his initial enthusiasm gave way to actual daily duty. He wrote Frank Hicks from his post at Curtiss Aircraft in the fall of 1918 advising against going into government service. "I am thoroughly sick of it myself and would like nothing better than to come back there and make things move in the Hicks Iron Works."[29]

Hill's first stint in the service came when he got telegraphic orders in late February 1918 to report to his former boss, now Major (shortly Lieutenant Colonel) E. J. Hall at the Dayton-Wright aircraft plant in Dayton, Ohio. Dayton-Wright was formed in 1917, the Wright part of the name being purely for publicity, and constructed 3,500 airplanes during the war, mostly DeHaviland 4s. It came under criticism for low production and was in the awkward position of having one of its founders, Colonel Edward Deeds, become also a major government official. Such a cloud developed over it during the war that it was bought by General Motors in 1919 for a little over $1 million in debenture stock as part of William C. Durant's expansion program. In the 1920–21 downturn in the economy and in aviation, it was dissolved altogether.[30] However, when Hill arrived, the mood was upbeat, and Dayton-Wright looked like a coming concern.

His job description was aeronautic mechanical engineer, his salary was to be $1,800 a year, and his unit for the moment was to be the army signal corps.[31] Hall, conveniently, did not notify the navy that he was commandeering a naval enlistee. Actually, there had been considerable maneuvering while Hill was awaiting military orders and also still working the Hicks deal. It might have been impossible to trace except that in 1918 he took up his diary writing again in a five-year "Daylogue" ledger book, which he diligently filled with the brief entries the space allowed before quitting again. Appropriately it had on its cover a quote from Alfred Lord Tennyson: "So many worlds, so much to do, So little done, such things to be." The contents illustrated that.

As 1918 opened, Hill was working at Hall-Scott again, introducing more efficiency into that company's inventory operation and serving as an inspector. Early in January he and his friend Scotchie Campbell heard that their applications for the naval aviation section had been turned down: "this leave us machinist's mates 2nd class." The news disappointed him sufficiently that early in February he asked the naval commandant of the Twelfth District for a discharge. Doubtless this was partly because he was already in contact with Hall about a job which, if not flying itself, at least kept him close to aviation.

Late in February came the orders and several letters from Hall. The problem was that Hill was forbidden by the navy from leaving the Twelfth Naval District, which did not include Dayton, Ohio. His first strategy was to try to resign from the navy altogether. That failing, he wired Hall to ask whether he should come anyway, naval release or not—a question to which Hall doubtless was unable to respond officially. On March 7, however, Hill recorded in his diary: "This PM I finally found one decent fellow among that bunch of fatheads in the Navy recruiting office. He pushed a permission to leave the District through in a half hour which I have." The next day Hill took a transcontinental train east, making the acquaintance of a lady with two children on her way home from China to divorce her drunken husband. The family informally "adopted" him, and they promised mutually to write. On March 12 Hill was at the Dayton-Wright Airplane Company factory looking over his new assignment. He wired his folks in California of his safe arrival and recorded in his diary two days later that he was "getting lots of dope on airplanes, guns & all other equipment."[32]

The work with E. J. Hall in Dayton was a critical assignment. Hall had become the head of the Bureau of Aircraft Production for the United States. At the time of the nation's entry into World War I in the spring of 1917, the total U.S. air force, then located in the aviation section of the army signal corps, consisted of 55 airplanes, all antiquated by comparison with the advanced fighters that had been developed by European countries during their three years of conflict. Outside of the Curtiss factory in Buffalo, New York, there was no aircraft manufacturing plant in the country capable of any level of mass production of aircraft, and even the Curtiss planes were so out of date that they were assigned to slow naval patrol and reconnaissance duties only. Total U.S. contribution to the war effort of complete manufactured airplanes was to be only 196 craft. One thing the United States did excel in, however, was auto production, and in those auto plants was the potential to manufacture thousands of aircraft engines, which could be installed under the supervision of the Bureau of Aircraft Production in British and European airframes.[33]

Particularly promising was a water-cooled V-12 called the Liberty engine, capable of 400 hp. Hall himself had co-designed this engine (first with eight cylinders) with J. E. Vincent of the Packard Motor Company when the two locked themselves in a hotel suite at the Willard Hotel in Washington for forty-eight hours late in May 1917. Only one week after the design was drawn, it was approved by the Aircraft Production Board and the first working models were available in June. In a short time the twelve-cylinder version was being produced by Packard, Ford, Lincoln, Nordyke & Marmon, Willys-Overland, Olds, and General Motors.[34] The plan was to focus American auto factories on producing this engine, and American aeronautical engineers on modifying heavy bombers, like the British DeHaviland 4 (DH-4), to use them.

Hill's assignment with Hall that spring of 1918 was to take charge of the DH-4 modification program. He designed modifications for the plane to replace the lower-powered, lower-production Rolls Royce engine that Dayton-Wright had been using with the Liberty and supervised the testing of the resulting hybrids, which were to threaten German cities with mass destruction from the air.[35] It was no easy task. The DH-4 itself was unreliable enough to be dubbed by its pilots "the flying coffin," while the Liberty engine, though promising, was not fully de-bugged during the war: one critic described it as an "unruly, underdeveloped adolescent."[36] Hall had a small staff of only five or six engineers, to which was soon added on Hill's recommendation his good friend from the university, Harold Crow.[37]

Hill's first project was to lay out a new generator drive for the DH-4 to be driven by a belt from the engine. By late March he was driving a Model T acquired with a friend and overhauling and timing the motor

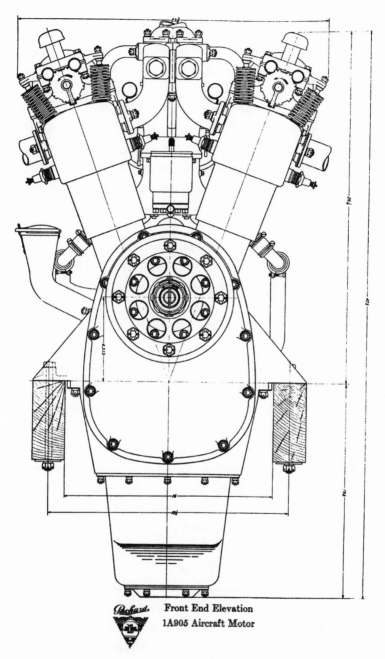

The engine Hill tried to fit into the DH-4.

on the first production plane. He designed larger radiators necessary for cooling the Liberty and experimented with the oil bypass system on the initial production run of four airplanes. He then took flights with the test pilots to determine how all these things worked and got them passed through inspectors from the Bureau of Standards.[38]

Unquestionably Hill was having a good time. When his friend Harold Crow arrived in the second week of April, Hill and Gus Wade took him into their room with them, making the cost each $2 a week. And though changing jets on the Liberty engine in the cold and snow was probably not always fun, the tone of the descriptions in the diary is always upbeat.[39]

The best was the flying. That April, Phil Rader, the test pilot, took Hill up in a DH-4 to check the oil bypass. To subject it to maximum stress, Rader did stunts at 10,000 feet, including tailspins that Hill relished in. So excited was Hill about doing the job quickly and well that he worked his employees until 3:00 a.m. one morning—"I guess some of those fellows haven't much love for me," he commented—to finish some electrical work. "This was a very interesting period," Hill remembered later. "All of us worked very hard without any time off more than was necessary for sleeping and eating."[40]

That charged and stimulating atmosphere was interrupted on April 6, 1918, when Hill got a telegram from the navy ordering him to report for duty at the Boston Naval Headquarters immediately. Although Hall claimed he could get Hill out of the navy soon, he could not prevent his reporting for duty. On April 12 he left for Boston on the train. After a layover in New York City, where he "went out and staged a lone party, taking in a number of cabarets, saloons, etc.," and was kept awake all night in his hotel by a gigantic flashing sign advertising Wrigley chewing gum, he arrived in Boston on the 14th.[41]

His naval basic training was a miserable time for Hill. He had enlisted in a fit of patriotism and enthusiasm for flying but had no interest in the deck swabbing and military discipline of World War I naval service at low rank. No sooner had he arrived than he was raked over the coals by a young officer for not saluting properly and was, as he put it, "immediately

E. J. Hall's World War I staff at Dayton. Hill is on the top row,
second from right.

bawled out by every officer I ran into."[42] The training group was awakened at 5:30 every morning with forty minutes of calisthenics and then allowed to shave and wash "if you can do it fast enough." Work squads were assigned, followed by breakfast, drill, knot-tying instruction, boxing drill, lunch, "drill, drill," supper, wireless instruction, study, and taps. His rating was chief quartermaster, and his pay was $60 a month with an allowance of $1.20 a day for eating in the M.I.T. cafeteria at Cambridge. He was working part of the time at the Aviation Training Center at M.I.T., but it was not the loose and creative situation he had experienced as second in command to Hall in Dayton. In fact, he found it was better not to let on in this environment that he knew anything at all about engine mechanics. And there was swabbing decks and cleaning latrines thrown in. "*Lots* of discipline," Hill wrote laconically.[43]

At close to the low point, it got lower. In the middle of April Hill got the flu. In that he was like a lot of other people during the virulent epidemic of that year, and luckier than the many who died of it. But it sent him to the naval sick bay, "which is a hell of a place," and where over 200 men, a number of whom died, shared the crowded military ward with Hill. The doctors gave him some medicine "that nearly killed me," and Hill began to "ditch" the doses he was instructed to take. Perhaps as a consequence, he recovered rapidly and in four days, with a weight loss of ten pounds, left the infirmary.[44]

Hill's illness was actually only the first wave of the terrible Spanish influenza epidemic of 1918 that killed 500,000 Americans and millions worldwide—more people than any previous disaster in so short a period. And it incubated first in Boston in a hot, dry, dusty summer and in the overcrowded condition of military occupancy in which Hill found himself. By September and October, 200 people a day were dying in Boston. The Public Health Service's sanitation officer singled out the navy facilities, where there were cracked toilets, no drinking fountains or soap, and myriad rodents. The prime pesthole was the so-called "Receiving Ship," not a vessel at all but a navy barracks and eating area in South Boston within "the drafty, odorous confines of Commonwealth Pier." It was to this Receiving Ship that Hill was sent upon his arrival after being "bawled out." It was a perfect breeding ground for a strain that had an especial propensity for pneumonic complications. Often soldiers, the strongest of young men a day before, would show up at the hospitals turning blue, their lungs filling, only to receive the only treatment known—tender loving care from nurses, fresh air, warm food, and blankets. There were no antibiotics. Upward of 20 percent of the soldiers and sailors in many units were sick, and autopsies revealed their lungs filled with thin, bloody, frothy fluid. It was lucky for Hill that he got out of Boston and back to Dayton in May before the worst of the epidemic struck. "No more war, no more plague," wrote Katherine Anne Porter after the influenza mysteriously disappeared early in 1919, "only the dazed silence that follows the ceasing of heavy guns; noiseless houses with the shades drawn, empty streets, the dead cold light of tomorrow."[45]

It was up from there. Late in April, Hill and some friends rented a Packard and took a sight-seeing tour around Boston. On the 30th he was called away from calisthenics and called before his commanding officer, who said he had a telegraphic order to release him and send him to headquarters in Boston proper. The officer provided a car and driver to attest to the urgency of the message. At headquarters, Hill was given his discharge papers, travel orders, and a railroad ticket back to Dayton.[46]

As though by way of a reward for being so suddenly free of discipline, on the subway back to training quarters to pick up his gear he met "a very beautiful girl" named Patricia (Pat) Brissette. They went out for dinner and dancing that night and met again the next day and every day thereafter until May 3, when Pat and Leroy had a fight at just the time Leroy ran out of money. Hill got a telegram from Hall arranging for his transport on May 2, the day he and Pat went to the movie of Polyanna, and still felt the way that optimistic girl did. "Pat is expensive," Hill wrote, but well worth it. Two days later he was on the train to New York City, bound for Dayton. He was so broke that he could not even afford a sandwich in the dining car.[47] Yet the romantic interlude, while short, was sweet, coming as it did at the end of an unpleasant, nearly disastrous interruption—neither combat aviation nor discharge but the kind of meaningless holding pattern on life's way that Hill abhorred.

Back in Dayton, Hall promised Hill that he would get him an army commission so that he could go to France and fly combat aircraft. However, there is no evidence that he gave the matter the slightest attention. He needed Hill and used him. Hill had clearance for virtually all the war plants. He visited the Standard Aircraft Plant in Elizabeth, New Jersey; the Ford Liberty Engine Plant; the Fisher Body plant that was making DH-4 wings and fuselages; and spent some considerable time at Hall's request at the Curtiss Airplane and Motor plant in Buffalo, where for the first time a U.S. manufacturer was attempting to build a war plane. The first combat craft built there were English-designed Bristol fighters, which were to be fitted with the Liberty engine, though that power plant was much too heavy and powerful for them. Later Curtiss manufactured the British SE-5.[48]

Glen Curtiss was an aviation pioneer for certain, and his company was an American original. The Buffalo plant, an offshoot of the main Curtiss plant at Hammondsport, New York, originated in 1914 because, as a Curtiss biographer puts it, the thirty-five-year-old aviator "chanced to be operating the only manufactory on the American continent which was geared to produce airplanes on a quantity basis at short notice." He had the largest and most competent corps of aeronautical engineers and mechanics to be found at any one spot in the Western Hemisphere, and was on the leading edge of experimental design as well as quantity production. In 1915 rented quarters in Buffalo were supplemented by a large factory structure of 120,000 square feet, "absolutely free of pillars or obstructions," and erected in thirty days. Wall Street money came into the company, and its capital stock went to $9 million. In 1917, when the United States entered the war, there was a further expansion of Curtiss at Buffalo, with the new $4 million North Elmwood plant covering 72 acres. Curtiss military orders stood at $150 million. It was a heady time for Hill to be there.[49]

Curtiss Aeroplane Co. Fuselage test from World War I.

Hill had a central role in all these activities and spent time in Washington as well during that very hot war summer of 1918 working on a spare parts inventory for the DH-4.[50] It was near hyperactivity, and if it was not what Hill really wanted to do, it was close.

Every day was an adventure of a kind. On May 9 the first Bristols came to Dayton from Buffalo—"they were awful heaps," Hill recorded. Jimmy Doolittle took one up, the fabric tore, and he hit some power lines coming down. The accident totally wrecked the machine, though the to-be-famous pilot was saved for a great role in another war.[51]

Hill got the job of fixing the Bristol "to make a good job to be used as sample for production machine." Tearing the airplane completely to pieces with the crew under his charge, he changed the radiator, the cowling design, the controls, the fuselage, the wings, "and nearly all details of construction." So satisfactory were his suggestions that in mid-May he was sent to Buffalo to superintend construction of the modified Bristol at the Curtiss plant. While there, he organized the plant in such a way that it became capable of turning out twenty completed machines a day, a not inconsiderable achievement for the times. Harold Crow got a similar assignment at Elizabeth, where the Standard Aircraft Plant was making DH-4s.[52]

Since the war was over by November, this American production was too late to have an impact on the conflict, but not too late to provide valuable training for Hill in aircraft design and the management of production and spare parts for aircraft that were intended to be produced in volume and flown and maintained by relatively inexperienced people. In the bargain he got a bad taste of working for other people, and particularly of government operations and government employment. It was to be nearly ten years before Hill made full use of those experiences, but they would be central to his career and way of thinking in time.

Hill was always somewhat embarrassed about his war service. "I felt pretty gloomy," he wrote later, "after having enlisted at the beginning of the war and ending up as a civilian without ever having an opportunity to have a chance to wear an officer's uniform."[53] He saw some aerial action, including the deaths of at least three test pilots killed in testing the old Bristols and observed the severe injuries of several others. One of the pilots told Hill how his accident happened even as he died. But it was not real war. In July 1918, Hill wrote a caustic and lengthy account about how the government should run production—anything but the way it was actually being run. In August, sweltering in Washington under the command of an "old woman," he railed at the bureaucracy: "Everybody here is asleep—the hours are 9 to 12 and 2 to 4 . . . . Sure costs a lot to live in this burg."[54]

One last try that fall at getting a combat commission while Hall was away failed. Hill's war ended on his standard north-central interfactory commute, often walking miles in a cold wintry Buffalo closed down with the flu epidemic and where all the movies and saloons, even the streetcar lines, shut down.[55] It was not his California youth at all, and, on the whole, he was not sorry to see it end.

The Salesman

*T*he first project Hill undertook after the war was working on a car engine. It was something he gravitated to at points of redefinition and maybe slight stress. He revisited his past too, going through Chicago and taking the elevated to Rogers Park and Evanston, as though reexamining and reassessing his life so far. After a leisurely visit with relatives in Sioux City, he finished a two-week trip home by entering San Francisco on the *Overland Limited* exactly at the end of the year 1918.[1]

His first instinct was to reestablish himself in an engineering job at one of the local manufacturing firms, living with his parents in the meantime to save money.

The return to the Hicks Iron Works was a great disappointment. Demarest, the new manager, told Leroy that Hicks and his sons were completely out of the business, that it was in financial trouble, and that there was no opening for him. Hill's own comment in his diary was: "Place is highly disorganized." Shortly, the Hicks company, for which Hill had such high hopes as a potential owner before his entry into the service, went completely out of business.[2] Hall-Scott was no more promising, though Hill's friend Hall did speak to him at the Hotel Oakland about perhaps putting Crow and him to work at an eastern firm he knew of laying out truck engines—a proposal without much appeal to Hill.

Hill searched for the right job for three months. He visited Standard Engine Works and studied its catalog and atlas. He toured Skandia Engine Works, Liberty Iron Works, and Enterprise Foundry with his resume. He went with a friend to Los Angeles, where he visited Harry Miller's shop and watched Miller and his assistant Offenhauser working on the automobile racing engines that were about to become famous at the Indianapolis Speedway. He revisited Hicks, at one point agreeing to start work the next Monday. However, when the manager who hired him changed his mind and asked for more delay, Hill quit talking to the Hicks organization completely.[3]

Typically, Hill was not simply job hunting. His entrepreneurial bent was strong enough that he was a hard negotiator on terms for working for someone else, and he was always thinking of what he might be able to do as his own boss in his own business. Harold Crow had returned with him to California, and he and Hill began working on a design for a marine engine—clearly an attempt to proceed from scratch to get into the business that Hicks, with its poor management, was abandoning.

Hill's prospectus, typed up at 1:00 a.m. on the morning of February 13 in his father's San Francisco office, was a request for financial backing.[4] It contained a complete report on the demand for marine engines on the Pacific Coast, including the value of the catch and the number of boats used. It surveyed the competition, concluding that their engines were unnecessarily complex and expensive and were offered in too many sizes instead of a few in quality. The management of the new engine concern was to be Hill as factory manager and shop superintendent, Glover Ruckstell as general manager, and Harold Crow as chief engineer. All had been in the Production Department of the Bureau of Aircraft Production in the war. Arrangements had been made to use the Liberty Iron Works shop for production. Hill created a careful pro forma of costs and potential profits and sent his requirement for $15,000 in working capital to several banks. He got no positive responses. Having finished overhauling his father's Dodge, he read Meredith's *Richard Carvel*, met Bee Warning ("a beautiful woman") at fisherman's wharf, and watched for the next chance.[5]

Late in March, running near the end of their self-respect, both Crow and Hill took jobs that were far from their ideal. Crow went to work for the Fageol Motor Truck Company in Cleveland, Ohio, and Hill started as chief engineer and general manager at the Hewitt-Ludlow Motor

Truck Company in San Francisco. Hewitt-Ludlow assembled a truck chassis using parts purchased elsewhere. Hill's responsibility was to supervise the assembly and road testing.[6]

That job lasted less than a month. Before his first week was out, Hill wrote: "I am getting disgusted with the place as old man Hewitt can't decide anything & won't let anyone else. He changes the trucks every day." The next day he recorded his decision to quit "in a week or so." On April 19 he did quit, effective the next week.[7] It was quite clearly a personal falling out with Hewitt. The backers of the Hewitt company, Rawlston Iron Works, spoke with Hill about coming back. By the time they did, however, Hill had moved on to a job as sale engineer for the A. H. Coates Company, the western representative for many of the parts used by small truck manufacturers like Hewitt. "Mr. Coates didn't know anything about engineering," Hill commented, "but he needed a good engineer to sell the stuff and I guess I was fairly successful at it."[8]

There was a month between Hill's hasty departure from Hewitt-Ludlow and his starting date at Coates. During that time, in addition to overhauling Fred Mulvantz's Saxon car, he did a consulting job for the Johnson Gear Company. There was a noise in the Doane truck differential, and Hill was to investigate it and recommend a fix. He was so successful in tracing the noise to out-of-tolerance parts manufactured by Johnson itself that his report ended any hope he had of becoming a permanent employee there. He collected his $50 for the report and moved on.[9]

The A. H. Coates Company was a happier experience. "Will like job," Hill wrote on his first day, "—lots of variety + will travel around outside a good deal."[10] Coates handled "some wonderful lines" and, being a pioneer sales representative on the West Coast, was usually able to get all the territory west of Denver—"many eastern manufacturers did not realize how big the West was." The Coates company was able to collect commissions on shipments into territory and to customers that no Coates person had even seen: it was like manna from heaven. Hill specialized in Timpken axles, Buda engines, Spicer Universal joints,

Brown-Lipe transmissions, Sheldon axles, Ross steering gears, and Morse roller chain and sprockets.[11] He delighted in understanding all about the qualities of these products and, like any good salesman, was such a true believer that he was sure he was doing customers a favor by selling parts to them.

Adding to the enjoyment was an active social life. Forty years later Hill could remember the names of most of the girls he dated—"I danced with them all." Food was cheap, there was good dance music in San Francisco, and "no one had ever heard of a cover charge." Hill recorded on June 25 that he had become engaged to "Irma" (probably Irma Benett). However, he got too busy filling the short diary spaces with his business ideas ever to explain how the relationship ended or why.[12]

Crow wanted to build a truck, and he and Hill worked on drawings on the weekends or evenings. However, the Coates work was teaching Hill both that he enjoyed sales and that there was money in it for a man who could explain the new technology that everyone seemed to need in language the buyers and users could understand. He became friendly with a Coates bookkeeper named Pete Adam, who had thoughts of going into the sales business on his own, and at the end of July the two started meeting regularly to plan a possible partnership.

Adam was quite a lot older than Hill and had a wife and two children. Hill had investigated selling Mosler spark plugs in the West and thought he could get a contract to do so. But Adam had a better connection. His brother-in-law was the manager of Baldwin Chain and Manufacturing Company in Worcester, Massachusetts, and wanted to establish distribution in the West. Adam was not prepared to quit Coates yet (and doubtless could not afford, with his family responsibility, to make precipitous moves), so he suggested that Hill quit and start the chain business. Adam would join him when the business got well established and he could make his peace with his employer.

In August Hill made up a letterhead for the Adam-Hill Company, sales representatives, and sent out sixty letters to different manufacturers offering to represent them. Even though the first group of answers were mostly turn-downs (Mosler plugs agreed to take them on), Hill quit at Coates on September 1 to start the company, and Adam joined him on the 15th.[13]

The Adam-Hill partnership gave Hill more authority and flexibility than he had ever had before, and he loved it. He hired a salesman to sell lamps for him, giving him 70 percent of the profits. He rented the basement of a cigar store building at 41 Market in San Francisco for $10 a month and began personally to do the heavy work of moving in the firm's main product, chain. Early in September he moved in and inventoried over seven tons of it. About the time that was done, the two businessmen received 1,000 spark plugs from Mosler on consignment.[14]

The company was successful. The sales were primarily in chain and sprockets for chain-driven trucks that used up these parts regularly on the San Francisco hills. However, Hill got the spark plugs adopted exclusively by the San Francisco Fire Department and typed out some letters every day to manufacturers to obtain new lines.[15] He added Detlaff transmissions, Dorman engines, Pierce governors, and Weidely motors. In October the two rented a store in San Francisco; Adam ran it, kept the books, and cultivated his network of contacts while Hill went out selling.

That fall, the partnership did well enough that Adam and Hill were able to pay themselves $300 a month each from clear profits.[16] In December they grossed $1,000 and netted $700, which gives some idea of the profit margin in the chain business. Early in 1920 they were receiving as many as sixty-four cases of chain a month by boat through the Panama Canal. Hill traveled to Seattle to sell to the Boeing Company there and expanded up and down the California coast. Hill's social life went up a step also. He bought a $65 suit and took Alice Clemo (Blue) to hear jazz in smart clubs. He seemed to fall in love, too, more often than usual.[17]

The partnership ended suddenly in April 1920, and, as before, the reasons were personal. Adam complained about the 50-50 split of the profits that had been the rule. The chain line, which had been obtained through his family contacts, was making most of the money, and, therefore, he thought he merited a larger cut. Hill calmly replied that Adam should go ahead and take two-thirds of the profit instead of one-half. But that night he wrote in his diary: "This shows him up as an ordinary piker. If an engine line showed 10 times the profit he would have hollered like hell if I had suggested taking 2/3. I will pull out as soon as possible."[18]

The opportunity to split came on June 1, with Hill taking the engineering lines and Adam the chain and spark plugs. "He sure is a welcher," Hill commented then. "It hurts him for me to have any lines." Hill had a new letterhead printed: "F. Leroy Hill—Sales and Engineering Representative," and at the beginning of July, just prior to his twenty-sixth birthday, he walked away from a most promising business.[19]

Hill always was on the lookout for engineering consulting jobs to supplement his sales income. In 1920 he designed a two-ton truck for the Goldman Automobile Company and worked on a design for an automobile, to be called the Heine-Velox, on an empty floor at the Heine Piano Company. Hill was proud of the chassis of the car "because its lines were far ahead of the time," and he got an order from Heine for twelve Weidely engines for the car. It was largely income from the Heine account that allowed Hill in August 1920 to take delivery on a Ford Model T coupe. His only transportation prior to this had been his father's Dodge, so that purchase was a liberating one.[20]

One day While Hill was working on his car drawings at the piano warehouse, in walked one of the most extraordinary and frustrating individuals he was to know in his entire life—Victor Lougheed (born Loughead). His visit was to sell steel disk automobile wheels, which he had designed. Hill recognized the name and asked Lougheed if he were the man who had written *Vehicles of the Air*. He was and seemed flattered that the young man should be familiar with his book. He told Hill that his name was pronounced "Lock-heed" but that people called him "Loghead" and "Luffhead."[21]

Lougheed was a great talker (and, as Hill later discovered, a consummate con man too), well educated and well read, and had endless engineering ideas that indicated genius. Right at the time he met Hill, for instance, he was installing hydraulic disc brakes of his own invention on his Premier automobile. His two half-brothers, Alan and Malcolm, had picked up on implementing Victor's book by building airplanes in Santa Barbara. This eventually led to Alan's founding the famous aircraft firm of Lockheed.

Hill was fascinated by Lougheed and became even more interested when introduced to his attractive wife Mary. Victor was about forty-five years old; Mary was twenty. Even Victor's mother, whom Leroy met in Los Angeles shortly, was a brilliant woman who could talk on engineering subjects with her boys. Sometime before his final split with Pete Adam, Hill rented a room on O'Farrell Street in San Francisco and began to see much of the couple, staying often two or three nights a week at their apartment and accompanying them on many social outings.[22]

Unquestionably one of the things the two men had in common was a vision of the future of the aircraft industry. Lougheed was never able to play a significant role in the Lockheed Company, perhaps because he hardly promoted a conservative business image personally, but in his *Vehicles of the Air* (1909) one gets a sample of what his early talks with Hill may have been like. In that book, Lougheed quoted these lines from Alfred Lord Tennyson's 1842 prophetic poem "Locksley Hall": "the heavens fill with commerce, argosies of magic sails, / Pilots of the purpose twilight, dropping down with costly bales."[23] This was an indication that he understood the romance as well as the mechanics of the new industry. Robert Wohl's *A Passion for Wings* documents the force of that vision in American culture. It was a "complex of emotions," Wohl states, as flights had been long dreamed about and "enshrined in fable and myth." As a cultural historian, Wohl was intrigued especially by "the compulsion that people felt to transform through the play of their imagination, the most mechanical of events—the invention and development of the flying machine—into a form of spiritualization."[24] It was just that combination of the shop and the romance that would have appealed to Hill—the reader, the diarist, the inventor, and the mechanic. To have something to do with making or selling a product so tinged with the romance of opportunity, so pregnant with possibilities for changing the world, was a heady thing.

Vehicles of the Air had said it all at the outset of the aviation age. A thick book containing literally everything that was known about aircraft in 1909, from construction to maintenance to takeoff and landing techniques, it was also a prophecy and a justification that was pure Lougheed. "Nothing but the utmost blindness to existing achievements can continue to belittle what it cannot comprehend," Lougheed wrote. "Aerial navigation today is no more a joke that was the railway eighty years ago . . . or the automobile ten years ago. On the contrary, it is already the basis of a vast and progressing industry, founding itself surely on the most advanced discoveries of exact science and the finest deductions of trained minds, and possessed of a future that in its sociological as well as in its engineering aspects sooner or later must stir the imagination of the dullest skeptics." There was resistance, he admitted, but "a gradual overcoming of the inertia of the mind appears to be an essential process in reconciling the generality of people to innovations."[25]

As a salesman, Lougheed was excellent at overcoming inertia, as Hill learned. In their earliest conversations Hill was sold on aviation, and though he never had an aviation project with Lougheed, he pondered the field from that time forward. Undoubtedly his interest in going into business with Lougheed made the separation from both Adam and his parents' immediate sphere easier. "Have been getting a real education from Lougheed," Hill wrote Harold Crow. "He certainly has a vast fund of information." In September he wrote again: "Have been spending a lot of time fooling around with the Lougheeds. Mary sends her best regards." To that Mary added a note: "Don't you think I am a swell stenog. Did this with my own hands. Guess you will see my Lord and Master soon."[26] (Victor was absent on a trip east.) It was to be a bittersweet but strong three-way relationship.

Lougheed was no respecter of traditional morality, and his penchant for young girls, sometimes using Leroy as bait, made life with this "thoroughly modern" couple a constant adventure. He was later imprisoned for a time for rape, all the while continuing correspondence with his wife and Leroy about the business.[27]

Although Hill's sexual vigor did not extend to such extremes, he did have another thing in common with Lougheed: a tendency toward decisive stubbornness and a willingness to create a scene, even a physical fight, over an issue. One night when Victor, one of his young girls, and Leroy were at the Bluebird Cafe in Los Angeles, the girl discovered a cockroach in her parfait glass. Victor shouted for the manager, stopped the music, and yelled to all the other customers what had happened. He described the cockroach-infested kitchen in gruesome detail. The girl nearly fainted with embarrassment, but Lougheed loved it. Hill ushered the young woman outside. When he returned, he found Victor backing toward the door pursued by a crowd of waiters ready to attack him with bottles and knives. They escaped with the help of Hill's expert wielding of a chair.[28]

Hill's similar style is illustrated by an auto accident he had at Gonzales, California, in August 1920. He was heading for Los Angeles on a sales call in his Ford. About 6:30 in the morning, after an all-night drive, he saw two cars on the road ahead of him and realized too late they were not moving. The drivers had stopped to look at a wrecked freight train, and Hill slammed into both cars, damaging his car severely and the others slightly. One of the drivers offered to pay for some of the damage, but the other demanded that Hill pay for the damage to his car.[29] That man, E. C. Bell, was an agent for the Southern Pacific Railroad and sent Hill a bill for $28.25 for repairs.

Hill's reply was strong: "I am returning these bills to you as I have no intention whatever of paying them for you." He denied that the accident was his fault and recommended that Bell, before taking further action, "obtain a copy of the Motor Vehicle Act and peruse it carefully, particularly that portion which refers to parking cars in the State Highway." If he heard from Bell again, he wrote, he would sue him for $62 damages to his own Model T.[30] Early in 1921 Hill received ever nastier letters from both Bell and the California State Automobile Association. He replied in kind, never admitting that he might have been drowsy or that there was any shared fault, and calling his opponent "belligerent."[31] About that same time he recorded in his diary: "had fight with Key Route Conductor at end of pier—3 others jumped me & spoiled it, but honors were mine.[32] Victor Lougheed no doubt approved.

Hill was, according to his own later claim, not a heavy drinker, but he was a regular drinker, right straight through prohibition, as was Lougheed. It was easy to get wine in San Francisco: the Italians there all had sources, and at Saturday afternoon poker games at the Adam-Hill company, the sales representative would bring in large bottles of vanilla, lemon, and other extracts that were mixed into cocktails. This type of session continued with Lougheed, and sometimes the excited talk was of engineering matters. When there was a question, Lougheed could call out the page number and volume number of the *Encyclopedia Britannica* from memory to prove his point. He would speak fluently in the most elegant English and then suddenly descend into gutter profanity. "He was a cheat," Hill remembered, "and thought nothing of passing bad checks or using his wonderful persuasive ability to victimize some innocent person," all the while preaching the most idealistic socialistic philosophy. The perfect model of the dissolute, unstable genius and a veritable outlaw in his own family, Victor Lougheed thrived on the attention from his new young partner, and the two remained friends to the time of Lougheed's death from a heart attack while driving his car in the early 1940s.[33]

Hill and Lougheed's first project together was the Duo-Disc Steel Wheel Company. Lougheed had developed an attractive-appearing steel wheel for the Model T to replace the plain spoked wooden wheels which came on the car. They were anodized in various bright colors and gave the utilitarian vehicle some real style. The problem was that they were not engineered very well and had a tendency to bend with the slightest jolt or bump on the curb. Hill discovered this quickly enough, both through experience and analysis, and advised Lougheed to redesign the

Test of Duo-Disc steel wheels. Contrast with the normal Model T Wheels on the front.

product before getting too far along with sales. It was, of course, not Lougheed's character to do so. He ordered all the machine tools for manufacturing while he kept on selling. Hill said he had a "hypnotic power" with customers, and apparently with associates also. "Am just scraping along, making enough money to eat on," Hill wrote in September 1920, "but I have large hopes."[34]

As an intellectual and social partner, Lougheed was great, but as a co-worker he was unreliable. Hill therefore worked hard to get Crow to quit Fageol Motors and return to California to join Hill in selling the disc wheels and other lines. Crow had a tremendous knowledge of manufacturers. In letters to Hill he would outline dozens of them and evaluate the strengths and weaknesses of their products and personnel. "If we could get a bunch of lines like [these] . . . ," he wrote once, "our combined resources ought to knock 'em stiff and we should be able to damn near corral the new business on the coast."[35]

Hill encouraged these upbeat thoughts: "Casting friendship aside for the moment and looking at the thing in a cold-blooded business manner, I assure you that the idea of combining forces with you appeals to me as an advantageous and profitable arrangement and not in the least one-sided. The income which I derive from my present accounts is nothing very stunning but if these lines were worked properly there will be a considerable income in the future. The fact is that one man's efforts are too scattered in getting started, to attend to correspondence, follow-up, etc. to chase new business in the right way. Every time I go on a trip, everything comes to a standstill in the home office . . . . Also being alone necessitates a heart-breaking attention to business which you as well as I are temperamentally unfitted to withstand."[36]

He painted an especially rosy picture to Crow of the Duo-Disc business. "These things are easy to sell," he said. Victor had sold 68 sets in two days in a trip down the valley, not touching Los Angeles or San Francisco. Hill estimated commissions in the next year would be about $10,000, and "I have only taken account of the business that we could hardly help falling into." Besides, "its nice & sunny & warm out here—not too cold and not too hot—makes you feel fine." He went so far as to promise to stop smoking, at least until Crow got there.[37]

In the spring of 1921 Crow came, and the two formed the Motive Products Company, a corporation, to handle their joint sales interests.[38] His arrival relieved Hill from a long spell of poker playing, drinking, and the blues ("I feel all in," he wrote in February—"feel rotten" in March). Both men were at that time completely broke, but Crow had made connections all the way across the country on his trip. The day he arrived, Hill was back in a confident mood, predicting "we will make lots of money this year." Between them they put together $100 for an office and furniture in the Atlas Building, at $20 a month rent, and bought a typewriter. Hill moved to the Congress Hotel, doubtless not an elegant address, and shortly to the YMCA clubhouse. He recorded: "We will have to be awfully economical for a while."[39]

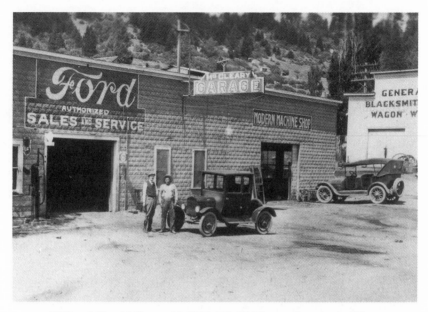

Hill and Harold Crow with Hill's Model T somewhere in the West
on their 1921 cross-country journey.

They got right to work. In mid-April Hill installed Duo-Disc wheels, painted light blue, on his own car and then did a second set of wheels "all nickeled and enameled dark blue . . . . They look very snappy." He employed some artists to come up with designs in different colors, grey and yellow first. Later he put maroon ones on his car. On his very first sales call at Burbank, and with his car as an example, he sold twelve sets to the dealer. Lougheed sold 200 sets on a single swing.[40]

The euphoria of these sales deteriorated when the dealers took delivery on the wheels, sold them, and then began fielding complaints about their fragility. The small factory in Los Angeles got a flood of returns and soon lost all credibility in the local market. Lougheed suggested the whole thing be transferred to a machine shop called the Universal Engineering Company in Maywood, Illinois (near Chicago). This shop was run by his friend Ray Acre. Lougheed's financial backers were disgusted "as he had been milking them for money right along," and one of them proposed that Hill and Crow go to Maywood to supervise the production of a reinforced wheel. It was with that destination that on September 9, 1921, Crow and Hill started east from San Francisco in Hill's Model T, complete with Duo-Disc wheels, on what became an epic journey.[41]

Although far from unprecedented, such a trip in such a vehicle at such a time was more than slightly adventurous. People who did it were prone to write about it, as did Henry Birdsall and Claude Blick, who kept a journal of their 1920 trip from Jackson, Michigan, to Sheridan, Wyoming, in a 1913 touring car modified into a speedster using cedar strips. Birdsall and Blick drove 1,400 miles, spent $36 for 87 gallons of gas and 32 quarts of oil, and took along a rifle and a revolver just in case. In the pre–Lincoln Highway days "most intercity roads, many mere trails out West, were quagmires after rains, dustladen when dry, and heavily rutted from car and wagon wheels." Travelers could take along maps provided by gasoline companies, but had to rely heavily on route advice solicited along the way.[42]

The Model T, while simple, was not durable or maintenance free in the sense a modern car usually is. It was assumed the owner should and would do considerable maintenance, and the owner's manual included instructions on pulling the engine with a stout rope, taking off the head, scraping the carbon from the top of the cylinders with a putty knife, and adjusting the valves, using a dime to measure the gap. The unique magneto electric system, the timer, and the planetary gear system were all simple enough for an individual to repair and complex enough to make it a rewarding challenge.

Even on the level of everyday driving events there was much operator involvement. There was a hand throttle and spark advance, which had infinite combinations of adjustments for various driving conditions, a three-gallon radiator operating at near boiling all the time on a Thermo-Syphon system without benefit of a water pump. Not only were there no "idiot lights" to monitor these systems, but the gas gauge was a graduated stick to keep track of the ten-gallon tank. Everyday things, like starting the car with a crank and avoiding a broken arm from improper spark advance, or repairing tires with a considerable package of irons, patches, and casing sleeves, involved as much art as science. The "splash" oil system had no circulating pump, and the level could be checked only with petcocks beneath the transmission housing. A new car used a quart of oil every 100 miles, older ones more—a considerable inconvenience on a long trip with few service stops. There was no heater, and even the common modification of diverting air from the exhaust manifold through the floorboards only warmed the T a little.

Every car had its eccentricities, and owners had various custom modifications to handle them. "Even if the motorist does not intend to repair his own car," advised a 1926 Model T manual, "he should be able to care for it intelligently and to locate the various troubles that are apt to materialize while the car is in operation. An engine stop on a lonely road will be a serious matter to one who does not understand the principles of action of the power plant, but only an incident to one who does."[43]

Hill was an engineer, so these things were doubtless more rewarding than frightening. Getting it all perfectly adjusted was doubtless thrilling. But the conditions were still the same conditions, and they could be tiresome on a cross-country trek. His diary was wordier than usual on the trip and some words he would have probably liked to have used were not written down.

"All roads are terrible," Hill wrote in his diary on September 11 after a miserable night in Winnemucca, Nevada. They had a 150-mile detour at one point, pushed the Ford at several points, bent their fancy wheels in every direction possible, and made most of the repairs in the Ford shop manual. "Frightful road," he wrote one day, "—Ford wouldn't climb one grade & we had to push." And the next day: "Ford making terrible noises." Two days later: "Spent day bumming & helping incompetent garage . . . to fix Ford. The universal joint was all chewed to hell. Shot pool to-night." Three days later the Ford was in the shop again while its drivers toured the temple in Salt Lake City. It overheated badly in a snowstorm outside Rawlins, Wyoming, but the two sold the Ford dealer there some wheels. On October 3 in Nebraska "Harold and I took Ford apart & scraped out carbon." About that time they finally hit a concrete highway and headed for Chicago. "Both rear wheels bent so badly that we couldn't sell to Ford dealers."[44] The pair spent from September 8 to October 14 driving their Model T on a journey they could have made by train in two days. The only positive thing about it was that in some little towns in Nebraska they had never heard of Duo-Disc wheels and thought they sounded great.[45]

The first thing Hill did when he got to Chicago was to visit the famous John Crerar Scientific Library. He then proceeded to go to work on new 18-gauge wheels that just might be strong enough to use. He lived cheaply and sent his parents money, but didn't care for the atmosphere: "Maywood is awful. Lucky it's near to Chicago. Only place to eat here—known as 'The Swede's'—dirty and expensive."[46]

Things went from bad to worse. Hill worked at the plant on weekends and evenings for lack of anything better to do, and said he was getting "chronically grouchy & irritable" due to the frustrations of the job. "Victor continuing petty grafting as usual," he observed. If it had not been for Victor, Hill thought the wheel would have possibilities. But as it was, it was a day-to-day struggle. He paid the last of the December payroll from his own money and had Christmas dinner in a cafeteria under bleak mid-winter skies.[47]

In January 1922, after getting the new wheel into production and after a fight with Victor over how a $1,000 capital input from California was to be used, Hill left the Duo-Disc Company. Malcolm and Victor Lougheed were even then starting a new company, the Four Wheel Hydraulic Brake Company, but Hill had resolved never again to go in on anything with Victor.[48]

As had been a pattern with him, however, Hill did not move on without some bridge from the job he had just held. His connection with the Lougheed family was to serve him well in later years in the aviation business. And he had become friends in Maywood with Ray Acre, who had promoted a new company in Grafton, Wisconsin, to manufacture portable electrical plants for farms. It was called the Lincoln Light Company.

Acre was persuasive. Universal Engineering had tried an electric light plant that had failed, and that was one of the reasons it ended up dealing with Victor Lougheed. Acre was certain, however, that he had it right this time, and showed Hill a demonstration unit fixed up in a glass case behind his car. Hill was already in the area, he and Crow were again near broke, and opportunity beckoned. Therefore the Hill/Crow duo decided to research the product and the market and to become salesmen for Lincoln Light.[49]

Understandably large territories were easily available to those willing to participate in this work. They stopped in Detroit where Hill spent several days in the library "collecting a lot of statistics re the lighting plant sales game." Then, after an icy trip to Grafton, the two became distributors for the states of Iowa, Nebraska, Kansas, and Missouri, with headquarters in Omaha. Hill built a cabinet on the back of his Ford, put a storage battery on the running board, and fixed up a reel with a long electric cord so that a light bulb could be taken into a farmhouse to show the wonders of electricity. Whether he continued using Duo-Disc wheels is not recorded.[50]

Their drive to Omaha with this rig was a disappointment. It was the center of the early 1920s agricultural depression, and in many places there were too many high lines to be prime light plant territory. The two plants they did sell were so defective that the customers refused to pay for them, and Hill soon had to return to Grafton and to Maywood (it turned out some of the parts were made at the Universal Engineering Company) to try to solve another set of manufacturing problems before he could make sales.[51]

There were personal problems, too. The head on the Ford had cracked at Grafton after abandoning it overnight in the ice, and on the way west the crankshaft broke. The shop "soaked" them, but Hill paid with a check he later stopped. On arriving at their headquarters in a hotel at Omaha in April, they were again out of funds altogether and elected not to establish their showroom and office right away. Hill had to wire his mother for a $50 loan so that the salesmen could even get out of town on some calls.[52]

The next month or so was a nightmare. The April 23 diary entry reads: "Clarinda, Red Cloud not a thing to do." The rear spring on the Ford broke, leading Hill and Crow no doubt to ruminate about the myth of that simple car's reliability. Often Hill and Crow were literally stuck in small towns for days at a time due to mud, and they stayed at potential customers' houses to save money. "Get terrible lonesome in Omaha," Hill wrote in June. "No money so can't get women. Walked around street till midnight." About the same time: "Nearly went crazy with nothing to do. Hot as blazes."[53] It was a far cry from the lush California days with Adam-Hill.

Hill's situation in the summer of 1922 was a near dead end. Sales were poor and the product was worse. Life was unpleasant and conditions grim. So in mid-June he returned to the factory at Grafton, leaving Crow in the field to handle any rush of orders. There and at Maywood, he worked on the manufacturing problems and drove Acre's Hupmobile around to see the company backers. These asked him to take a job as factory manager at $25 a week and some stock in the company. Being broke, he accepted. He had a date, the first one in a long time, with a long-distance operator. "Very passionate little girl but bum looking & a darn fool."[54]

Since things were at a desperate pass, Hill applied himself earnestly to this new chance. He ordered a Lincoln Light electric sign sent to Harold for their office in Omaha and then put in ten-hour regular days at the manufacturing facility (the workers were there from 7:00 a.m. to 6:00 p.m.) plus every night until 11:00 p.m. or midnight.[55] He not only did much manual labor, but personally was the area service representative for Lincoln Light, making trips through Indiana and Illinois trying to repair light plants owned by disgruntled farmers.[56]

It was to no avail. Although Crow returned east also to try to save the company, its creditors shortly took it over, and it was shut down, leaving the two out of even the tenuous job they had. They worked for a time again for Universal Engineering, but, as Crow commented, that was "out of the frying pan and into the fire."[57]

Hill again tried to make something out of the ruins. In one corner of the abandoned Universal Engineering machine shop, Ed Andrews, son of one of the wealthy backers of the Universal company, had set up a little office to market several devices he had developed for the growing market in amateur radio sets. He had a loop aerial and a gadget called a "Tiny Turn" to help with fine adjustment on the dial. He called the company Radio Units, Inc., and was selling enough by mail order to offer Hill and Crow jobs. Ironically, Andrews was an outspoken communist, and Hill doubted that his enterprise would last long. He noted laconically, though: "We did get eating money from him."[58] His surviving correspondence file from this period, in contrast to the full folders for other eras, consists mostly of resumes, which he was circulating in hope of a better job.

Such a low time seems an odd one for getting married, but that is what Hill did. He had been isolated from his slick dates in California, had energy to burn, which was not well applied to meaningful business projects, and no doubt needed the confidence that an affectionate companion could give. Since his marriage to Melba Mayer of Grafton was both short and often unhappy, and since what can be known about it is filtered through sometimes bitter contemporary and later recollections by both partners, it is difficult to imagine accurately the atmosphere when they first met. But some good guesses can be made.

For one thing, Melba was physically attractive. In 1935, when the two were only in occasional correspondence, she sent Leroy a black and white snapshot of herself sitting on the porch with her mother (after the divorce, she had moved back to her home in Wisconsin to save money). The woman in the saddle shoes that looks back is strikingly good-looking with straight black hair, smooth skin, and a body only tending a little, in a voluptuous way, toward avoirdupois. She was sending the photo, Melba wrote, "so you can tell I'm not beginning to show my age as you probably hope—and I hope you are very unhappy because I certainly am."[59] She was, at the time of their meeting and quick marriage, very young—barely sixteen, while Leroy was twenty-nine. That, too, became a sore spot with her in later years. In the Depression she would write Leroy, by then an aviation firm executive, asking for money and would sometimes get in a dig. "Have a good time with all your girl friends," she once wrote, "but have a heart next time and don't pick on any 16 years old."[60]

But for all the recrimination, another thing that is certain was that there was initially some magic and considerable adventure in the relationship. Their romance peaked in December of 1923, when Leroy sneaked away to see Melba at her married sister's house in Milwaukee. There they arranged to meet in Chicago a few days later, on December 31, and get married. Hill was close to broke but borrowed $50 from Ray Acre, who also arranged a justice of the peace, all the while advising against the whole thing. Another $20 went for a diamond ring, and the rest for a three-day honeymoon at the Atlantic Hotel in the Chicago loop.

Melba's side of the later correspondence indicates that she stayed in on New Year's Eve for years afterward and was nostalgic and sentimental about their wedding on that day. "My! My!" she wrote Leroy in 1934, "I bet you chew nails before you write to me—or else you have eaten a lot of things you shouldn't have . . . . Did you realize it was almost 10 years ago last N.Y.'s Eve?"[61] She sent Leroy a valentine every year until at least 1940, and he sent her a Christmas gift, usually clothes or accessories of the type she had when they were well off in the late 1920s. Hill was not inexperienced with women and had never found it necessary to get married before. "I guess if she had been 18 or 20 or so," he wrote years later, "we would have gotten together and had it over with. But as it was I kept my distance and confined myself to simple admiration which was no doubt flattering to her."[62] There was something, and the memory of something, special.

Reality set in quickly in 1924. The couple moved into housekeeping rooms on the second floor of a private home in Oak Park, Illinois on "a very small and unpretentious road." He had to use his Ford to get to work, leaving Melba more or less stranded for lack of car fare. Shortly

On left is Hill's first wife Melba. She sent him this photograph some
years after their divorce to demonstrate she was still attractive.

they moved to Maywood near the factory, but, wrote Hill, "the poor little girl must have been disappointed and miserable at the outcome of the great adventure." Melba's older sister was sympathetic, but her parents were outraged. The family forced a remarriage in a church on March 12, 1924, and shortly after that Melba discovered she was pregnant—"a frightening surprise." Hill's pay at Radio Units was about $40 a week, and he often had trouble cashing his checks because the company's account was overdrawn. When they held about $700 in due paychecks, both Crow and Hill quit Radio Units. By summer Melba was hunting a job, Leroy was sending to radio companies a prospectus he had written for manufacturing an improved antenna, and things were "getting hungry and desperate." In August there was a breakthrough. Two companies accepted Hill and Crow's proposition on the same day: the White Cross Electric Company and the Bodine Electric Company. They elected to go with Bodine.[63]

Bodine Electric, founded in 1905 by Swedish brothers, specialized in the manufacture of small fractional-horsepower DC motors (the Model "D" was its best seller), shortly adding AC motors and complete machines using these. Small motors were difficult to manufacture well, and Bodine was able to establish a niche reputation for a quality product. Expansion during World War I was rapid, as demand for everything electric increased. The factory to which Crow and Hill reported, at 2254 W. Ohio Street, Chicago, just across from the Mitchell School, had been built in 1914 just in time for the war boom and the demand for motion picture projector and washing machine motors. The twenties were a time of diversification and expansion.[64]

Central to the planning for that diversification was Leroy Hill. The official company history notes that Hill, "momentarily nonplussed, but not disillusioned" about the failure of the company formerly manufacturing his device, was that September "a persuasive-talking young man with an odd-looking gadget which he called a folding loop aerial under his arm and a detailed prospectus and cash forecast of its sales potential." Ads in ham radio magazines produced good orders. In December 1924,

Applications for Bodine Types "SA" and "SD" Motors

The number of applications for these motors is almost unlimited. It has been the constant aim of the Bodine Electric Company to perfect this line of fractional horsepower motors for applications requiring a high-grade motor that is electrically and mechanically correct and so well proportioned and finished that it will improve the appearance of the installation. Bodine motors offer these advantages to manufacturers of motor-driven machines, and new applications are constantly being made.

Trahern pump operated with Bodine Type SA Motor

Household machines, office equipment, small pumps, valve control devices, twine-tying machines, therapeutic machines, traffic-control signals, and hundreds of other devices are now Bodine-equipped to the entire satisfaction of

the manufacturers of such motor-driven machines and their customers. The quick interchangeability of the two types of motors appeals to the designer, and it enables a manufacturer to sell his motor-driven devices in any alternating or direct current market.

Inquiries are solicited from manufacturers interested in solving their motor problems. The experience of Bodine engineers is of inestimable value to motor users.

Bodine motors are guaranteed to be free from mechanical and electrical defects. The Bodine Electric Company will replace or repair, at its option, any motor which may prove defective within one year from date of its purchase, but will not be responsible for repairs made or attempted by others.

Bodine Motors are used on McIntosh Therapeutic Machines. Reliability is always essential for hospital equipment.

Ives and Stern Timer for heavy-duty traffic signal control, equipped with Bodine Type SD Motor.

Page from Bodine Electric catalog, January 1927.

less than three months after the launch of the aerial business, sales totaled more than $20,000, a larger number than the gross income from all the motor sales together. They dropped off radically as competitors entered the market, but it was a promising sign.[65]

According to the original deal, Hill and Crow were to get 50 percent of the profits from the loop aerial and a $60 a week drawing account against these profits. During the best antenna sales months, Melba and Leroy rented an apartment in Oak Park, bought a little furniture on an installment plan, got around on public transportation (Hill had to sell his Ford during the starving times), and greeted the arrival of their daughter Beverly in a fairly settled situation.[66] When Hill applied for a job at the *Chicago Tribune* in April 1925, he said he had a small child and expected a salary of $5,000.[67]

However, in the spring of 1925 an accounting showed that profits from the antenna were barely enough to cover Hill and Crow's drawing accounts. Crow resigned and went back to California, where he later worked for Caterpillar Tractor. Hill himself was "pretty disgusted" and interviewed with Acme Steel Company as well as the *Tribune* before deciding to stay with Bodine when he was offered a position managing the sale of their electric motors as well as the radio accessories. Under the new arrangement he got 5 percent of radio sales and had a company car during the day for sales calls. He raised the selling price of the aerials to cover the overhead better and designed a new deluxe model that sold for $12.50 retail. He did well with the electric motor sales, as he had studied electrical engineering in college. In addition, he designed new products (the most successful was a radial frequency coil called the Bodine Twin-8), all of which made him good money and kept him long hours at the office.[68]

Hill put one of the results bluntly in his "Recollections": "Things were getting quite unhappy in our new home." Melba often would leave to see her sister in Milwaukee or her parents in Grafton, and Leroy struggled with arranging child care. Soon he placed the infant in weekly care at a nursery in Evanston, where he visited her only on weekends.

Beverly Hill was to spend her entire young life "parked" in day care or at private schools and very few hours indeed with either of her parents. Near the end of 1926 the Hills decided they would have no more children and would eventually terminate their marriage. In mid-April 1927, when Leroy joined Ray Acre for a trip to California, Beverly and Melba moved in with a friend of Melba's, Melba took a job at Wiebolt Department Store, and there began a series of on-and-off separations.[69] The rising executive and the young girl with no higher education increasingly appeared a mismatch.

However sad his personal life may have been, the business thrived, and Hill with it. He became sales manager at Bodine, shaking up what had been a fairly conservative, specialized organization. He had been watching the competition between the talking machine and the radio receiver. KDKA in Pittsburgh started broadcasting in 1920, and in 1924 NBC started the first national broadcasts. Hill was one of the first to predict that the radio and phonographs would eventually be marketed in a combination set. He also thought that the electric motor would replace the hand-wound spring motor—an idea the Bodine brothers resisted. It took considerable urging by Hill to get them to build an improved turntable motor, but when they did so in 1927, sales were enormous. Hill was assigned the job of improving it, and the result was the RC-10, which appeared in 1928 and within a year was Bodine's top seller, almost 21 percent of the company's total motor sales.[70]

Hill rated his businesses in categories. A category 5 was one at which he profited between $10,000 and $100,000. Bodine Electric, where he worked from 1924 to 1928, was the first category 5 listed.[71] The extensive sales literature at Bodine gave Hill experience in cataloguing and inventorying as well as mail order, which was to place him in good stead later. And while there he improved on the experience with customers and troubleshooting that he had gotten with Duo-Disc and Lincoln Light.

In addition to marketing and putting into production the loop aerial and the radial frequency coil, Hill improved Bodine's line of motors to make them more competitive with those of General Electric, Westinghouse, and others. He designed and built the prototypes of the reduction gear motors that became the main product of the company and adapted them to driving phonograph turntables, which were at that time usually driven by hand-wound spring motors. He handled the sales correspondence, built up the manufacturer's agent organization, wrote copy for the house organ (called *Motorgram*), and developed a new advertising program.

He proved a good judge of talent, too. At a trade show at the Stevens Hotel in Chicago (now the Hilton), the manufacturers were having trouble converting the DC power supply to AC to run their new model radios. Several electrical manufacturers, including Bodine, provided DC/AC converters, but all of them made a terrible noise when running the AC radios. A young man, the assistant to the show manager, came over to Hill and said that he could eliminate the noise easily. Hill took him aside and invited him to the plant next day. The fellow worked on it for two or three days and produced a perfectly successful filter circuit, which Hill then installed in a portable unit and used it to get a substantial order immediately. The young man was twenty years old at the time and his name was Bill Lear. Hill and Lear became friends there and then, and some of the first of Lear's income was derived from royalties Hill arranged for him on the filter unit. Of course, he went on to develop the Lear business jet among many other products.[72]

On the negative side, Hill was more an entrepreneur than a manager. Bodine's early advantage in the radio business, for example, diminished when the company failed in the late 1920s to keep up with the changing technology. The Bodines, the company history records, were primarily motor men "and Hill had but an elementary understanding of the problems and technicalities. He might have kept abreast of developments had he been so inclined but increasingly became interested in motor application problems (by his own admission he was a better mechanical than electrical engineer)." He was, however, by all accounts an excellent sales manager. His "alert and vigorous mind" and engineering background made him good at understanding the power problems of customers and proposing motor solutions. He would design an application and then sell the company the equipment needed to implement it.[73]

There was also his powerful persona. A classic letter from Hill to his employers at Bodine survives from 1928. He and Bodine's Brooklyn representative, John Barker, called on a businessman named Webster Tallmadge, who had been complaining about his motor installation. "First," wrote Hill, "I want to say that Webster Tallmadge is the most disagreeable, overbearing, ignorant Boob that it has ever been my misfortune to meet." When Hill pointed out to him that he had ignored earlier recommendations about how to use his motors (he was running them at 6,000 rpm under almost no load and enclosed away from ventilation), it only made Tallmadge mad. The customer said that the motors should stand up under any conditions and he had no responsibility at all for their failing. Hill's conclusion was simple: "I do not think that it will pay to argue with Tallmadge about his faults any more than I have already done. I told him plenty and we had a hot and heavy argument from which I finally backed down as I saw that he would never give in, in any argument, whether right or wrong . . . . It looks to me as though we will have to play along with him for the sake of reputation."[74]

With the success of Bodine, Hill's personal finances improved apace. He had a spate of investment accounts with several brokers in New York and Chicago and bought stocks regularly in the late 1920s stock boom—Reo Motors, Radio Corporation, Chrysler.[75] In the spring of 1927 he bought a Model 60 special Chrysler coupe with a rumble seat. He and Acre actually bought it from a California dealer, but he took delivery on it in Detroit. Hill recalled it had four-wheel brakes and was "a real sporty car." Later that year an invoice went into the archives for a Hudson seal coat for Melba with ermine collar and cuffs—price: $500. Melba had charge accounts at all the large Chicago department stores.[76]

His marriage, however, continued to deteriorate. A friend of Melba's moved in with the couple at their furnished apartment on Diversey Parkway (they had "broken up housekeeping" and put their own furniture in storage against the inevitable in 1927), and there was a brief time when they were a "happy group," according to Hill's memory of it. One night the three were followed by two toughs who shouted abuse from their car. Hill invited them to pull their car over and get out. "I peeled off my coat and got out and took them both on. I was lucky enough to flatten the first one temporarily and I had a busy time with the other one and then eventually with both of them." A double-decker bus stopped and a whole audience of people, including Melba and her friend, were cheering the bout. All ended up at the police station. That night "the girls were very attentive and admiring of me," Hill wrote, but not for long. The friend moved out, and Beverly stayed farmed out—sometimes with the friend, sometimes with others—until in 1928 the not-so-standard family of three moved into the Wacker Hotel, "not a very high-class hotel" on the near north side of Chicago.[77]

Hill was restless again. Partly it was for personal reasons. It was only a matter of time before the marriage ended formally, and doubtless new skies looked attractive. Partly it was the entrepreneur built into him. As early as the spring of 1927, he was corresponding with Crow in California about deals that might take him back to his home ground and put him in business entirely for himself again.

Crow was in contact with a man named Lowenthal who was working on the idea of something that could be sold by crews of salesmen without much training on a strict commission basis. He had thought of ladies' hats sold door to door and shipped by the manufacturer direct. Women to sell these would be recruited through want ads, and the price would be split between salesperson, promoter, and supplier. Lowenthal also had a large display card with little envelopes that sold retail for five cents and contained things like a few aspirin tablets or breath sweeteners. The card sold to the dealer for $2. The salesman made forty cents and Lowenthal twenty cents. "This sounds silly at first," Crow wrote, "but consider the mass of cigar-counters, etc. that are prospects for the cards, consider that the sales can be made for cash, and consider that there are a lot of folks that will go out on a proposition like this." Lots of people would answer the ad. Most would not work out. "Handling a proposition of this type means simply being hard-boiled. You know that out of 100 men that start out on your proposition, 90 will not make enough to live on, 8 will make enough so that they will continue for some time—hoping that they will break better in the end—and perhaps 2 will stick. Of the whole 100, though, it is probable that every one will sell something, and that by constantly dragging in new men the proposition can be kept going." Crow quoted H. L. Mencken: that no one ever lost money underestimating the intelligence of the American people.[78]

Hill did not seem especially interested in that prospect, but he kept his feelers out for something. Toward the end of 1927, with no clear alternative goal in mind, he announced he would terminate his employment at Bodine Electric as soon as replacements could be trained. "I had decided," he wrote later, "to change my lifestyle."[79]

Air Associates

*I*n May 1927, Charles Lindbergh flew his Ryan monoplane from New York to Paris alone and caused a sensation that made aviation the hottest business in the United States. Hill had connection enough with the field, dating from his World War I aircraft modification experience and, even earlier, his work with aircraft engines at the Hall-Scott company. However, it was not so much intention as accident that shortly led him into the center of it.

In April 1927, Hill and Ray Acre drove to Los Angeles with a side trip to the Grand Canyon. A walk down the canyon led to near disaster when Acre collapsed from heat prostration, and it was all Hill could do to get him out. From there, however, things improved. In Burbank Alan Lougheed showed them the prototype of the Lockheed Vega, which was to be a famous airplane. His chief draftsman, Jack Northrop, was an architectural draftsman and mechanic who had started in the Lougheeds' garage/factory in Santa Barbara and was soon to start his own near legendary company. Acre, who had once built an experimental airplane of his own, became quite excited about the Lockheed company and became the company representative to find a distributor in the East. Hill was satisfied at Bodine for the time, but the exposure to the cutting edge of aviation on that trip could not have failed to have an effect on him, especially when reflecting on it during that "Summer of Eagles" when flight was on all the front pages.[1] It was doubtless more of interest later in the year when he decided to leave the Chicago electric company.

In February 1928, while Hill was still training his replacement at Bodine Electric, he heard from Acre in New York. Acre had done his job for Lockheed by appointing a young man with good financial backing as a distributor for that company, and the man had advised Acre that his company needed a business manager. Asked to find one, Acre recommended Hill. The full text of Acre's initial telegram to Hill was: "Will you be interested in position as business manager for new aircraft distributing organization in New York. Future prospects look excellent to me. Financial backing unlimited. Salary six thousand and bonus and possibility of entering firm. Wire if not interested. Otherwise I will phone you at eight thirty eastern time tonight at my office." Hill was nonplused. Didn't they want to interview him? No, they put entire confidence in Acre. Hill did ask for some written confirmation from the company and got another wire, which read: "Glad you will be with us. Expecting you next week. Give regards to Ray. Signed, Air Associates, Inc."[2]

To a more settled personality, this move would have been disruptive. Hill had a new Chrysler in which daughter Beverly got carsick at nearly every opportunity, and the prospect of a long auto trip with her and his estranged wife at this point was probably not in itself attractive. But he packed the family belongings and had them shipped by express, and he, Beverly, and Melba headed for the Big Apple.[3]

The more Hill learned about Air Associates, the more interested he became. The proposition was attractive, he wrote in his acceptance letter, "because it appears to present an opportunity to apply such business talent as I may possess in the field of my primary interest."[4] Moreover, Air Associates was the kind of company that boom times produced. Hill found that its store in New York was at "a very fancy location" on the ground floor at the corner of 44th and 5th Avenue (where the Hill family arrived after Beverly threw up in the car in the Holland Tunnel) and that its backers were the financial and social elite. The company had been organized by Haven Page, president of the Yale class of 1922 and son of a prominent New York banker and broker. Page had been a navy test pilot and was carried away by the romance of aviation after Lindbergh's flight. He put in $20,000 or so of his own money and got several of his Yale classmates to go in with him: Gilbert Colgate of the Colgate soap fortune; James B. (Jimmy) Taylor, a World War I pilot from a wealthy family; and Beauregard (Bo) Sweeny, grandson of the Confederate general and son of the corporate and rail attorney who was once Secretary of the Interior in the Wilson administration.[5] As Acre advised Hill, they were no pikers. They were taking on rental of a huge hangar at $1,400 a month, had agreed to take twenty Lockheed ships for resale at $11,500 net (the Vega retailed for $50,000), and had a bank balance of $22,000 with immediate access to $150,000 on call.[6]

Bo Sweeny had some operating experience, having worked for Otis Elevator and Wright Aeronautical, but even so, Hill's initial impression was that the situation was "pretty hopeless." "They didn't seem to know what they were doing. They didn't have any sales volume. They were selling helmets, goggles, magazines, books and trying to book students for flying instructors on a commission basis and operating from an expensive ground floor store in the middle of New York City." Taylor had gone to England and made arrangements for Air Associates to sell the Avian airplane. He had ordered around forty Avians in addition to all the Vegas coming in for resale. "Their attitude towards me," Hill wrote, "was that I was a business manager and therefore they turned the whole thing over to me and expected results."[7]

Acre was happy-go-lucky about it, as apparently was everyone else that year before the great crash when everything was turning to gold. Acre wrote, "I told him [Sweeny] that you were leaving $9000 job because you had reached the limit of your possibilities." Acre predicted Hill would be promoted from business manager to general manager in a few months and that all the managers would be taking advice from him. "This seems to be the first business venture of these folks, and confusion and heavy overhead reign. You can straighten out the confusion rapidly and reduce the overhead gradually, and diplomatically. I am sure you will find them sensible and reasonable and glad to have somebody assume the burdens, which are burying them, and which will be boy's play for you."[8]

Harold Crow was similarly upbeat. "You'll have lots of fun playing with the airplane business," he wrote, "and you'll make more dough than a not-so-good proposition in this territory would bring in. You're getting in the business at the right time, too. After watching the great increase in interest in flying here [California], I'm convinced that the growth of the airplane business during the next ten years is going to be as remarkable as the growth of the automobile business during the last fifteen to twenty years . . . . I think that aviation has struck the popular fancy—that it is one of those things that is automatically popular, just as radio was popular. The type of folks that rushed to buy Chrysler roadsters will all be prospects for airplanes in a comparatively few years." Air Associates, Crow speculated, "is the type of organization that might become a Manhattan Electrical Supply Company in the airplane field."[9]

It was hardly "boy's play," but Hill got busy trying to "do something to justify the salary they were paying me." He rented hangar space at Curtiss Field (shortly renamed Roosevelt Field to accord with an adjoining plot) and hired a mechanic and several helpers to operate this building and to schedule customers' airplanes for service. He raised the storage rates on the hangar they had and attracted more customers with an offer of better service. Hill decided on the mission of building an aircraft supply jobbing business and organizing a repair service for aircraft and engines. He established a store in the corner of the Roosevelt Field hangar to sell supplies for the repair of airplanes and for the sale of flying equipment, instruments, and accessories. With these innovations and attention to limiting overhead, the company began to make some money.[10]

It was a fast life, figuratively and literally. Hill commuted between the downtown office and the field and his changing homes (a hotel, then an apartment in Flushing, then Garden City). There was a private two-lane tollroad with no speed limit that fit his route, and Hill took full advantage of it in a sport model Chrysler 60. Once when he was going "as fast as my Chrysler coupe would go," a steering knuckle broke and he and Sweeny had to crawl out from under a car that ended up on its top. Sweeny was shortly in an airplane wreck when he hired the wrong pilot in California to ferry a Vega back to New York, but it was all part of the pace.[11]

The Air Associates store at Roosevelt Field New York.

Famous people and publicity stunts abounded around the company. Amelia Earhart was backed by George Palmer Putnam (whom she married) for a transatlantic flight. On that flight the plane was handled by others, but on her return Earhart took flying instruction with Taylor at Air Associates so that she could fly herself. Haven Page, who had a penchant for publicity, convinced Art Goebel, who had won the Dole race to Hawaii in a Travel Air, to fly the Air Associates Lockheed Vega to Washington where he was to get a medal. Hill went along to watch the company's property, and so did Melba, who promptly got airsick. The Hills showed Goebel, a "Kansas farmer boy," the sights of Washington as it should be seen. Page organized a New York dinner for Bernt Balchen and Vilhjalmur Stefanson, who had piloted a Lockheed Vega over the North Pole. He promoted an ultimately unsuccessful deal with a group of New York politicians to enter a Vega in the 1928 transcontinental air race with New York mayor Jimmy Walker's name painted on both sides. In 1932 the company tried to gain publicity by flying the film of a prizefight held in Miami to New York in one of its Vegas. It would have been a great stunt in those days before electronic transmission, and Hill was to be aboard pumping gas from the auxiliary tanks into the main gas tank to ensure a nonstop flight. However, weather scotched the trip. Air Associates, in short, always had an eye out for publicity, and its imaginative logo, showing a high-winged monoplane amid artistic lettering, was familiar nationwide in aviation circles.[12]

Hill's work was much appreciated by his associates. In June 1928 Page wrote him: "In appreciation of your being with us, of the way in which you have built up our merchandising business—and your happy personality—I am having transferred to the books of the corporation, from my name to yours, twenty shares of our no par, voting, Common Stock. Perhaps we can thus discount the future a bit." At that time also Hill arranged a bonus based on 2 percent of profits. In August Sweeny resigned, and Hill was elected to fill his place on the board of directors of Air Associates with the title of vice-president in charge of sales. A month later it was agreed that Hill should regularly receive 1,000 shares of common stock for each year's employment.[13]

His personal life was less upbeat. Just as he became an officer and director, Melba, who for a time had taken a temporary job in New York City, left to visit her parents and relatives in Grafton, Wisconsin.[14] This practice became so frequent that Acre wrote asking how he enjoyed the "single life."[15] Victor Lougheed was in jail for rape. Mary was trying to get him out on grounds of ill health, but when Hill visited him, Lougheed was "ornery" to him and seemed to count their friendship for little. Beverly, who was again placed in various forms of child care, moved to California that August of 1928 to stay with Hill's parents at their home on Russell Street in Berkeley.[16] Doubtless this was at the insistence of Leroy's mother Nellie, who did not approve of the context of Jazz Age New York business and a broken marriage for raising a young girl. Beverly grew up in her grandparents' California home and remained there, attending a nearby nursery and then elementary school and

Air Associates, July 1928.

expensive, but sometimes lonely, summer camps until she went to boarding school in her teenage years.

This arrangement led to an extended, detailed, and warmly personal series of letters to Hill from his mother (his dad only added a note occasionally) documenting the progress of her second family and at the same time the deterioration of the grandparents' own health, strength, and personal finances as they aged in the hard times of the Depression. Leroy sent money for Beverly's support, and his mother, with apologies sometimes for being from another age, did her best to provide the rest.[17]

Hill's business life in 1929 became frenzied as Air Associates grew and prospered rapidly. The company sold twenty Avians and eight Lockheed Vegas rather quickly. Page got some new financing through Lehman Brothers, and in 1929 the directors agreed to create branches. "In 1929," Hill commented later, "everybody was enthusiastic about the aviation business and our directors were talking about establishing a chain of aviation repair and supply stations all around the country."[18] Hill opposed this shotgun approach strongly, but agreed to personally take responsibility for starting one branch in Chicago, with the understanding that further expansion would depend upon the success of that venture. His space was on what is now Midway Airport. At that time there was no commercial air service from New York to Chicago, so when Hill did not drive, he took the train to Cleveland and the Universal Airlines flight from there to Chicago. In 1933 a second branch was established at Glendale, California, to try to capitalize on proximity to a growing aircraft industry there by becoming a wholesale supplier to it.

More interesting to Hill than the idea of establishing branches was the publication of a catalog by Air Associates. Hill hired Stanley Harzfeld, who had experience in the automotive supply business, and went about getting new lines to handle, much in the way he had in San Francisco with the Adam-Hill company years earlier. The first Air Associates catalog was published in 1929; it grew every year until, by the mid-1930s, it was literally the bible of the aviation supply business. Hill used his knowledge and connections in the radio business, for instance, to assure that Air Associates became the exclusive distributor for RCA radio equipment for aircraft, a very profitable line.[19] Hill was pleased with the catalog not only for its marketing potential, but as an internal aid. "With this catalog," he wrote to Crow, "we can turn to a particular line and do some selling, whereas the old system was to wait for the inquiry, look dumb, run upstairs to get a piece of literature, go in to a huddle about the price and let the customer get away, then go upstairs and say 'Gee we ought to carry some of those things in stock, I could have made that sale if we had had one of them here.'"[20]

Hill's closest personal friends and advisors were Ray Acre and Harold Crow, both of whom he was able to bring into the management of the company. Bill Lear often wrote from Chicago, but, although Lear averred that Hill was "one of the few fellows I got any real joy out of palling around with,"[21] Hill doubted that his friend would make a good organization man in a subservient position. There were enemies, too.

On right James B. Taylor, Mrs. Taylor and Haven Page, officers of Air Associates, in front of the General Aristocrat, which the company sold, 1929.

Hill said of a director of an associated aircraft company: "We heartily disliked each other."[22]

Hill's lifestyle was mixed. He had "no regular home" in these years, staying in small hotels in Chicago and rooming houses when he was in New York. He was sending money both to Melba and to his mother, but still had the income for a rather lavish lifestyle. He bought stocks, especially Lockheed and a Kansas City company called Jesco Lubricants, dated regularly, and dined well. In 1930 he sold his Chrysler coupe to Harold Crow and bought a two-seat Auburn from Jimmy Taylor. Commuting from New York to Chicago was made somewhat more pleasant by being able to do it in this American classic sporting vehicle.[23]

Toward the end of 1929, as Hill was trying to convince Crow to quit his job at Caterpillar in California and come to join a business with "nothing humdrum about it . . . and very few pikers in it,"[24] came the last of the fast-growth phenomena for Air Associates prior to the Great

Depression. Hill had set the priorities—service first, sales of supplies and mail order second, and sale of airplanes third. In fact, he was trying to get the company sold out of its overlarge inventory of aircraft, though he ended up in the Depression with formerly expensive Vegas which, with Lockheed itself in bankruptcy and parts in short supply, he had to auction at any price offered.[25] Wall Street analysts were telling the board of the trend toward mergers, which was the dominant feature of the aircraft industry at the time. Giant concerns were absorbing smaller ones (the creation of United Technologies and Curtiss-Wright were two prominent examples), and it appeared that each segment would be controlled by a few in oligopolistic competition. Perhaps, one of these analysts said, if Air Associates were to merge with another company, more service would come its way and the overhead expenditures connected with aircraft sales would be justified. In order to be an attractive merger candidate, however, Air Associates was advised to build hangars in Kansas City and Los Angeles at a minimum. To be left out of the merger movement would be a disaster. Wrote Gilbert Colgate to Hill: "Because so many others have merged, . . . the small independents will find hard pickings. The big companies will imitate them (as Curtiss is imitating us now) and even though they do not make money they will at least prevent us from making money. If, however, we are powerful enough to be a factor in the industry, we could either combine or remain independent with a close alliance with some large company." Colgate suggested that price should be sacrificed for speed in negotiating a merger right away. "The industry is moving at about the same rate of speed in proportion to average industries that aeroplanes move in proportion to average means of locomotion. Whereas it took the automobile companies twenty years to form big groups, it is taking the aeroplane companies barely five and this rate of combining is increasing."[26]

The prime prospect for an Air Associates merger in 1929 was a company called Bredouw-Hilliard in Kansas City, one of several major competitors of Air Associates. The others were Nicholas Breazley Company in Marshall, Missouri, which was the main source for World

Commercial ad for the Aristocrat, sold by Air Associates, 1929.

War I surplus parts; Johnson Airplane and Supply at Dayton; and Pacific Airmotive Company in Los Angeles. Hill had extensive talks with Bredouw-Hillard and less extensive ones with Pacific Airmotive about a merger.[27] However, as with the matter of creating branches, he was less desperate to move than some and would not make what he felt was an unsound business decision in order to get on a bandwagon trend. Therefore, the merger talks fell through just about the time the Depression hit. Hill wrote to a friend at Lehman Brothers at the time of the October stock market crash that he had been anticipating a slump and was glad the Bredouw-Hilliard deal had not gone through. "I think there will be many opportunities to acquire such companies before next summer."[28]

In the late fall months of 1929 it became increasingly clear that the entire strategy of Air Associates was going to have to change toward surviving a major business downturn. Hill wrote Page that the pleasant Jim Taylor was an ideal president for such times. "There is no use trying to make Jim over. He can't work and never will. We like him the way he is, so why not leave him alone. I think he makes a fine president. The responsibilities bear lightly on him because he doesn't realize he has them." Hill had gotten a tip from New York that the entire air industry was due for a big crash and that Curtiss Flying Service would be the first to go. There would be many disappointments for Air Associates directors and stockholders in the next few months, Hill wrote, "and Jim is a good man to do the explaining."[29]

But while leaving the public relations to the political types, Hill as operating manager became extremely intense in trying to establish strict internal controls and cost-saving measures in the field. "I've been ruminating on this business considerable in the past week," he wrote Page late in November, "and things look pretty blue. This should not be a surprise to us as I have been looking for this condition of the business for many months. However, it is no easier to bear than if we weren't expecting it." Hill believed the next year would be a bad one, but the year after, when many competing companies would have failed, might be better. "What we should do is to pull into our shell as much as possible.

By that I mean reduce expenses to the point where they are in line with our income even if we have to stop growing for a while. If we can go through this winter and a possible depression period lasting a year without losing money, we will be far ahead of the other fellows who have operated over the same period at a loss, and we will be in a much better position to go after new business when it is there to get." The managers would have to "use to ax" on expenses: "If it is impossible to run the business we have at the present time without the high overhead that we have, we might as well shut up now."[30]

Every part of inventory, stock, and equipment had to be examined. Although the aircraft supply business was a problem because a large supply of diverse parts had to be stocked and turnover was small, there could be improvements. Almost in the manner of a modern computer-aided inventory manager, Hill suggested that the turnover rate in inventory be carefully studied to see which items sold fast enough to be profitable at the markup the company could get away with under current market conditions. He wanted Air Associates to get the manufacturers to cooperate on slow turnover lines by consigning goods or giving the selling company extended dating. He also believed that the company needed to convince operators to let Air Associates carry their stock for them instead of their doing it themselves and, further, that the company should work on the manufacturers to keep them from selling direct to customers and bypassing Air Associates, thus building the sales volume in Air Associates that was so necessary to profitability. All office staff was to be cut to the bone.[31]

A good deal of the implementation at the main hangar in New York was done by Crow, and he communicated the problems to Hill in discouraging detail. He wrote in November that "sometimes I get so damned discouraged here that I hate the sight of the place. I wish I had more patience, or wasn't so damned nervous." One of the engineers was ill and, Crow said, "running down, something like a clock." But it was just as well as he had little energy or technical knowledge and "keeping [him] moving around is like pushing on an elephant." The key to profit was simply quality work, and no amount of hype would substitute for it in such times. "The thing that infuriates me about the shop is that it is apparently such a simple thing to run it right, and still it is so hard to get it run right. The group of men we have here has been narrowed down to a pretty good crew. They're willing, and most of them are competent, but they have to be watched all the time, as every workman seems to naturally tend to go haywire if he can. If we had the right leader there, to sort of catch them up with enthusiasm, and to keep them in line, we would have a damned good organization." Air Associates had just lost its Pratt & Whitney distributorship, Roosevelt field was dead ("no flying at all"), the company's display ads had had to be cut way back to avoid what otherwise would have been a $10,000 a month loss, and Crow wished for Taylor's sunny disposition. He and most others around him, he said, were suffering from stomach trouble. "This is a depressing business all right," he concluded, "and it's easy to get to be an old crab in it."[32]

Even the company Christmas parties did not go well in 1929. Hill held the one in Chicago with few mishaps, but Haven Page's car slipped off the road on the ice while trying to deliver ten-pound turkeys to every employee at Roosevelt Field. When he finally arrived at 5:00 p.m., the employees "fell on me like kids." The turkeys were lined up in the superintendent's office, and each person marched by to get a turkey and a Lily cup of Scotch that Page had smuggled to them. Soon they were all singing, though for reasons that were not totally clear.[33]

The year 1930 was a worry in every way. In January, Melba and Leroy made a final decision in Chicago at the Greenview Hotel, where he was living, to terminate their marriage. Roy drove her to the Allerton House, a hotel for women where she was to live until she got a job to support herself. Hill agreed to pay her maintenance for a period, and she agreed to get an uncontested divorce. However, the divorce was not final until 1934, the custody of Beverly was never made entirely clear, and there were years of recriminations in both directions.[34]

The Depression was no time for a single woman to find work, and Melba, who had married at sixteen and never received any education, was not the best prospect. Then, too, the transition from the life of the wife of a top executive was a difficult one. She wrote Hill in November 1930 inquiring about Ray Acre and Haven Page and about the wives of some of the executives. "When we separated I not only lost one friend but all the other interesting people I knew. Of course I knew they only tolerated me because I was Mrs. F. L. Hill but just the same I miss them." She was angry that Leroy did not send more money and asked him to imagine what it was like living with her folks in Grafton: "I know it is none of my business what you do with your money, but when you can finance a trip east—have all your friends and relatives come and stay with you in a house with a maid, pay their various hotel and restaurant bills—take innumerable people to speakeasies and then refuse to send me even ten dollars a week to make things more bearable there is something wrong some where." She wanted money to buy an interest in a beauty shop, but by 1935 she wanted Leroy to hire her as a secretary somewhere at Air Associates. "Even if I wasn't terrible efficient—don't tell me that a great big organization like yours would miss one $16 or $18 a week pay check." The two did exchange presents and Melba remained concerned that Leroy eat right, but in general the situation was confusing and painful for both. Hill was upset when Melba showed up once in California and stayed with his parents and Beverly for a time without warning him of it. Melba imagined all the "girl friends" Leroy must have and missed no chance to mention them. She could not be sure how to sign her letters to him. "As ever," she wrote at the bottom of one in 1932, "(or what ever the appropriate thing to say to your x husband is)." Often she just signed them with "love," but her letters became less frequent and there are none in Hill's files after 1939. "Of course I am not angry," she commented once, "but what could I possibly write that would interest you?"[35]

About the time of the sad hotel meeting in New York with Melba in January 1930, the Air Associates board discontinued the sale of aircraft and the city office operations, both of which were major losers, and tried to focus on the lines that Hill had largely established. The profit and loss statement for 1929 showed a $600 profit with those elements eliminated, so there was hope. However, Hill admitted that he lay awake nights worrying about the complex service jobs at Chicago and about the myriad items in the catalog.[36] As the financials through September 30, 1930, appeared, Hill tried to make the best of it. "This is a pretty bad looking statement and balance sheet, but remember that there has been no effort to make it look good, and plenty of things have been written off that might have been carried as assets in inventory accounts." Hill told Acre, who was in California working for Lockheed and developing ulcers that would make him a near invalid in a few years, that he did not accept responsibility for many of the losses at Air Associates and that the Chicago branch was okay, with a net profit of about $2,000 for fiscal 1931.[37] Hill was recognized as an expert on shop methods for airplane servicing and gave a speech on the subject to the American Society of Mechanical Engineers, which was printed in the group's trade journal in 1931.[38] As more tangible recognition and evidence of confidence, in 1931 Hill was elected president of Air Associates.

Even in this period, the company grew. Net merchandise sales were $139,000 in 1929–30; $153,000 in 1930–31; $158,000 in 1931–31; $229,000 in 1932–33; and $430,000 in 1933–34. The total net loss for fiscal 1933 was held to only about $1,000.[39] By the end of 1934, Hill estimated that Air Associates' yearly sales volume was greater than that of any other company in the world in its line. Its wholesale sales department was handling 3,000 dealer and subdistributor accounts and its manufactured products included everything from flying clothes, goggles, and personal equipment to special tools, aircraft hardware, radio and electric equipment, aircraft instruments, airport beacons, wind cones, and various navigation and landing lights. Most of this was manufactured in the company's own shops, and some of it had been invented and developed by Air Associates. In addition to its own products, it held exclusive sales rights on the aviation products of a number of prominent manufacturers, including RCA Victor, General Tire and Rubber, and American Plywood. The 1935 catalog would be 9 × 12 inches and 140 pages. Crow wrote that "the work that we are doing in placing in the hands of the foreign buyer a complete and easily-understood catalog of American materials and accessories is one of the finest pieces of propaganda that has ever been done for American products."[40]

Still, Depression strategy meant tight financial controls, corporate and personal, and that was as frustrating for Hill as anyone. Friendships were important to him, and in the 1930s many of his friends needed money and thought Hill should be the source of it. In his files is a folder called "Girls," and most of the girls were thanking him for loans. Alice "Midnight Blue" Clemo sold him shares in "Blue, Inc." and wrote him long, vibrant letters about her radio programs, club dates, auditions at CBS and MGM, and her experiments with "how to look well in cheap clothes." She sometimes signed letters "Joblessly Yours" and once sent a clipping of an ad she had placed in the newspaper: "YOUNG woman trained studio, secretarial & radio script desires position as secretary to writer, lecturer or movie star."[41]

Hill's father was increasingly in debt. He did not seem to be able to adjust his outgoing deal-making to the new market conditions. Hill wrote his sister in the spring of 1933 that he had gotten a phone call from "Pop" asking for $6,000. Hill refused partly because he did not want to encourage his father's excesses and partly because he didn't have the money: "I am ashamed to admit [it], after all these years of work." Frank Hill was always mysterious about the details of where the money was going, and increasingly Hill found it necessary to go around him and send money directly to his mother, which she kept in a secret account. In 1933 he was sending her about $125 a month. His sister, Isabella Hill Perkins, who was married to a principal at Paramount Pictures and living in China, was sending the family in Oakland money also.[42]

Of course, there were the Lougheeds. Victor always had a new invention, and that was the ostensible business reason for loans from Leroy, which were really an expression of compassion. Hill was not the only salesman Victor convinced to advance him money, and letters from him and Mary regularly came from Europe where they were touring.

Typical was a gushy letter from Mary from Paris in May 1935. She had been to a nude show at the Moulin Rouge, where "a nigger" asked her to dance. She counted nineteen blacks with one white woman at a party. Would Hill take her to a Harlem dive when she came through New York? "I must see if the white-black dancers *can* do *such* a rhumba as they do here!" There was some sympathy: "You poor dear—you sure sound like Santa Claus—and I feel more than conscience stricken . . . . This is the first time in my life I ever did a foolish stunt where money was concerned! . . . . Isn't Victor the splurger? He always did have a yen for using the phone for long distance—sort of flatters his ego—to think he really has enough cash in his jeans to pay for telephone bills."[43]

Victor's half-brother Allan was developing a new $20,000 executive airplane called the ALCOR. Hill was impressed by it but could not advance much money. Eventually Allan crashed the prototype and had to ask Hill for a job, any job, at Air Associates. Hill wired him money regularly.[44]

The stress of all this led Hill to his usual palliative of engineering work, but the aircraft engine he designed in his spare time in those years was nixed for production by Air Associates under Hill's own rules of economy and conservatism.[45] So his "stomach troubles" got worse.

His friends, of course, did more than borrow: the relationships were warm and supportive even when slightly cracked. Alice Blue visited Hill's mother and daughter and wrote him loving notes about them ("You've fooled your mother a long time, if you're not O.K. She adores you"). "I liked holding your hat on my knee too . . . some hats are just hats . . . but yours is something else . . . part of Life's crazy quilt. And for once I didn't mind not being beautiful. It didn't seem to matter much." Clearly she had loved Hill "harder than I've ever loved any other man" and still did. But her romantic hopes were in the background in the 1930s, while her simple caring was at the front. She wrote in 1940: "Leroy, I'm so proud of you, it's just funny . . . You've traveled the straightest path to a goal of any man I've ever known. This is brought on by my having just looked through your catalog #18. I think that's the most wonderful proof of achievement . . . I'll never forget that you said I'm too goddam sentimental but lord . . . that book gives me a thrill. I remember a little mimiographed [sic] thing you produced at college which was used as a text book . . . This big catalog has grown from that. No matter how many rich and beautiful women you marry, or don't marry . . . there'll always be me sitting back in some obscure corner being proud of you. Please don't laugh at me. I'm ridiculously sincere . . . If I had family and wealth I'd give a few other women something to think about . . . at least, get in their hair . . . But I'm perfectly harmless . . . Take care of yourself. Love, Alice."[46] Such friends were a gift, and Hill knew it. He wrote Acre in California in 1937 recommending that he go hear a "great pianist" and an old friend of his. "She's kind of sentimental and an introvert, but I am sure you will be nuts about her music and you will probably like her as she's the most kind-hearted and considerate girl I ever met."[47] In the large folder of Alice's letters is a typewritten slip reading "To Be Retained."

Ray Acre was more matter of fact but no less helpful. Hill depended on him for his common sense, engineering knowledge, and a friendship as sincere if not as long-standing as that of Harold Crow. Acre knew Victor Lougheed well and could reminisce with Hill about the old days at Duodisk. "I, too, can overlook his [Lougheed's] morals," Acre wrote, "but can't forgive his disregard of you. However, he has always done this kind of thing to me, also." Victor's old flames were always shaking Acre down for money—"if he only had enough sense to use condoms."[48] Acre's correspondence with Hill was an encyclopedia of practical knowledge from the experience of both, set forth in the completely forthright fashion of men who had absolute confidence in each other. Hill gave detailed advice about how Acre might improve the Glendale branch, where he was working, but added: "Don't let me influence you . . . you go ahead and make any alterations that you think are justified. I will not criticize you or reproach you in any way on such matters. You should know by this time that I am perfectly willing to trust your judgment and I want to let you do you job in your own way."[49] To have that kind

This is ...

Air Associates

Catalog No. 15

1933

In this catalog we have listed most of the standard items that you will need from time to time in operating your airplane, and some of the accessories and extras that will enable you to get more pleasure from your flying.

We have space to list only a few of the hundreds of aviation necessities that we regularly carry . . . it would require a catalog many times this size to list them all. Please remember us whenever you need something that you do not find listed, we probably have it right in stock, ready to send to you; if not, we'll be able to get it for you quickly . . . and at the right price.

You will notice that many prices are much lower this season, and that our prices are considerably below those of any other supply house. We have taken the lead in bringing down the prevailing high prices on airplane supplies; your operating expenses this season will be much lower than before.

AIR ASSOCIATES

INCORPORATED

BOX 333
GARDEN CITY, NEW YORK
Telephone · · Garden City 4374
Located on Roosevelt Field

5300 WEST 63rd STREET
CHICAGO, ILLINOIS
Telephone · · Hemlock 4600
Located on the Chicago Municipal Airport

Send your orders to the nearest branch

Introducing the Air Associates catalog for 1933.

Radio-Aire AIRCRAFT RADIO

Combined Radio Beacon Signal . . Weather Report and Entertainment Program Broadcast Receiver

Flying becomes infinitely more pleasurable when you know you're on the course . . . when you know what kind of weather to expect at your destination. Dull moments become bright when you tune in on the game, or listen to your favorite entertainment program. The Lear Radio-Aire gives you everything you want in aircraft radio . . . at a price so low that you will not care to be without this insurance against tiresome or anxious hours in the sky.

Radio-Aire covers the entire frequency band from 235 to 720 kilocycles. It gives you perfect reception of beacon signals and weather reports, broadcast from 240 to 410 kilocycles, and the Naval communication band from 410 to 550 kilocycles. It also covers 17 channels in the entertainment broadcast band, from 550 to 720 kilocycles . . . all by single control—no coils to change when shifting from one frequency to another. The dial is marked in frequencies, you know exactly where to tune for any station.

Radio-Aire is unusually sensitive; a pilot flying above Detroit reports receiving beacon and weather clearly from Chicago, Cleveland, Jackson, Columbus, Cincinnati, Pittsburgh and Buffalo. It is highly selective; it easily separates all radio beacon stations without being too sharp for easy tuning, and it is possible to tune from a weak signal to a much stronger one without experiencing uncomfortable eardrum blasts. The set is thoroughly shielded to insure clear reception, and has a patented, built-in ignition interference suppressor that effectively reduces the ordinary noises. This highly important feature is found on no other aircraft radio.

Radio-Aire fits all airplanes. It is small and light, and easily installed. It operates from your regular aircraft storage battery and uses the standard aircraft lightweight "B" battery. A "B" Eliminator is furnished for a small extra charge.

Previous to the introduction of Radio-Aire, and of Air Associates Magneto Shields, the cost of aircraft radio was prohibitive. Now it is possible to make a complete radio installation for only a small part of the former cost, that is why so many commercial operators and private flyers are now installing Lear Radio-Aire, the set that is endorsed and accepted by the U. S. Navy and by all the leading flyers.

Enjoy Radio-Aire . . The Real Aircraft Radio

Radio-Aire is only 7″ x 7″ x 8½″, and is usually mounted in the cockpit and operated directly; where remote control is necessary, Type R Radio-Aire is furnished, it has precision remote control of both tuning and volume.

The standard Radio-Aire is 12-volt; 6-volt sets can be furnished at the same price on special order. The set weighs 9 lbs.; the complete installation, including "B" battery or eliminator, antenna and headphones, weighs 19 lbs. There are jacks for 2 headphones, one headphone comes with each set.

The Radio-Aire Interphone Kit, for inter-cockpit communication, can be added at any time. With it, you have a special anti-noise microphone in each cockpit, connected to the radio. Without detuning the radio, or throwing any switches, you just press the button on the microphone and talk; the other person hears you louder than the radio signal.

Small in size, Radio-Aire will out-perform large sets

Radio-Aire is beautifully made, with the finest precision workmanship throughout, that is why it can be depended upon for clear, sensitive reception and trouble-free service. It is designed so that the chassis slides right out for instant removal; if inspection is ever required it can be made with the chassis out of the ship.

Radio-Aire will out-perform much larger and heavier sets, because of its special, highly efficient circuit—licensed under RCA patents. Radio-Aire is a 5-tube tuned radio frequency receiver incorporating the latest automotive type tube equipment: 3-39 Screen Grid Amplifiers . . . 1-36 Special Detector . . . 1-41 Output Pentode Tube. It consumes low filament and plate currents, with negligible battery drain . . . less than 9/10 amperes at 12 volts.

Standard Lear Radio-Aire	**$195.00**
Complete with Tubes and 1 set Headphones	
Type R Lear Radio-Aire	**$234.50**
With Remote Control, Tubes and 1 set Headphones.	
Radio-Aire Interphone Kit	**$54.50**
With 2 Anti-Noise Microphones, Transformer, Leads and "C" Battery.	

Special 135-Volt Light-Weight Aircraft "B" Battery	$7.50	Complete Aircraft Antenna Kit, No. A.	$3.50

When ordering sets, state whether for 12-volt or 6-volt operation. Prices of sets do not include batteries, engine shielding or installation.

Radio-Aire is Precision-Built, Simple, Compact and Sturdy

Radio-Aire "B" ELIMINATOR

This replaces the ordinary "B" batteries, and furnishes an unvarying, dependable "B" current supply. It operates directly from your storage battery, and is available in two types, to fit either a 12-volt or a 6-volt battery.

It is small and compact—only 7″ x 10″ x 3¼″, weight 9½ lbs.—and is easily installed. It is perfectly safe, and has no moving parts and contains no liquid; it requires no attention after installation. It is tested, proven and guaranteed, and is the ideal source of "B" current for aircraft radio.

Only . . $29.50 Complete
Specify your storage battery voltage when ordering.

Radio equipment page from the Air Associates catalog, 1933. Note the association with William Lear, whom Hill met while at Bodine Electric.

of letter from the boss and know that it is heartfelt is the dream of many an employee. Of course with it went the admonition to increase production by 40–50 percent in the next year.

Haven Page was all business, but understanding. "I admire your patience with your family," Page wrote in 1934, "your sales 'plunge' with the coast branch; the dope on the catalog; the R.C.A. radio contract; your new Roman-face machine (typewriter) type; your perennial 'yen' to design that engine; and your bonus . . . . I *don't* admire your stomach ulcers . . . and the other fatigue symptoms . . . . Seriously, I know a lot about fatigue symptoms, since I am perpetually enervated myself, and you can't fool me with that 'from butcher boy to bank president' stuff. The trouble with you is . . . you never take a rest, and you spend all your time with people who are not on your intellectual level." Page could joke with Hill about their associates. "How [Jimmy Taylor] got an honest salesman's job is beyond me. His mind is a cross between a corkscrew and a rainbow. For a brief period I was his highball & pot o'gold. Don't believe anything he says which would have a tendency to result in something passing from you to him."[50]

Probably Hill's best friend was a near invisible one—his mother. "If there is any possibility of your getting sick," she wrote in 1932, "I want you to make a bee line out here. I can take care of you and make you comfortable. The expense of coming out here is nothing compared to the expense of hospitals and all. I hope you will not make light of the advice I am giving you. Come right away—no dallying."[51] She sent Bev's school papers with a scrawl on the back—"Dear Daddy XXXOOOOXXXXOOOO Love from Beverly"—and took the young girl to plays, on shopping trips, and to the library, as well as making sure she read the numerous books her father sent her.[52] "I think you are crazy to say I do not approve of your being on good terms with Melba," Nellie wrote in 1933. "I think it is most fortunate that you can be. Even if I didn't like the idea I hope I would have sense enough to keep it to myself, so don't make any more insinuations like that again." And in the same letter: "I can hardly make myself believe that you are 39 years old . . . . I wish I could give you a

An Air Associates hanger.

fine birthday dinner & a big cake."[53] She had her private bank account. "Sometimes I feel guilty, but as I have never known how we stood financially I have resolved to be a little secret myself. He is very generous when he has money but some way or other he never could put any money aside for a rainy day. I am not keeping anything from you & if Pop has to have any money on short notice let me know & I will send what I have to you & you can send it back to him. I think it best to be coming from you. I feel like a conspirator but 'needs must when the devil drives.'"[54] Nellie Hill was strong, independent, and articulate. She had her "darky," as she phrased it, to help with some of the heavy housework but was otherwise on her own in straightened circumstances. "Don't worry about my financial affairs," she wrote cheerily in 1939, "I always keep a penny in my pocket for good luck."[55] Her letters were filled with reports of everyday things, but her personality glowed in them and doubtless communicated to her son in New York that there was a rock of love always in California.

Hill gave personal advice and support as well as getting it. The most notable thing about his business correspondence with subordinates is its entirely casual, open, and personal tone—never forgetting for a moment that he is addressing a human being with a psychology and stresses. Hill put Ted Lynn in charge of the Glendale branch and soon found that this was not a wholly popular decision with Lynn's employees. Lynn had vision and enthusiasm: his letters to Hill are almost giddy with excitement. But he had a tendency to be brash, even cruel, in carrying out business decisions, as well as a penchant for company politics. Hill supported him, but not without constructive personal criticism. Once when Lynn wrote him of a no-risk insurance deal offered by Lloyd's of London, Hill replied: "I have heard of investments that bear returns of from ten percent to twenty-five percent, but when I hear of one that involves absolutely no risk of any kind as you state, I am naturally suspicious and I would advise you to be that way also." Hill advised him not to write to the Air Associates board about the insurance deal as "it would damage your prestige." He told Lynn that he needed to evaluate percentage of profit, not just volume or prestige in sales, and needed to watch writing letters "which express impatience, sore headedness and other emotions which result in an antagonistic reaction on the part of the recipient. Some of your critics are inclined to laugh it off, some take it good naturedly and some get sore. You can never tell who is going to get sore and how much damage it is going to do." On the other hand, he did not want Lynn to become so subtle that he was not forthcoming. He said of one man in Lynn's organization that he did not talk straight: "He talks to me like he would to a purchasing agent that he is trying to sell stuff to."[56]

There were technical as well as human problems with which to deal, and Hill handled those also. In 1936 the manufacturing capacity of Air Associates was strained in getting out brake orders for Sikorsky and Pan American for their new Douglas DC-2 airliner.[57] Hill and Crow (who had become vice-president of Air Associates) became increasingly frustrated at not having employees with sufficient technical knowledge or initiative to free the two top executives from constant direct supervision in the shop. As equipment became more complex, more and more inquiries ended up with Hill, Crow, or Acre. "This business is never going to be reduced to a routine," Hill wrote Acre, "and, therefore, the organization must be developed to maximum resourcefulness." It was dangerous to centralize so much authority. "It is especially necessary to pay more attention to organization when a company gets big. With a million dollars in business going through the outfit, no amount of ability in one individual can be very important, and the dependence on the ability of an individual is dangerous to the company and tough on the individual." Crow was getting depressed in 1936 and talking about quitting. Hill told him to keep hiring and firing until he found a man as good as himself to help him. He wrote Acre: "I do not think that long friendship with me would keep Harold from leaving me in a hell of a spot if he took a notion to beat it . . . . I am personally in a hell of a fit of depression, bogged down with a thousand jobs to get done and nobody to turn to. I would like to get on a boat and go to Bermuda or Nassau for a month."[58]

Among important problems Hill faced in the fall of 1936 was a refinancing of Air Associates and the persuasion required to bring all the stockholders in and to get the right underwriter. Preferred stock would remain as it was, but the over 14,000 shares of common would be exchanged one to four for new common, and $400,000 in new stock would be sold to the public for $6.[59] Haven Page was particularly difficult to deal with in the final stages of the refinance, and it put a strain on his friendship with Hill, which that friendship proved strong enough to survive. "It's a rotten shame I'm in my present fix," he admitted to Hill, "—I could be quite helpful to you instead of being just a destructive critic."[60] Hill, as usual, was patient but clear in explaining that all deals were compromises. "Considering the fact that the preferred stock can hold up the progress of the company indefinitely, about the best thing to do is arrive at a division by which nobody is very well satisfied. The preferred stock won't get as much as they expected, the common stock won't get as much as they expected and the management won't get as much as they expected. And that is what we are approaching now . . . and I forgot to say that the bankers won't get what they expected. It looks to me that such a deal will come pretty close to being fair all the way around, —and if it isn't it's better for whoever thinks he isn't getting enough to take it anyway and let the company go ahead as he will lose more by delay, even if he wins the argument."[61] Page eventually agreed and put some of his pride as a founder and need for cash aside. "I thoroughly approve of the way you have handled those various birds," he wrote Hill, "and know what an accomplishment it is to work up such a deal."[62] Altogether Hill was annoyed by the proceedings. He lost Ted Lynn to another company because, Hill thought, the president was too busy with the financiers to make Lynn comfortable in a new New York job with Air Associates. "You can see why I am not enthusiastic about having active directors to take an interest in the company," he told Page. "I would like to have a board of directors that knows nothing whatever, has no interest in the company, and never gets together for a meeting."[63]

The refinancing gave management stock options in Air Associates. Specifically Hill had the right to purchase 8,500 shares of Air Associates at $8.50 a share. By the end of 1938 the shares had reached a market high of 12⅞.[64] Hill moved to apartment B-35 on the second floor of Hilton Hall, 67 Hilton Avenue, Garden City, at an annual rent of $960.[65] He bought a 1935 Fairchild 24 aircraft, cream with international orange wings, at the same time that Acre, suffering intensely from a perforated ulcer, bought a Waco.[66] Hill traded his Auburn for a Ford V-8 Club Coupe in 1937, but by 1939 his car connoisseur tendencies were getting the better of him again and he bought an "airliner gray" supercharged Graham-Paige six, Model 97, with a specially installed Warner overdrive (magnetic control) and a custom-installed tachometer.[67] He borrowed a Zeiss camera from Victor Lougheed, while kidding

Leroy's Graham-Paige supercharged car at Air Associates with his daughter Beverly at the wheel 1937.

that "I guarantee to get tired of it within thirty days and return it all to you intact."[68]

But while he kidded, the fascination with new and fine things, particularly on the leading edge of technology, were a passion with Hill which he had, for his spirit's sake, to indulge when he could afford it. He attended the National Air Races at Cleveland regularly and in the summer of 1937 watched the Grand Prix race at Roosevelt Field, where Rudolph Carraciola and Bernd Rosemeyer dominated in their twelve- and sixteen-cylinder streamlined Mercedes and Auto Union cars. He found all this stimulating, and it kept him refreshed and focused on his own goals. "Those German cars are certainly miles ahead of anything ever before seen in this country."[69]

The completion of the refinancing allowed Hill to turn again to organizing the business. "I guess I had the idea that you were feeling depressed and discouraged," he wrote Acre, "but I see now that you are

simply recognizing troubles, evaluating them, and laying plans to eliminate them systematically, which is certainly the essence of good common
sense." By the middle of 1937 there were 2,000 stock record entries to
be made each day at Air Associates, all without the aid of a computer.
"I have noticed," Hill wrote, "that the best route through our organization is from the stockroom, through the stock record system, into purchasing and then into sales. The business is so complicated that a salesman
starting in at sales is so unfamiliar with so many things that he practically
has to spend years learning . . . . Buying in a business like ours is like
buying in a department store, in that most buying is done for resale rather
than for use or production requirements. You have to buy what can be
sold at a price such that a profit can be made." This required trading
instinct in people and a through analysis of the card inventory and sales
record history.[70]

Things at the company improved rapidly in the late 1930s. Hill rented
another building at Roosevelt Field to double the size of the shop and
ordered new machine tools and modern electric furnaces. He went back
to his own inventing, patenting an overload release device for relieving
stresses of torsion when transmitting power between a driving and driven
shaft.[71] Air Associates began in 1937 declaring substantial dividends,
and Hill bought shares for his sister Isabella.[72]

In January 1938 came the merger that had been hanging fire since
1929. Air Associates took over the assets of Nicholas-Beazley Airplane
Company, Inc., one of its major competitors in the aircraft supply
business.[73] The company had started out in a garage in Marshall,
Missouri, selling World War I surplus aircraft parts. It later built several
successful airplanes of its own and was sole export agent for such products
as the Swallow airplane from Wichita, the Warner Scarab aircraft
engine, Kendall oil, and equipment from Consolidated Instruments. But
the day of an aircraft company in every small town was over. There were
lawsuits pending against Nicholas-Breazy, and it could not make up for
losses in one line or location with profits from another. So it too joined
an increasingly oligopolistic industry.[74]

That year also, came the beginning of the war contracting boom and its positive impact on Air Associates. The stress went from worrying about sales to concern about losing men to competitors as wages rose.[75]

It seemed that the promise glimpsed for Air Associates in 1929 was to be realized more than fully ten years later and that Hill's salvage and survival operation in the depths of the Depression would pay off richly for both stockholders and management. The catalog was a marvel. Hill wrote in December 1939: "I do not think that anyone will ever match the catalog that is now being printed. We will never print another one like it." As of that date, all the machines in the shop were running on a two- shift and many on a three-shift basis (135 hours a week).[76]

And Hill's personal life was more stable. As though to close an era, his father died late in 1939, depriving Hill of a friend but relieving him of a care at the same time. Frank Sr. had occupied the same office on the Embarcadero in San Francisco for thirty-one years after leaving the Manitowac Aluminum Company and moving west.[77] "I have had much sympathy for him," Nellie had written during her husband's final illness, "but I would have had still more if he hadn't done so much grunting & groaning. Men are such boobies when they have anything the matter with them." For Leroy, she made an exception to this rule, saying that he was always patient, even when he was a little chap, and "I don't forget it." After his father's death, following several strokes and a hospital stay, Nellie Hill took a trip to Hawaii (out by Matson line and back by Pan Am Clipper) to visit her relatives, doubtless with her son's financial aid. She could hardly realize, she wrote that July 1940, that Leroy was forty-six years old and Isabella forty.[78]

In those final days, Isabella pitched in too, traveling from Shanghai to help out trying to find a sanitarium for "Pap." She wrote Leroy that she was glad to find from his letter "that I am not such a strange creature after all and that your mind works along the same channels." She said knowingly of their mother: "She certainly doesn't shirk responsibility; I think to be without it would kill her." Isabella kept up a regular correspondence with her brother after 1937, often sent by Clipper air mail, and so was not long out of Leroy's rich support network even in Asia. She sent him Chinese rugs and studied publications to find the best school for "Bevy."[79]

Beverly became less of a worry as she grew older. She was tall and overweight, and had not entirely enjoyed the Anna Head school in Berkeley or the Drew Seminary for Young Women in Carmel, New York, where she was placed for a time to be nearer her father while her grandfather was in the hospital. She was also, after all, a teenager in the care of an aged woman, who objected to her use of lipstick, disliked Bing Crosby, and said that Claudette Colbert made her sick to her stomach.[80] In the spring of 1940, no doubt as an adjustment to her grandfather's death, Beverly went for a year's stay with her Aunt Isabella and her family in Shanghai, even as Isabella warned of Japanese bluster and incursions. She enrolled at the American School there, took riding and French lessons, and lost weight on a heroic diet monitored by her aunt. She even had her own printed stationery: Beverly Hill, 69 Great Western Road, Shanghai, China. She chided her dad occasionally about not writing. "As a correspondent," she said once in 1940, "you're a swell business man."[81] Hill later claimed that Bev's purchase of an immense handmade Chinese wardrobe gave her "a recklessness about money," fostered by his sister. But in general Beverly seemed happy with her travels and regimen in a strange country, even at Christmas, when she noticed it was a little remote from home.[82]

At best, the divorce and the shuttling between different sets of relatives had been confusing. Beverly had both Nellie and Isabella, for instance, pushing her to achieve. Isabella wrote to Leroy in 1934: "She is as smart and intelligent as she can be, extraordinarily so, but if she doesn't have it directed in proper channels, she will be worse than a dumb kid. And just because she is out of the ordinary she needs twice as much attention and handling as the usual child." When Beverly was with her mother and her family in Grafton, Wisconsin, she was told that Melba had complete custody of her, could do with her what she pleased, and might take her back permanently. Isabella concluded while visiting the Mayers in Wisconsin that she no longer hoped Melba and Leroy could patch things up. "You are right—she is dumb—and I think very selfish & self centered—but golly she certainly is beautiful when she is dressed up. Too bad she has such enormous hips." She noted as well that "Bevy can be the nastiest most disagreeable brat I have ever known, and I like kids. And I think Melba brings out the worst in her."[83] There was a regular furor between California and Wisconsin at every vacation time about where Bev should be and when, with Leroy Hill often, at a distance, in the middle of the negotiations. To confuse things more, Hill got his mother and daughter an airline discount card and flew them fairly regularly to New York for short visits with him.[84] When Beverly was in Grafton, the family there explained the relationship between her father and mother to her according to their own lights because "somebody needed to tell her." Bev told her Aunt Isabella during a visit: "I don't care what they say, they can't make me hate my daddy." Isabella commented to Leroy: "Isn't that a heck of a thing to put a kid through?"[85] It was indeed.

Hill saw Ellen Mayo socially a few times. She had come to Air Associates to get some solo hours and ended up with a job in the advertising department, including correcting the vast catalogue. This relationship was to lead to a second marriage in 1942. Ellen was the daughter of a New York attorney and herself a Smith graduate who had worked at McGraw Hill as an editorial assistant in the school textbook department. She had lots of overtime at Air Associates, did not need to borrow money from Leroy, had an independent and take-charge personality, and was clearly, compared with most of his female associates of the 1930s, a stabilizing influence. She was also much younger than Leroy and at first did not consider him a romantic possibility at all.[86]

It seemed that only some force external to the company itself could ruin progress on all fronts, business and personal.

The Picket Line

The Air Associates strike of fall 1941 was an exceptional event, leading not only to a takeover of the plant by federal troops, but the ousting of Hill and others from the management of his own company through governmental pressure justified by a war emergency. There was context for such action, but the Air Associates events themselves have been little studied in secondary literature. They definitely belong in importance alongside those, such as the North American Aviation strike, that now serve in the literature as exemplars of emerging wartime labor policy. The situation at Air Associates developed slowly, but the movement there grew by what it fed on, internally and externally. The explosion, when it came, was violent.

It may well have been true that the concept of "industrial democracy" was one whose time had come and that, as Milton Derber observed, "during the war many management leaders gradually abandoned their long struggle against the collective-bargaining model and decided to accommodate to it . . . . They realized that resistance would be futile in the light of public attitudes and the distribution of political and economic power." No doubt some managers from intimate contact with labor leaders during the war saw "that most American unionists shared the same underlying values about the capitalist system and were reasonable and responsible men."[1] But Hill was a production efficiency expert, not a social planner, and as a manager he grated at worker self-government beyond a certain minimum. He had been the right man at Air Associates in the 1930s, when the bloated company needed to be disciplined, pared down, and driven to the market. But he was the wrong man in the wartime

1940s when "accommodation to the program," a program largely political, was the key to corporate prosperity.

Governmental seizure of plants during war emergencies, as happened with Air Associates, was a rare device in American history, having happened only seventy-one times by the late 1960s. The justification was the superiority of public over private interest in times of national emergency. "Labor-management negotiators," wrote one observer, "who ought not to be allowed to cross the street without a seeing-eye dog are free to inflict hardship on millions of their fellow citizens through sheer incompetence at the bargaining table."[2]

Presidential seizure was used once during the Civil War, when Abraham Lincoln by executive order seized the Philadelphia and Reading Railroad during a strike in July 1864. It happened in three instances during World War I, the most prominent of which was federal operation of all U.S. railroads for the duration. It was more commonly used during the Roosevelt and Truman administrations, but only four times by Roosevelt before Pearl Harbor: North American Aviation, Federal Shipbuilding, Alcoa Freighters, and Air Associates. Only twice—with Federal Shipbuilding and Air Associates—was the seizure because of defiance of a government board order by management. And only once was the principal manager a personality like Leroy Hill.[3]

The impact of the strike—the events leading to it, its climax and aftermath—on Hill personally was monumental. In that cauldron he became a nationally known figure and then an obscure one by turns nearly overnight. He was perceived at best by his friends as a brave and articulate defender of the lost cause of company autonomy, and by his enemies as a kind of monster. The strike drove him out of Long Island and to the town of Rockford, Illinois, to start a new life with a new wife managing small intrastate businesses not subject to union organization. It took him out of the top echelons of corporate America, first by necessity and later by philosophical choice. It transformed his focus and social psychology. Although always one of strong conservative views, he now became a considerable political philosopher, activist, and financial supporter of organizations on behalf of individual freedom. The things that tempered his soul to the change made him into a kind of Ancient Mariner, telling to whomever would listen the story of his shipwreck and with it, he thought, the destruction of the best ideals of America.

Hill had never been particularly active or interested in politics. His concerns of invention, engineering, and then business management were enough to occupy fully his skills and interests through his middle forties. But the economic changes of the second New Deal in the late 1930s, following as they did the "Thunder from the Left" occasioned by the rhetoric of the likes of Huey Long and Father Coughlin, were hardly standard fare. The National Industrial Recovery Act, the Banking Holiday, and the Agricultural Adjustment Administration of Franklin Roosevelt's first one hundred days seemed to conservatives a severe enough wrenching of traditional free enterprise. To them the legislative and administrative events following the confirming election of 1936 appeared to herald an absolute and not attractive revolution. The late thirties was the era of Social Security, of the Tennessee Valley Authority, and, most telling for Leroy Hill, the National Labor Relations (Wagner) Act. The Wagner Act passed in 1935, the same year that saw the formation of a new labor organization with which Hill was to become intimate, the Congress of Industrial Organizations (CIO).

The Wagner Act, sometimes called the "Magna Charta of Labor," was the culmination of a series of federal actions regarding labor, which together represented a purposeful attempt by government to encourage "countervailing power" in the U.S. economy by strengthening the trade union movement. Section 7(a) of the National Industrial Recovery Act, passed during Roosevelt's initial hundred days, guaranteed labor the right to organize and bargain collectively "through representatives of its own choosing," but, like most of the NIRA structure, it depended on vague voluntary compliance and had ineffective enforcement machinery. The Wagner Act, in addition to providing more specific rules, created the National Labor Relations Board, which could evaluate the fairness of union elections at company plants and even estimate and correct the degree of "good faith" with which management was bargaining. It outlawed many techniques that had been used by corporations to discourage unions, to encourage company unions, or to impose even seemingly ordinary management discipline, by designating these "unfair labor practices." It required noninterference with union organization in company shops, recognition of unions that won supervised elections, and then "good faith" collective bargaining with them. Theoretically it did not require that a labor agreement be signed, but many managers felt that the "closed shop" (i.e., one in which all employees must join a union) would be universal in manufacturing firms in the future. Certainly a stated goal of the Wagner Act was to get rid of company unions, which had flourished since World War I. In 1935 about two-thirds of these relied on the employer for financing, and less than one-fifth of companies had any type of labor agreement. Clearly businesses could no longer ignore politics or the impact of regulatory agencies upon their day-to-day operations.[4]

The CIO was a national organization of industrial unions. It had split with the American Federation of Labor, which since the 1880s had been the dominant labor federation, over the issue of craft or skill versus industry unionism. The CIO's member unions, such as the United Auto Workers (UAW), organized assembly-line workers in industries which, because the workers were not skilled and were therefore easily replaceable, had been largely nonunion previously.[5]

The UAW had an aviation division, and it was that organization with which Hill soon became familiar. Although aviation never became the mass-production/mass-sales industry that the auto industry was, there were similarities, particularly as the aircraft industry, its technology, and its manufacturing methods matured in the 1930s and 1940s. In the late 1920s there were a series of large mergers in aviation, making it look much like the automotive oligopoly. Where there had been "three hundred aircraft factories, including those where you had to shove the cow aside to see the airplane," the formation of the enormous United Aircraft and Transport Corporation and North American Aviation,

Inc., in 1929 suggested a structure more susceptible to industrial union-ism. In fact, some auto makers had major stakes in the aviation combi-nations. While the Depression temporarily interrupted this growth, by 1940 aircraft production was again at its 1929 level and again an attractive target for union organizers.[6]

The difference between aviation and automobiles was that aircraft plants in the 1920s and early 1930s did not use the machine tools typical of the auto industry, did not have nearly the volume (in 1935 2,000 airplanes were produced in the United States versus four million autos), was beyond the handicraft stage but short of the large machine tool stage, and required a high percentage of skilled and semiskilled workers. This last factor was often critical in the location of plants, and some of the prime centers, like Los Angeles, had strong anti-union traditions. A last factor making unionization difficult in aircraft was that the industry was a relatively small-scale employer, employing about two-tenths of one percent of the manufacturing work force in the 1930s. Wages were comparable to those in the auto industry, and strikes in aircraft were rare before 1937.[7]

Because the CIO unions were broader-based than earlier labor organizations, because their members' lack of extensive apprenticeship and skill required more radical methods to threaten employers into concessions, and because they originated in a time of special governmen-tal support for the rights and privileges of organized labor, the negotia-tions and strikes of the late 1930s and early 1940s were some of the most confrontational and violent in American history.

It all began, of course, with the sitdown strike of 1936–37 at Fisher Body Works in Flint, Michigan—the defining watershed and original organizational victory for the UAW in the automobile industry. That strike, where workers remained in occupation of the plant to prevent the company from replacing them with a ready supply of quickly trainable unemployed, represented a confiscation of company property that was illegal (as the Supreme Court declared in 1939). It was also a form of civil disobedience, and as such relied on a just cause and the pressure of public opinion to allow it to prevail on the "higher issues."

As such, it created a passionate response in the country. The reaction of management was well summarized by *Business Week* in 1937, which commented that "by means of sitdown strikes, the country has been put at the mercy of thoroughly irresponsible groups which in effect have no leadership, no control, no authority that can restrain them. Great industries, whose operations affect the daily welfare of millions, are confronted with demands to sign contracts with groups which day by day and hour by hour, demonstrate that they have almost no control over their own people, no respect for property rights or for rights of any kind except their own."[8]

The Communist Party was active in the early CIO, complicating responses further. And the communist influence was especially strong in a series of what one author calls "precipitous and ill-managed strikes" in 1940—the most disruptive being at Allis Chalmers Corporation in Milwaukee, the Vultee Aircraft Company near Los Angeles, and at North American Aircraft in Englewood, California.[9] Communist membership among the United Auto Workers went from 630 in 1935 to 1,100 in 1939, when the Communist Party had perhaps its peak influence in American unions.[10]

The war era of the 1940s was important to labor policy. These were the years in which "business and labor firmly established the industry-wide collective bargaining that would prove routine throughout most of the postwar era" and the time in which was consolidated "the dimension of depression-era insurgency that sought a fundamental transformation of power relationships in the factory, mill and office." In addition, the war created great home-front pressures for social order, predictability, and political orthodoxy. The creation of the National Defense Mediation Board and later the National War Labor Board were steps as important as the Wagner Act in introducing a heavy federal hand into the new "industrial jurisprudence."[11]

Aviation was affected. The Wagner Act and the creation of the CIO also encouraged the International Association of Machinists, the UAW's primary union competitor in the aircraft plants. There was a sit-down strike at Douglas Aircraft in California in 1937, which brought union recognition. That same year, Lockheed accepted the IAM as bargaining agent for its employees.[12] All of these developments were moving things away from Leroy Hill's attitudes and philosophy about management.

Hill's first major contact with the CIO was in 1938 when it organized fifty-seven employees at Air Associates, negotiated inconclusively for a contract, filed charges with the National Labor Relations Board, and then, in the words of Hill's careful chronology, "disappeared until 1941."[13] He wrote his friend Ray Acre in February 1938 in a tone that reflected his deep concern and his acute awareness of the larger implications. The CIO had organized some of the shop and stockroom men, he reported, and tried to get him to sign one of its exclusive bargaining contracts. "I said *NO* very emphatically but quite carefully as I hope we can avoid giving a lot of lawyers a Roman holiday. It's a hell of a condition when the government actually and deliberately endeavors to wreck business and reduce production for the purpose of raising the standard of living—pure insanity . . . . I am getting into a nervous condition where I can't sleep nights but my stomach is O.K."[14]

A month later his stomach seemed to be worse. "This god dam labor business has got me down," he told Acre. "You would not believe what it is necessary to go through to comply with the law as now written and administered. I have heard it said and I most emphatically agree that the major cause of the present depression is reduction of production due to labor trouble. It certainly is reducing production around here. I think that about the only way that we will be able to operate is to gradually let the shop run out of work and shut it down until times get better." The plant, however, could not close up suddenly, as that was against the law. The company could not fire a man for gross inefficiency or refusal to work because the NLRB would issue an order forcing the company to reemploy the man with back wages. "The National Labor Relations Board IS the C.I.O.," Hill stated. He observed that almost all cases were decided for the union and against management and a case cost management a bundle to defend as well.[15]

With Acre Hill waxed broadly philosophical about the issue: it was a question of belief as well as one of strategy and tactics. "I know you always feel a lot of sympathy for your fellow men, but if you had to put up with what I am going through I am sure you would lose a lot of it. It isn't only the administration of the act that is partial and unjust. It is the Wagner act itself that is vicious. It was apparently cooked up to enable organized labor to get control of practically the entire industrial vote . . . and turn it over to the Democratic party. It was probably doped out by a lot of impractical uplifters and some practical labor organizers and made possible by some Democratic politicians getting behind it for vote getting purposes. I don't think they realized what they were doing, which has been the case with a lot of other New Deal schemes. It is based on the fallacious conception that all industry can be divided into two classes of people—capitalists and laborers. This conception confuses capital, which is stored up product of human effort, with people who possess it; and labor which is human effort, with laborers, who make the effort. Capital and Labor are two separate and distinct things, but capitalists and laborers are the same people, since practically everybody works and practically everybody possesses something which is the product of human effort—even if it [is] only a few cents out [of] last weeks pay check and a broken down Ford and the clothes on his back." The Wagner Act, Hill believed, regarded capital and labor as in a natural state of conflict and the "uplifter" thought the laborer should be helped in his fight against the capitalist while the politician knew that there were many more laborers (read "votes") than capitalists. Hill was tired of "loose talk on economics" but wasn't sure what he could do about it.[16]

But he was determined to do something and to stand fast by his principles. Others assured him that his "stubbornness" about the right and the true was a significant liability given the times. Acre, for instance,

wrote Hill in 1938 that, yes, he was right in his concerns about the
Wagner Act but "I doubt if an organization the size of ours is in a position
to put up much of a fight against such forces as the C.I.O. Why not work
cheerfully with the boys and tell them that they are going to soon find out
that adjustments will have to be made or we will lose our business, which
means they will lose their jobs. In the meantime, let's figure what can be
done to carry on through this period of adjustment."[17] Hill understood the
appeal, but it wasn't in his temperament to play the game that way.

This was the pattern straight through Air Associates' union negotiations. Hill was philosophically at odds with the demands of the unions
and the government and insisted upon defending his rights and those of
the company as he perceived them. However, even the directors of Air
Associates increasingly advised Hill to "play along" or "make some accommodation." In the end only one director defended Hill in his stand.[18]

It was not that Hill was such a willing ideological warrior. While later
he averred that he had "fun" in the struggle, every indication at first was
that he abhorred the role. Certainly he always pointed out that the
public/government relations and negotiation part of his job, which was
increasingly prominent in these years, was a nonproductive use of time
that damaged the company, its stockholders, and its employees by diverting
his attention from direct profit-making and wealth-creating activities.

He certainly did not relish needing to deal with the government. "I
most certainly will enjoy sitting down with you," he wrote Haven Page
in Washington, "but you know that I am a little unsympathetic towards
activity in Washington that isn't absolutely necessary. Please don't
misunderstand me—I appreciate your helpful attitude, but from where
I sit, I can't think of a thing to take up in Washington with anybody, that
would result in any increase in revenues."[19] However, he ended up doing
it all—from direct negotiating with the union, to press interviews, to
networking with other executives, to testifying against the Wagner Act
in Washington. He did it because he had to in order to remain himself.

The NLRB complaint of 1938 was Hill's first major experience in
labor negotiations with the CIO. The UAW local made a complaint

against Air Associates charging unfair labor practices in the discharge of employees Joseph Seifert, Warren Thompson, Charles Werner, Joseph Geoghegan, Ted Rodilitz, and Walter Betz from the Roosevelt Field plant. Air Associates had begun to be vulnerable because of Hill's policy of increasing the manufacturing end of a business that had, to that point, largely focused on distribution through its famous catalogue. The union claimed that the men had been discharged for their union activity and that Air Associates had "urged, persuaded and warned its employees . . . to refrain from becoming or remaining members of the union; has threatened said employees with discharge and other reprisals if they became or remained members thereof"; and had kept union meetings under surveillance.[20]

Hill insisted that any meetings between himself and his executives and the union be recorded either on a Dictaphone or by a stenographer. He distributed these transcripts to other employees, to the interested press, sometimes to politicians, and even to his family, on the grounds that only a verbatim record would reveal the actual dynamics to those interested in the truth.

In March and April of 1938 several meetings with union members at the Air Associates shop were thus documented. The shop committee said that the men were not laid off because of economic conditions but rather as "a medium of intimidation or coercion on the other men in the plant." Miner Tuttle, the Air Associates counsel, said that Hill's policy was not even to know the union membership in the plant and that the company wished the union cards to be checked independently of management. The immediate cause of the dismissal of the men was that they had left their jobs at ten o'clock in the morning without permission. The company thought that to reinstate these men immediately would be not only tacitly to admit that they had been wrongfully discharged but to set a precedent for people leaving work willy-nilly. Actually, it was more complicated than that. The men were union shop stewards and said they had asked their foreman for permission to leave for a union meeting in New York City concerning the issues at the plant. They were denied permission and decided to leave anyway. It was a case of technical insubordination, but hardly one of random absenteeism.[21]

Hill argued that the story was still more complex than this. He had talked extensively with Seifert when the union was first organized in the plant and told him, as he told others, that there was a grievance procedure and that compliance with the kind of contract they had submitted "would make it impossible for me to operate the company as I would not be able to exercise control over the employment policy of the company. I further pointed out that the seniority provisions in the contract would make it impossible for us to build an efficient organization because promotions and re-employment after layoff could not be made on the basis of individual work and ability." Seifert, according to Hill, saw the point, at least as an individual: "He seemed quite friendly and understanding and stated that he did not particularly care whether he belonged to the union or not but that he felt he had to 'go along with the boys.'"[22]

On the day the workers left their posts, Art Carrington, foreman of the stockroom, told Hill that Harry Lee had requested permission to leave at 10:30 a.m. to attend a union meeting. According to Hill's account, he told Carrington to deny permission and tell Lee he was endangering his job. Carrington reported back that Lee had decided to leave anyway. Hill then went to the machine shop himself on the suspicion that people there might want to leave. The foreman said that William Hartman and Joseph Seifert had announced they were leaving for a union meeting. Hill claimed that the men announced their intentions rather than requesting permission and that the foreman did not think he was being asked a question he could answer negatively.

Hill said that his unwillingness to let the two leave was not random spite. Hartman was working on a propeller de-icer slinger ring for Pan American Airways that was urgently required for shipment by air express to the West Coast. Seifert was working on some urgent parts for an order for Bellanca Aircraft Company. The foreman intercepted them after talking to Hill and reported back that they insisted on walking out and "had remarked that the union would protect their jobs regardless of his orders." Hill agreed to talk to any of these men personally who had questions about his policy. When one did ask, Hill said, "I told him that we could not operate a business with employees walking out on their responsibilities without notice and that we would therefore have to get other employees who would take the responsibilities of their jobs more seriously."[23] Hill stated that there had been a previous agreement that union activity would not be carried on during working hours and that the employees on the first disputed occasion had not made an attempt to see him or give him an opportunity to contact their union officials to arrange for some other time for their meeting. In his mind, "Failure to discharge these employees because of their membership in the union would be positive discrimination against other employees not members of the union."[24]

Seifert ruined a considerable amount of work on his milling machine a few days after he was reinstated following the absentee charges. Ordinarily this was cause for immediate dismissal, and Hill said the union had approved dismissal on those grounds. Because of Seifert's position with the union and the prior difficulty, the company kept him on for some time until, after further union assurances, he was again dismissed. The union then brought unfair labor practice charges before the NLRB in this second dismissal, introducing technical evidence about the operation of Seifert's machine from a man Hill said had an "utter ignorance of technical details and manufacturing methods."[25]

Hill talked with these men and about them extensively over the next months. The company carried the case through the NLRB hearing process in the fall of 1938 at a cost Hill estimated at $25,000 and then appealed the decision reinstating the men to the circuit court on the grounds that the NLRB examiner was prejudiced in favor of the union. Hill wrote to an Illinois congressman about it: "The ostensible purpose of the hearing was to reinstate six men in jobs for which they are not suited, displacing six men from these jobs who are making a success of them. The real purpose of the hearing, however, is to penalize this company for its failure to make an agreement with a union on terms which they dictated . . . . The whole proceeding has been a bare-faced and shameless attempt to blackjack this company into submitting to the union, and it has already been hinted that more charges will be filed if we have not yet learned our lesson."[26] A decision upholding the board's decision was rendered in court in the fall of 1940.[27]

The detail of the transcripts on the 1938 negotiations and hearings with the union was revealing not only of the trends of the time, but of Hill's particular character and method. The demands of Aircraft Local 365, UAW, CIO, were (1) a closed shop, (2) application of a strict seniority rule in firing, (3) a ten cent per hour across-the-board increase for all plant personnel, (4) a forty-hour work week with time and a half for overtime and the first eight hours on Saturday; double time for Sunday work, after the eighth hour on Saturday, and on certain holidays, and (5) involvement of the shop steward in discharges and grievances and impartial binding arbitration in cases where the foreman and the steward were unable to agree.[28] Hill disagreed with these and told the men, the attorneys, and the arbitrators exactly why.

On the matter of the closed shop, Hill said he could not understand what reason the union found that this would advance the welfare of its members. Abner Rubien of the UAW replied that with the closed shop there could be a "more solidified group of men, more in accord." It was also argued that closed shops protected the company in that it prevented other unions from coming in and "raising hell in the shops," as well as ensuring management would have only one union to deal with. Did it increase production? Hill asked. It seemed to him it would hamper it by denying management its choice of men. What was the union willing to offer the company in return for a closed shop? Was this a bargaining session, with give and take, or just a listing of union demands? Perhaps there could be some wage concessions, Rubien replied. Hill picked up. How much? Rubien would not say. Hill: "If we can save a lot in wages which would help make up for all the time spent in the bargaining, that might be a consideration which might make us favor closed shop."[29]

On the seniority question, Hill thought that with a closed shop seniority might not be so important. He argued that the company generally worked on a seniority basis anyway. The union people said that strict seniority made for "tenure of position," so the men would not feel afraid or insecure. Hill response was: "I can't see that an able employee needs any such guarantee. I have never had it and can't get it. I should think an able employee would be opposed to a seniority rule because it might prevent his advancement . . . . Look at your own organization. You fellows haven't been there so long, but talk to any old employee in our organization and he will tell you seniority has always been used after consideration has been given to the individual ability. . . . The only way I can see we can improve the efficiency of our organization is through the selection of particularly efficient individuals, and the only way we can find those particularly efficient individuals is through trial and error. . . . Unless I can see some advantage to such an arrangement, we wouldn't want our judgment hampered in any way. It seems to me that anything that is good for the Company ought to be for the good of all the men . . . ."[30]

Rubien had brief responses to this. "That isn't in accord with the labor movement throughout the country," he said. And then later, and more telling, "I am afraid, Mr. Hill, that the unlimited discretion of the Corporation, not only in your industry, but throughout industries in general, is a thing of the past."[31]

Hill was not ready to accept either that he was, as a manager, of some other class than his workers or that it was time for him as president to abandon his sole responsibility in order to join in team decision making. "When it comes to the final decision, that is what I am paid for. I am paid to make decisions as to who is fitted to do a job, who is to be given new jobs and who is considered inefficient, and to decide when new people shall be put to work and when people shall be laid off. That is my duty. Now you are asking me as an individual to hand decisions of that kind over to somebody else. I can't do this. I haven't the power to do it."[32]

He offered, unasked, several lessons in basic market economics. There was this on extra wages: "You can't just say the Company will make it up to you. It is just as difficult for the Company to get money in as it is for the individual to get it in. If you lay down a positive time and a half overtime and limit us to 40 hours a week you are going to limit production. The extra cost to the customer eliminates your opportunities to do work, to earn extra money."[33]

His attorney pointed out a Hill basic: "Mr. Hill feels that it will not help in arriving at an agreement, to set up a fence and have you sitting on one side and he sitting on the other side. His feeling is that this Company is one organization and that everybody in it from the lowest salaried employee to the man who owns the most stock in it have the same interest, and that is to have the Company function economically and successfully. By successfully I mean that it may make a profit. If it can make a profit everybody is going to prosper. If it can't make a profit nobody is going to prosper."[34] Hill himself elaborated this point in a remarkable exchange:

Hill: I am a worker. I am not the owner.
Field: You are the President. You represent the stockholders.
Hill: And so do all the other employees. I am here as a representative of the Company and everybody connected with it, its stockholders and employees. It hasn't been proven to me that all of them have joined your Union.
Fox: We can get a lot farther if we don't ignore the economic realities. Those fairy tales about the interests of the employers and the employees being identical, those are just fairy tales.[35]

The parties were miles apart, and the differences were basic. Hill thought people ought to love to work, as he did. He wrote to Acre that he could not imagine limiting working hours except in dangerous occupations where health was at stake. "However, in most occupations no harm is done to the individual to let him work as long as he pleases. It is good for the individual to let him work as long as he wants to because he earns more and it is good for the country as a whole because the production is increased . . . . In a business, the value of an individual is measured by how much he produces, not by the time he spends. A business is a community—a group of individuals banded together for their common good . . . . An individual who works long hours and works

137

Hill at about age forty, at the zenith of influence as president of Air Associates.

efficiently will earn more and get further ahead than an individual who does not. The same is true of business . . . . No individual believes in a share the work program when it comes to dividing up his own income."[36]

Morris Field, an international board member of the aviation branch of the UAW, disagreed: "Nobody takes any interest in a job nowadays. It is monotonous and tiresome." Hill insisted that the company was a wealth creator and that if management's ability to create wealth and to sell competitively to customers were compromised, workers as well as stockholders would suffer. The union response was "where you get that money is really not our problem. It is a management problem." The union said that Hill was being stubborn, fulfilling the requirement of the labor laws to bargain, but with no intention of coming to any conclusion. Hill said that there was no exchange, only demands, that principles were at stake that would damage all his workers and that he could not afford to be dictated to. The union argued that competition was not an issue, as there was an "evolution" that would bring everyone around to the same rules. Hill was afraid it would not happen quickly enough to save Air Associates.[37]

Testimony that fall before the NLRB by the dismissed men gave a sample of Hill's casual style with them in the plant. He seemed eager to talk to them individually about their grievances, but loath to make these discussions into a formal union procedure. When he had dismissed the men, they claimed he had intimated that he was testing the Wagner Act and did not want any union "telling me how to run my business." He spoke of one particular employee, Thomas Berger, who had been dismissed after many discussions with him concerning his temper and his violently suspicious attitude regarding management. "There is a union fellow for you, " Hill was reported as saying, "cursing and throwing tools around." Supposedly when asked about signing a contract with the union, Hill had told the men, "I am too old, and I am not going to change."[38]

One upshot of the 1938 troubles was the institution at Air Associates of a written employment agreement. "Although this may seem like a needless formality to many of you," Hill wrote in a circular letter to his employees, "it is a fact, as you all undoubtedly know, that employer and employee relationships have been considerably complicated during the past few years by federal and state laws creating possibly considerable confusion in the minds of many of us as to the respective obligations of the company and the employee." The letter stated that the company was not interested in employees' personal affairs and that this included union membership, religious and political opinions, social activities, and personal relationships. However, the condition of employment was that the work the employee did should be satisfactory in the opinion of the president and that this determination rested solely with the president or

Air Associates appeals for workers at its new Bendix plant, about 1941.

his designees. Union critics later called this employee agreement a "yellow dog contract," a contention that Hill vigorously denied.[39]

In the relatively calm interim on the labor relations front between these 1938 dismissals and the more serious 1941 confrontation at Air Associates, Hill pursued legislative change by supporting those in Congress, particularly Senator Edward R. Burke of Nebraska, who were pushing amendments to the Wagner Act. Hill wrote Burke late in May 1938 after Burke had sent him a radio address. Hill disagreed with Burke's viewpoint in that he thought the Wagner Act should be repealed entirely. It was "wrong in principle, is vicious in its effect." The key flaw was the class division assumed. "The Wagner Act created conflict because it decreed bargaining, and since bargaining presumes a conflict of interest, it therefore decrees conflict and provided that this conflict shall exist between employers and employees." Hill was upset that under the Wagner act a union organizer could come into a plant and recruit at any time and by any means. It guaranteed noninterference from employees who refused to join or who disagreed with the union creed by classifying these employees as "employers" and "denying them both the right of free speech and the right of membership in the same organization that it guarantees to the other workers. This makes it easy for Union spell-binders to lead large numbers of people of lesser intelligence, with the promise of something for nothing, into actions which result in just the opposite."[40]

To Hill what was important to the welfare of employees as a whole was not what job a certain individual held, but having as many people as possible producing efficiently. Welfare, he said, was measured by the satisfaction of our wants, and "prosperity is simply having more of the things that we want than we had at some previous time. Since the only way to have more things is to produce them, it follows that prosperity is the effect of increased production." The NLRB, in Hill's opinion, was not interested in increasing production and employing more people in that way. Rather, it was concerned with the protection of individuals and organizations whose creed was more pay for less production. According to Hill, at Air Associates a simple organization had been divided by the

Wagner Act into two opposing groups, "both of which now have less than they had previously." Hundreds of hours and thousands of dollars had been wasted "bargaining." Production and employment had been reduced. The only answer was entire repeal of the Wagner Act.[41]

In March 1939 Hill wrote Burke again giving a summary of Air Associates' experience with the NLRB and offering more philosophical comment. "We have been operating for just about a year," he wrote, "under the handicap of Labor Board persecution." The NLRB complaint had resulted, he said, in 2,500 pages of testimony, which the company paid for at a rate of forty-five cents a page, not to mention the attorneys' fees and the time. Hill believed that the board purposefully dragged out the proceedings to penalize the company and that the trial examiner had showed "obvious and shameless" bias. Hill had just learned that there was another discriminatory discharge case pending against Air Associates, the third, and concluded that "their system is to slug us with labor board cases until we acknowledge defeat and come to them on our knees." His defense was the written employment contract that required employees to report immediately any violations of the law at the plant. He hoped this would avoid dredging up "overheard remarks" as evidence of company policy in hearings months or years later. Hill did not know how many union members he had in 1939, but suspected that there were very few and that some who had joined in 1938 had resigned. Nevertheless, he said, the NLRB would continue to regard the UAW local as the exclusive bargaining agent "for whatever they choose to consider an appropriate bargaining unit and will continue to persecute us until we consent to cooperate with their chosen union to force our employees to join and pay tribute to us." He confessed that his policy might be tough on stockholders and present and future employees, "but there are some principles worth fighting for."[42]

On June 7, 1939, Hill testified before the Senate Committee on Education and Labor concerning his views of the Wagner Act given his specific experiences with it. Hill said that his company had always been willing to bargain with any group or individual at any time or place and on any subject, but it would not "make concessions nor pay tribute to any group or individual in return for the promise of protection or immunity from prosecution or persecution by the Labor Board." He said that in his twenty-seven years as a worker in industry, he had never opposed or expressed opposition to labor unions and that there was no evidence in any of the transcripts that he ever had. After the controversy over layoffs, Hill took away all power to discharge from managerial employees and handled every case himself (incidentally, with his usual meticulous written documentation of the exact circumstances). When told by an executive of the NLRB that "every $15 a week stenographer always looks down on the man who works in the shop," Hill expressed amazement, saying, "We do not operate our business nor treat our employees in accordance with the conceptions of such $15 a week stenographers." Again he suggested the repeal of the act that in his view encouraged such class distinctions.[43]

Hill expanded his views in a letter to the *New York Herald Tribune* in October 1939. The letter was a sort of primer in market economics, and Hill was direct indeed in expressing his logical and moral concerns with the new age. "Progress and prosperity in America has been built upon free enterprise—the right of the individual to trade the product of his effort for as much of the products of others as they are willing to pay." The New Deal threatened that. "We deliberately destroy things that people want that have been produced. We discourage further production by robbing some of the people through high taxes of some of the product of their effort, and giving it to other people in return for not producing things that are wanted. We encourage organized ignorance to produce less as a means of getting more of the products of others. We restrict free enterprise." Wage and hour laws were the worst of the lot, as they prohibited many from trading their efforts for anything at all and more efficient workers were forced to contribute through taxes to their support. Hill always defended the twenty-five-cent-per-hour jobs for boys at the Air Associates plant and said that average wages were competitive and advancement swift for those who learned well and applied themselves. Most restrictions upon individual choice, whether the individual was a manager or an employee, were ultimately damaging to all. "Let's tear up the deck and quit making believe that government is a game of cards."[44]

Still another expression of Hill's general philosophy, pithily stated, came in a letter to Senator Rush Holt in September of 1940. Holt had given a speech against the draft. Hill was not against the draft if necessary for national defense, but he did think a great deal of equipment would be needed before more men would be useful in the war effort. He went on: "Why has no one proposed a draft which would be limited to members of the C.C.C., N.Y.A., W.P.A. and other government charity agencies?" Ironically, though, army pay of $30 a month would be illegal for any private industry to pay under the minimum wage laws. Perhaps if the minimum wage law was reduced to army pay, the draft would eliminate unemployment. "Maybe you could persuade the New Deal to try this as a final experiment. At least it would not discourage production— and production is one thing that is needed more than anything else for defense." Hill added that it was not only the details of New Deal programs that were damaging the country's defense, but the spirit it engendered. "France's capitulation is an example of the weakness generated by idealistic social uplift laws on false premises. Prosperity and power result only from an increase in the supply of things needed to satisfy material wants; —an increase as compared to the supply at some previous time or to that possessed by someone else. The only way to *increase* the supply of *things* is to *Produce more* things. Laws which reduce production, therefore, are against the national interest, even though they might benefit a special group."[45]

Of course, a law he specifically mentioned was the National Labor Relations Act. The unions were benefited by it, he wrote, but they stood ultimately for reduced production and more pay for their members. "They place a premium on inefficiency. They seek to better themselves by creating an artificial scarcity of the things their members produce. They sell memberships and collect dues from the unintelligent on the promise of 'more for less' or 'something for nothing.' They have convinced their members with the help of the government that they belong to a distinct and mistreated class. They are backed in their sales campaign by the Federal government, which, through the N.L.R.B., denies the right of free speech to workers who dare to expose the fallacy of the union creed. Producing organizations are wrecked through Kangaroo court proceedings and back-wage penalties levied without regard to logic, justice or national welfare, and aimed only at promoting union membership sales and dues collections. The N.L.R.A. is a proven deterrent to production. It promotes strife. It discourages individual initiative. It encourages loafing. It has wrecked discipline in shops throughout the country. It has weakened the industrial and military strength of our country. No nation—no army—no corporation, whose leaders are powerless to exercise discipline, can compete with a disciplined organization."[46]

Air Associates contested every labor case and appealed every decision at great cost in time and dollars. Hill wrote letters to editors and joined organizations protesting violations of the Constitution. The company's attorneys argued bias; they argued that there was no substantial evidence introduced that the company was culpable under the law; they claimed that due process was violated in the passion of the moment of crisis and the desire for restitution of perceived general wrongs; they pointed to their verbatim records and they distributed them for all to see. Irritation of a foreman, they said, was not in itself an unfair labor practice. Neither was economic conflict. Nor were random comments. In 1940 the Air Associates brief pointed out there had been no labor dispute of any sort at the plant since 1938. "Its participation in the national defense program is proceeding smoothly and on schedule. The local union involved in these proceedings has been dissolved. The employees of 1938 are largely gone." All that could be achieved by further enforcement was to "disrupt [the] respondent's business and create industrial strife and unrest where there is now peace. That is not the purpose of the Act."[47]

Still, it was sure that neither Hill nor his attorneys nor his managers were certain that it was over, given the trend in fundamentals and the deep division over the way things should be between the operating head of Air Associates and union and government representatives. Hill clipped a piece from a New York newspaper in January 1940, presumably because it represented something of his view. "It really does no good," the reporter wrote, "to argue with those who are devoted to the C.I.O. because they start from the premise that majority rule cancels minority rights and that organized labor must engage in politics. Anyone who does not concede these things as a beginning is a Fascist."[48] Also in one of his file folders was a CIO poster, torn from a bulletin board at Air Associates in 1938. "By joining this 'Brotherhood' you keep out unions which are not incorporated—and by so doing you are masters of yourselves . . . . Don't you think it is about time you 'aircraft workers' had someone to represent you in Washington and elsewhere? . . . . WE MUST ORGANIZE. The protection of the Government is ours; why not use it?"[49] That "why not?" rang as strongly in the 1940s as before, and the war crisis raised the stakes for both sides.

There was a lull, however, before labor relations dominated the horizon at Air Associates again. Hill read books on the general issues of how the economy should work in relation to government—for instance, Connor Ross's *The Sphere of Individualism*—and the subject was never off his mind again.[50] And with each pause Hill continued his program of building the company and its prosperity according to his idea of what was good for all elements of it.

Actually the Depression—coming as it did before Hill, who took the presidency in 1931, had time to deal completely with the high overhead and optimistic practices of the young Yale founders—caused serious damage to the company for only a short period. The catalog grew and continued to be a wonder. In 1934 the company made a profit, and Hill's salary was raised to $12,000. In 1934 the profitable California branch started, and the same year he took up manufacturing in a corner of a hangar at Roosevelt Field with a lathe and a couple of drill presses left over from the repair business. In 1935 he discontinued the repair of airplanes, as he had discontinued the sale of them in 1932. There were only twelve men in the manufacturing shop as late as 1937, but with additional capital and more markets, that part of the business, with its accompanying labor difficulties, became ever more remunerative thereafter.[51] The company manufactured airplane seat buckles and seat belts, needed more and more by the commercial airlines. It made airport beacons, special tail wheels, lighted wind cones, radio-shielding equipment, and spark plug shields. Its export business grew, and Air Associates became the exclusive sales agent in the United States for a number of foreign manufacturers. Air Associates gained some basic U.S. accounts too, and were direct representatives for American Steel and Wire Company, General Tire and Rubber, and American Plywood. In 1935 the company declared its first dividend.[52]

The numbers in the annual report show the financial gains. In 1933 there was a loss of $968.98 on sales of $250,296.21. That was the last loss. In 1934 there were sales of $454,215.73 and net profit after taxes of $31,013.10. In 1935 sales were $688,271.82 and profit $40,512.50. Sales in 1936 were $1,045,114.18 and profit $65,033.08. In 1937 sales were $1,450,366.88 and profit $82,290.19. The year 1938 saw sales of $1,844,522.42 and profit of $104,808.80. In his presidential statement for 1938 Hill noted that "the broad diversification as to both customers and products which has characterized the business of the Company has been maintained. Customers include every branch of the aviation industry in all parts of the world and the company either manufactures or distributes practically every item needed for the manufacture, operation and maintenance of private, commercial or military aircraft."[53]

The outbreak of war in Europe only made steady growth exponential. Sales for 1939, including branches at Chicago, Dallas, and Glendale, were $1,860,774.04 with net profit of $126,939.52. There were unfilled orders amounting to $400,000, a record.[54] The next year, 1940, was a year of national preparedness and enormous expansion of the aircraft industry and all its ancillaries. As the Air Associates Annual Report put it: "With the eyes of all America focused on one industry— aviation—as our hope for impregnable defense and national integrity, we might well look upon the story of its growth—the growth of an opportunity and a vision—as it is reflected in the development of one company from a small store, offering the first unified aviation service to the groping plane builders of fourteen years ago, to a million dollar organization supplying the complex, special equipment demands of today's commercial, military and private aviation manufacturers." Air Associates in 1940 had 600 employees in manufacturing and 150,000 square feet in four strategic marketing plants; it was earning in a few hours the $5,000 that represented the company's entire business receipts in its first year of operation. Sales in 1940 were $4,065,111.80 and profit $409,265.56.[55]

From that time throughout the war, the curve was to be straight up. Hill's only disappointment was that the stock price did not quite follow suit.[56] The company's 1941 sales were $7,410,746.19 with net earnings of $456,554.78. Sales peaked at $12,512,296.57 in 1945 with additional branches in Atlanta, Kansas City, Los Angeles, and Seattle, before dropping to just over $5,000,000 in 1947, leading to losses for the first time since 1933.[57] During the war years Air Associates experienced its peak, guided by the mission Hill and his associates had set for it. After the war the company focused more and more on electronics, after making its first electronic product in 1939. So transformed did it become that in 1956 it moved to St. Petersburg, Florida, and in 1957 changed its name to Electronic Communications, Inc.[58]

The prosperity of Air Associates was not solely due to external conditions: in the 1930s external conditions were terrible and the competition great. Much of it must be attributed to Hill's innovations, his personal strength, and his management style and substance. It was Hill, not the directors, who took the initiative to drop the airplane sales and repairs, thus cutting a major loss point just in time. It was Hill who pushed the Glendale branch in 1934 and negotiated the merger in 1938 that added the Dallas outlet. Hill got interest rates lowered to 2 percent from the 3.5 percent at which the company had been borrowing. He was primarily responsible, with a lot of help from Harold Crow, for expanding the catalogue, using the significant Hill and Crow experience in handling inventory and attracting sales lines, going all the way back to their World War I service.[59] And Hill's personal touch and force of character were everywhere. That the results were so good, and that the man was seen as so important to those results, is an important fact to keep in mind in understanding why, during the 1941 strike, so many Air Associates employees were so loyal not only to the company but to Hill personally, and why the attempt to split the organization along class lines was unsuccessful.

One Hill innovation in management was his unified central control system from Roosevelt Field, New York. He insisted on loyalty, to the point that Acre accused him of exaggerating and of pulling the old Victor Lougheed trick of trying to tell people what they were thinking. Hill wrote to the Glendale branch: "If there is someone in the organization out there who is going around continually griping about the stupidity of the home office organization, their mistakes, their shortcomings, etc. it will permeate the organization and will not make for efficiency. I have noticed that the smaller the man, the more indignant he gets at the home office or the branch organizations as the case may be. What we want is a spirit of co-operation and a feeling that we are all one organization and that the problems of the home office are also the problems of the branches and vice versa. It does no good for the Glendale office or any part of it to treat the Garden City office as though they were a vendor and try to teach us a lesson on quality of material by making us pay transportation charges on it all the way across the country. The problem of this rejected material has to be dealt with. It is just as much your problem as it is ours."[60] Hill balanced the need for centralized control with that for decentralized action by instituting Form 405 at the company. This created small supervised groups and made the supervisor responsible for the actions of these groups to the central management.[61]

He insisted on absolute honesty. He refused to be a part of any shady industry practice to get business or to retain any employee, valuable or not, about whose character there was any question. He refused to send

Air Associates stock to Acre to be used as a kind of bribe to get a contract at the Lockheed plant. "If we can't get Lockheed's business by legitimate methods we will just have to struggle along without it. I am not going to argue the point as to whether the legitimate methods are more costly—I think they are not in the long run—but regardless of that, I am through with that kind of funny business. . . . At any rate I am willing to take the consequences of our depending on the quality of our products, our prices on them and the service we can render alone and if we can't sell on that basis we had better fold up."[62] Acre had an employee in Glendale whom Hill absolutely demanded be fired, despite the difficulty of getting good salesmen during the war emergency, because he had stolen from the company in the past; furthermore, he was an uncontrollable drinker and a man whose word could not be relied upon. "I don't dispute [his] ability as a salesman," Hill wrote, "but I'd a hell of a lot rather sacrifice the sales than have the guy in the organization." After several exchanges in which Acre argued he could control the man, Hill dispatched a short note. "[He] may be all of those things that you say—I don't dispute it. But I'd rather let the Glendale organization rot and disintegrate and let the company go busted than keep him. I really mean it. Sorry."[63] Mighty clear!

In addition to the evolution of specific policies, Hill was important to Air Associates for his uncanny sense of the proper combinations of lines to carry as well as the right prices and margins to remain both competitive and profitable. He pioneered the idea of "just in time" inventory, criticizing his managers both for hoarding too much inventory in anticipation of increased sales and forgetting that the goal was profit, not sales volume. He was involved by the 1940s in the financing of Air Associates as well as every other aspect of the business and therefore saw the whole of the picture as he pieced the puzzle together. It was important, Hill often noted, to do a level and kind of business appropriate to the company's capital, manufacturing capacity, market contacts, and people.[64]

When complaints from customers arose when Air Associates raised the price on bolts in 1940, Hill wrote his managers that no doubt the chagrin was exaggerated. "We expected to lose business when we increased the price of bolts. That was what we wanted. We wanted to reduce the amount of orders we were taking down to what our capacity was, and at the same time substantially increase the profit that we were making on the volume of business that we can do." How he determined pricing, Hill could not exactly say. "I can't tell you how I do it; maybe it is the workings of the subconscious mind, but I have been guessing at these things for many years and the fact that we are still in business and making money in a business that has been very difficult for anybody else to stay in makes me think that maybe my guesses are pretty good." As for the customers, there was a subtle psychology involved. "Subconsciously they will feel that our bolts are better because they cost more, and it will be very much easier for a salesman to convince a customer of the superiority of our products if we can brag about the fact that it sells at a higher price than [a] competitor's bolts. Then when the competitors raise their prices to meet ours he can go back again and say we are selling a superior bolt and that it actually costs no more than the competitors.' In other words, it is often easier to sell something if you don't try too hard, especially when you are in the enviable position of handling all the orders that you can handle anyway."[65] This kind of savvy advice, issued in a personal manner to managers, combined with successful implementation, built a close management team at Air Associates.

His attitudes and practices regarding labor seemed for the moment workable also. Hill used individual personnel problems, more frequent as war orders poured in, to expand on his general philosophy of dealing with people in an organization fairly but firmly. He pointed out in later letters that any use that could be made of a dishonest employee was small compared to the damage that was done to the organization. "I have impressed on . . . supervisory personnel around here, that suspicion of dishonesty, sense of distrust, general unreliability of an individual, are all sufficient causes for dismissal. It is not necessary to have absolute proof. We should give ourselves the benefit of the doubt and operate the company on our opinion and judgment. When an individual is employed by the company, that individual does not thereupon have a vested right to continuance of employment. On the contrary, he is continually selling what he produces to the company, and the company still has the right to stop buying at any and all times for any or no reason (except as specifically prohibited by the screw-ball labor law, which is a bureaucratic infringement on individual liberty)."[66]

Hill did not believe in Christmas bonuses and thought that company parties should be operated by employees, not by management, lest they seem paternalistic substitutes for fair reward for hard work. "I believe the average employee appreciates the fact that every one in the company is employed on the same terms and conditions except for rate of pay which is determined by the individual's contribution to the enterprise."[67] Wages needed to meet the competition for all, and for certain key individuals, it would be necessary to pay top dollar, all the while recognizing that "higher expenses will necessitate higher margins of profit." The president continued to be concerned about the mental and physical health of these key people. "I know how high strung Dick is," he wrote to Acre in the Glendale office. "He has been working under pressure and carrying a great deal of responsibility. I think he is going to pieces and will have a nervous breakdown if you don't take some responsibility away from him . . . . This business of ours is hard on the nerves because we handle so many thousands of different items and particularly now when we are having so much trouble getting deliveries of materials . . . . There is no use going haywire about it."[68] Above all, Hill wanted to avoid the impression that peoples' fate in Air Associates was determined in any way by an inflexible system independent of human judgment traceable to an individual manager, or, worse, to politics. That type of process had become particularly repulsive to him, and he would rather be accused of being hard-hearted than to move in a direction he considered inherently unworkable as well as ultimately unjust to the majority.

All this was sensible from his perspective and admired by many fellow top managers. But events beyond Hill's control soon created a result at Air Associates beyond his imagining.

Explosion

*I*n 1940 President Roosevelt called for the immediate manufacture of 50,000 airplanes for national defense. Every aircraft manufacturing plant and aircraft supply business was overwhelmed with orders (Air Associates had $2,000,000 in unfilled orders in the summer of 1940) and was expanding facilities. The Japanese were moving into Shanghai, and Hill advised Isabella and Beverly not to take any chances if trouble started.[1]

Thus began one of the most extraordinary and rapid defense buildups in the history of the world. Understandably it affected management and union relations centrally. Writes historian Joel Seidman of the atmosphere in U.S. companies at the time of the fall of France: "Many leading employers still dealt with unions because they had to, holding them at arm's length and restricting as narrowly as possible the scope of their influence." A no-strike agreement by the major labor federations during the war, the wage controls of wartime, and the inflationary wage-price spiral of the postwar reconversion culminating in the Taft-Hartley Act of 1947, with its "cooling off" provisions for strikes and open-shop protections, would seem to make the war a down era for unionism. But labor emerged from the decade with a membership of fifteen million compared with nine million in 1940, and in many relatively new industries, like aviation, thousands of workers were hired who had had not only no experience with unions before but no experience with employment at all.[2] "Shift change," wrote one observer, "resembled a high school dismissal." Their paychecks were fat, profits were high, and they could see the benefits of joining a group to protect and advance those interests.[3]

Still, at first blush it appeared that the defense crisis would resolve labor disputes temporarily in favor of management. The number of work stoppages in 1937 was 4,740, more than double the previous year and far over the previous record from 1917. However, over the next two years strikes declined and there was "a growing public impatience and irritation with the labor movement" as winning the war became a central concern. The primary student of wartime labor policy calls 1941, the year the dramatic strike at Air Associates took place, "a period of relative peace in labor-management relations."[4] The view emphasizes the significance of the word "relative." From Hill's perspective there was no peace at all.

When there were work stoppages, the public tended to blame the unions, and relatively minor interruptions became front-page news. The first strike to threaten defense production was that of the CIO's Industrial Union of Marine and Shipbuilding Workers against the Kearny, New Jersey, plant of the Federal Shipbuilding and Dry Dock Company. The union tried for a union shop and ended up with a compromise clause in which the company agreed to give each new employee a copy of the contract. Shortly several "wildcat" strikes, carried out despite the no-strike agreement between the unions and Washington, hit the West Coast aircraft industry. In November 1940, 3,200 workers went out at Vultee in an attempt to raise the company's hourly wage for beginners from fifty to seventy-five cents. There was a seventy-six-day strike at the Allis-Chalmers plant in Milwaukee early in 1941 and strikes also at International Harvester and Bethlehem Steel.[5]

The federal response was immediate and strong. Franklin Roosevelt by executive order established the National Defense Mediation Board in March 1941. The board, consisting of three public, four labor, and four employee representatives, was charged with mediating labor disputes affecting the national defense. That spring Ford Motors, long a union holdout, entered into contractual relations with the UAW, and "Little Steel" followed the trend.[6]

In general, compulsory arbitration was popular at the time. In 1941 more than half the strikes in the United States were settled through the intervention of government officials or boards. The National Defense Mediation Board settled usually through public recommendation, though sometimes by direct mediation. Theoretically its public recommendations had no binding force on the parties, but the actuality was different. "The parties understood," concluded a 1943 study, "that failure to agree involved a gamble as to what the Board would recommend. The parties understood also that public opinion and even governmental force might compel acceptance of the recommendation." That might take the form of threat of loss of government contracts or seizure of the plant by the government either for a period, until things changes, or for the duration of the war. These givens made those recommendations, to understate it as the study did, "quasi-compulsory."[7]

In the field of aviation, perhaps the most telling labor incident of 1941 was the wildcat strike at North American Aviation in June. The UAW in 1940 had authorized an organizational drive in the aircraft plants in California, a point away from the traditional geographical strongholds of the union. But the strike at North American was neither authorized nor approved by the national UAW rank and file; rather, it was an exercise in autonomy by a Communist-oriented Los Angeles Local 683 during a time when a wage increase issue for North American workers was before the National Defense Mediation Board. Richard Frankensteen of the UAW was hooted down by the North American workers as he advised a return to work.

The final result was a meeting between Franklin Roosevelt, Sidney Hillman, and William Knudsen of the Office of Production Management in which all agreed that the army should be used to take over the plant and reopen it. This was done with 2,500 troops on June 10, 1941. Some defended the action, noting that strikes like that at North American were "not real Labor strikes. . . . They were strikes against the government." However, William Z. Foster, a Communist leader, said the federal troops used at North American provided "a taste of Hitleristic terrorism that Wall Street capitalists have in mind for the working class."[8]

Whatever the controversy about Communist influence in the North American strike, and whether the wage dispute justified it, the spectacle of soldiers marching on and injuring strikers was widely interpreted to

One result of the Air Associates strike in the fall of 1941.

be the end of legitimate striking for the duration of the war and to effectively suppress political dissent in the union movement. It was the first use of troops to break up a strike since the Pullman strike of 1894. In the case of the Employers Negotiating Committee, involving a strike in fifty-two Northwest Lumber camps, the head of the union charged the National Defense Mediation Board with "trying to bulldoze our workers" by simply rewording management's offer as its recommendation.[9]

The situation at Air Associates, where another of the rare violent interventions by the federal government occurred as arbitration broke down, followed a different pattern. There, too, in October 1941 troops were used to stop a wildcat strike at a defense facility, but on that occasion the action was not anti-union; rather, it resulted in a forced change of management and not too subtle pressure on the new board for recognition of the UAW. Something similar happened at a strike at the Federal Shipbuilding and Dry Dock Company in August 1941, when the shipyard was temporarily taken over by the navy due to management's refusal to change its position on labor issues, and company control was returned only several months later.[10] Such cases strongly suggest that while stabilization of defense plants was the goal of these extreme interventions, it was not so much inflexible ideology as the specific circumstances of the work stoppage and the personalities and claims of the individuals representing management and labor that dictated the labor-management balance after federal force was applied.

The events at Air Associates are particularly important precisely because they are anomalous. They illustrate the more ideological/intellectual nature of mature militant trade unionism in the immediate New York City vicinity.[11] It is a further demonstration too, if any is needed, of how deeply the force of Leroy Hill's personality and policy could influence events with which he was connected.

The Air Associates Company, unable to expand sufficiently at Roosevelt Field, moved to the Bendix airport in New Jersey and constructed a new plant with 12,000 square feet of executive, sales, and engineering offices and 63,000 square feet of manufacturing area. The new facility opened with great ceremony on October 1, 1940. At the same time, land was purchased at the Los Angeles Municipal Airport, and plans were under way to construct a new 40,000-square-foot building there.[12]

Hill reemphasized his advice on appropriate scale. "I don't want to pass up any chances to make money except for surer chances to make still more money. However, we have to pass up lots of chances because we don't have the money to finance them and the cost of financing would take the profit away . . . . We are doing a tight rope act with our financing now and it gets on my nerves. I don't want to be destructive in my criticisms or suggestions but we have got to make money faster or pull in our horns."[13] Hill had arranged further financing, but before it was final, labor troubles again put Air Associates in the headlines and out of the business mode.

Though union activity since 1938 had been minimal, government relations had remained strained. In 1940, for example, a federal grand jury indicted four airplane fabric manufacturing corporations, including Air Associates, on charges of agreement to rig prices on that material. One of Hill's friends wrote him in jest that "you're fast gaining a reputation which in time will place your name in the annals of criminal history along-side those of Jesse James—Dillinger—yes, even Moe Annenberg. Just one of those guys who is persistently attempting to thwart the government."[14] Amid all the expansion there was a constant Damocles' sword of which everyone in management at the new Bendix facility was painfully aware.

The union later said that Air Associates had "fled" to Bendix to avoid union organization. If so, it was not a successful tactic. On June 17, 1941, a CIO representative appeared at the new plant, claimed to represent a "vast majority" of the workers, and demanded that a contract "satisfactory to the union" be signed. The company agreed to an NLRB-supervised election. This was a concession because the Wagner Act did not require a certification election unless the union could show that it had collected authorizing signatures from at least 30 percent of the nonmanagerial employees, which in this case was not done.

The election was held July 1. The "bargaining unit" was defined to include only 428 of the 650 employees at the Bendix plant and none of the 250 at the branch plants. The UAW/CIO won the election with 206 of the 401 votes cast, hardly an overwhelming mandate, and there were recriminations charging that the election did not fairly represent opinion among workers then, and especially not after the strike began.[15] The new laws gave the union some advantages, not only in gerrymandering the election pool to identify pro- and anti-union workers (something which, if done by management, was an unfair labor practice), but in promising the workers things when the company was not allowed to make its own promises.[16]

On July 3 nine men in the sheet metal department were laid off because of an aluminum shortage, and the union demanded their reinstatement. On July 8 the union presented a contract including provisions for a closed shop and a checkoff. On July 11, with little time for negotiations, a strike was called and a picket line established, ostensibly on the sheet metal layoff issue.

That morning a member of the shop committee stood up in the factory and made a speech attacking another employee. When an attempt was made to reprimand him, he insisted that the entire committee be present. This committee left work and convened, but refused to talk in Hill's office if a record of the meeting was made. Later that day the committee entered the shop in a body. One committeeman pulled the quit-work whistle cord while the others shouted "strike" and ran through the shop, stopping machines and in some cases trying to pull men away from their work. One manager claimed that the union representatives at this time actually made the ultimate statement of industrial democracy, claiming that "the government had granted them an interest in the business which they were going to protect."[17]

To counter this action, the company cut the steam from the whistle and locked unguarded entrances. The Bendix police officer ejected them, but they were joined by others in a short time. Within an hour a picket line had been formed on the road outside carrying signs reading "AIR ASSOCIATES EMPLOYEES LOCKED OUT." Hill sent a telegram to Loren Houser, regional director of the UAW, which read: "Your committee of our employees left their jobs this afternoon and forced a number of other employees to join them. Is this a strike and is it authorized and approved by the U.A.W., C.I.O.? If so, state reasons by telegraph immediately as we are engaged on National Defense Work." He did not receive a reply. He then sent a telegram to about thirty absent employees: "Claims of lockout by the company false. Plant still operating. Your job waiting. Report immediately. Protection guaranteed."[18]

While the company claimed that there were never more than fifty employees on the picket line, there were hundreds of imported ones. CIO spokesmen reiterated that the government had provided them an interest in the business which they intended to defend and asked that negotiations be conducted without a written record. Hill thought that this strike, which lasted eighteen days, was a "pretext strike of a small minority with accompanying violence" designed to get the case before the National Defense Mediation Board, a group Hill considered friendly to the union movement and the closed shop idea.[19]

Whatever the motive, the strike was effective, not in shutting down production (the plant maintained 85 percent to 90 percent production through this first disturbance), but in focusing press and management on the labor issue. Acre wrote Hill: "It is obvious that you were framed. They've undoubtedly been laying for you." He said that the company was getting bad press in California, with the "godam lie" being circulated that Air Associates paid the lowest wages in the industry. "Attitude of large customers was interesting—they wished us success, but warned us they didn't want it to interfere with service . . . . Odds against you are great. Wonder if they could stop us from getting government work?"[20] Hill's opinion was more mixed. "I have the C.I.O. on my neck again," he wrote Isabella. "It is taking a lot of time, but I know the ropes a lot better this time and am going to be very careful not to get slapped with one or more of those labor board cases which are the strongest weapons they have . . . . I will have to stick with this C.I.O. battle till it's finished and I am not sure just how long it will take."[21] Hill retired his Graham-Paige to secondary duty and bought a new Cadillac Model 62 Deluxe with Crow. Neither had much time to enjoy it in the next months.[22]

The record of this strike, especially of Hill's view of it, is extraordinary because of his lifelong habit of reflection, careful record keeping, and retention of business and personal papers. He started a rudimentary diary for the first time since 1923, and this was the beginning of a diary-keeping habit that lasted the rest of his life. He recorded early exchanges with union people on a Dictaphone hidden in a drawer in his office before he finally prevailed in getting an official transcript. In addition, Hill helped form company documents summarizing events.

One of these, "So That the Facts Are Clear," became a bone of contention when the union got hold of it, as the company seemed, for some reason, interested in keeping it to itself.[23] Of course, there was also considerable newspaper coverage, and Hill kept a large scrapbook that captured the local as well as national press.

Tension increased. On Sunday, July 13, it was found that several kegs of roofing nails had been spread on the driveway leading to the plant and punctured tires of police and sightseers. Employees were threatened with "dire consequences to themselves, their families, and their homes and cars if they showed up for work on Monday." One hundred employees called in the next day saying they were too frightened to come to work. On July 15, 600 pickets, about 50 of them Air Associates employees, stoned cars that tried to enter the plant. Workers willing to work asked the company to hire private guards to protect them. On July 16 these guards escorted them in and out of the plant. The union threatened to bring 1,000 additional pickets to "clean up" the guards.[24]

On July 17 the picket line was again violent. Early in the morning six were injured by tear gas as pickets battled steel-helmeted police over access to the plant. That afternoon sixty-seven cars with 300 employees crashed the line, but were booed and threatened by pickets whom a company spokesman called "a howling mob." Most of the vehicles were prevented from entering the plant by 500 rock-throwing pickets at the entrance, and a bus was dented and all its windows shattered. The local sheriff requested troops from the New Jersey governor. So did Hill by telephone and telegram. The union now promised to bring in 2,000 outside pickets to shut down the plant entirely on the grounds that 100 thugs and "professional gunmen" had been hired by the company as strikebreakers. Hill himself cruised the picket lines in a car with some of these "guards" that morning and slept in the plant with 25 men that night.[25]

The only detailed secondary account of the Air Associates strike, Charles Baird's article "A Tale of Infamy," which appeared in the Foundation for Economic Education's magazine *The Freeman* in 1992, takes a jaundiced view of this union activity and, as the title suggests, regards the whole sequence as an outrage—which from the libertarian perspective it certainly was. Baird wrote that "it is important to understand that there was no legitimate strike. There had been no refusal to bargain, and neither side had declared a bargaining impasse. The union had claimed discriminatory firings, but some who were allegedly fired were already back at work." The company attorney, Walter Chalaire, met with the federal government's Office of Production Management, according to Baird, and reiterated the company's willingness to bargain, insisting only that a record be kept of the negotiations.[26]

However, there was more to it than that. From the union's perspective, Leroy Hill was not bargaining "in good faith." From Hill's perspective, it looked like "good faith" was taken to be consenting to demands and nothing else. William Grede of Grede Foundries, a well-known opponent of unions and management member of numerous wartime tripartite panels, always emphasized that the law required signing a document only when "total agreement" was reached and did not coerce that agreement. He suggested to his managers that they be frank in the negotiations, enjoy them, and meanwhile appeal to public opinion and to the local police for protection of property. As far as he and Hill were concerned, it was a struggle to keep control of their businesses, and without control, they felt, no one would benefit in the long run, including the workers.[27] Grede, however, was much more of a publicist and glib negotiator than Hill. Hill's "trouble was always he was a kind of do it yourself guy, not good at judging people and delegating." Had he not been rather "stagestruck" and shy about speaking in public, one close to him believed, "he could have been famous."[28]

It was damaging to the company's stance that thirty-four employees of a Newark detective agency were found in the plant. Hill explained that these had been hired by the nonstriking employees as protection and that he had insisted they be unarmed. The company dismissed the "private guards" on the afternoon of the July 17 at the request of the local sheriff. It always denied that they were strikebreakers specifically, but the union pointed out that they were men "of the fighting and not working type." Hill had to give a talk to the stockroom employees on the 18th, assuring a group of doubtful men that they would be adequately protected by the police. But the hiring of these guards, especially in the context of the notorious role that the Pinkerton Agency, for instance, had had in violent labor disputes since the 1890s, was fuel for the union fire.[29]

On July 19 the Department of Labor assigned the National Defense Mediation Board to mediate the Air Associates controversy, and management was told to appear on July 22 to begin the process.[30] Francis Perkins, the U.S. secretary of labor, sent telegrams both to the company and the union advising both to do nothing in the meantime to aggravate the situation.[31] Things did remain calm on the picket line, though a call by the CIO for the government to seize the factory, as had been done with the North American aviation plant in Inglewood, California, drew a comment of "ridiculous" from an obviously aggravated Air Associates public relations director. The *New York Herald Tribune* called this takeover suggestion "not only premature but an impertinence of the first order."[32] That same day, 350 Air Associates employees petitioned the National Defense Mediation Board, demanding protection for their right to work and requesting a new election.[33]

Mediation began July 22, and the next day the board recommended a solution involving (1) a return of all workers immediately without discrimination, (2) submission of all questions of back pay to an arbitrator, and (3) a stipulation that negotiations toward a first contract begin right away and that, if not done by August 9, the contract be set by binding arbitration. Hill accepted all these conditions except binding arbitration, and on July 28 the board agreed that this was "substantial acceptance." On the 29th picketing stopped and employees went back to work.[34]

There remained plenty of questions and plenty of stress. The company announced that 379 employees had signed a petition asking permission to maintain an open shop. Local newspapers called for the police to acquire machine guns and fire extinguishers and to abandon the wishful thinking that "it can't happen here."[35] Hundreds of telegrams from

Oct 23, 1941

To: President Franklin D. Roosevelt

Rep. J. Parnell Thomas

Gentlemen:

We, The Entire Night Shift At Air Associates, At Bendix, N.J. Do Hereby Protest Against The Loss Of Our Right To Work At Our National Defense Jobs, Because Of A Strike Called By A Small Minority Group Of Agitators Under The Guiding Hand Of The C.I.O. These Striking Hoodlums Have Never Numbered More Than A Small Percentage Of The Force Employed, And Are Keeping Us From Our Jobs Solely By The Importation Of Outside Thugs.

The Brutal And Violent Methods Used By These Pickets, Have The Local Police Either Helpless Or Unwilling To Do Anything For Us. We Therefor Ask You Gentlemen, As Our Legally Chosen Representatives, To Do Whatever Necessary To Return To Us The Right To Work, Without Fear Of Injury Or Terroristic Reprisals. We Believe In The Management Of Our Firm, And Back That Management 100%. We Have Been Working Under The Best Of Working Conditions, And Wish Only To Return And Be Left Alone To Do Our Jobs.

Albert Casano

Anna Motley

John R. Hess

Frances A. Heinriche

Thomas Gordon

John R. Sarno

Frank Albanse

Petition by non-union Air Associates workers, 1941.

nonunion workers in the Air Associates plant were sent to President Roosevelt or members of Congress in Washington with messages such as "Where I work is my business. When I work is your business. But where when or how I work is none of the CIO's business" or "Demand American Right to Work CIO Gangster-like methods employed at Air Associates strike by non-workers."[36]

"I don't believe this strike has meant a thing," Hill told the press. "I believe we are right back where we started from."[37] Hill had notified the Selective Service director when the strike began, suggesting that it might be time to change the draft status of the men on strike. He did not withdraw the request when they returned to work and publicly stated that none of the CIO men involved held important jobs in the plant and could be spared if needed in the army. This was not a public relations move calculated to make friends among the union members.[38]

The bargaining sessions, under the aegis of the National Defense Mediation Board, were held on July 30–31 and August 1, 4–5, and 7–8, mostly at the Hotel Pennsylvania in New York City. As in 1938, Hill participated for the company, and a verbatim record was kept (though not without extensive opposition from the union).

The transcript reveals much about the broad as well as specific differences that led to pickets on the road and intransigence in the executive offices. "We are glad to have your suggestions and ideas," Hill said at the opening session, "but remember I have had a great deal of experience in shops from a good many different positions. I have worked in shops myself from a sweeper on up, and I know something about relations between employees and management, and I know what kind of shop works efficiently and I know what causes disruptions in shops too."[39]

The union wanted a union shop, mandatory dues checkoff, a grievance system that prohibited workers from working out even small misunderstandings directly with supervisors, and binding interest and rights arbitration. The company would accept binding arbitration, it said, if the union would accept the same on questions of property damage by the union in the first strike and the legitimacy of the July 1 certification election.[40]

Hill was active again in the August 1 session held at the law offices of Scandrett, Tuttle & Chalaire. He insisted that the grievance procedure first involve just the worker and the foreman without a steward. "They can talk to as many stewards as they like outside of working hours and talk their grievances over with them and find out whether they have a legitimate grievance or not, but what we ask is that they first try to settle the grievance without having a third party come in on it and then if they are not settled, then bring in your third party." Frederick Yakel of the union responded, "If you had a steward in that place you would have real shop discipline and not the way I've seen it. It is none of my concern . . . but as far as I can see, some of these foremen that you have around there belong in the Mexican army."[41]

A large issue at that session was the closed shop. Hill thought that asking the company to make employees belong to the union was in conflict with another clause of the contract saying that neither the company nor the union should discriminate against, coerce, or interfere with any employee. Yakel explained that this was to protect the company, and then the exchange got rough:

> Hill: We want to ask you if we have a man that has been working in our Company for 10 or 12 years that is in that unit. Would you really expect us to go to that man and tell him that after working there for 10 years that if he wants to continue in the Company's employment that he has to join the Union? You really seriously expect that?
>
> Yakel: I will counter with this—
>
> Hill: I asked you a question.
>
> Yakel: Do you really expect one man to live peaceably amongst neighbors in a majority for the rest of his work day life—
>
> Hill: That doesn't answer my question. Do you seriously expect us to go to such an employee—
>
> Yakel: Why not?
>
> Hill: You still don't answer my question. Do you expect that?
>
> Yakel: Yes.
>
> Hill: It seems like a hell of an unreasonable expectation.
>
> Yakel: Those are your viewpoints.
>
> Hill: I am expressing them. We have a lot of people there that have been with us a long time and we are not going to coerce them into joining any

organization, any more than we are going to coerce them into not joining any organization.

Yakel: You are saying you are going to have one union. That clause tells you right up and down cold turkey you are dealing with one bargaining agency. Of course if you would want your way, go ahead and have your way. After all you are the owner of the business, and we are not dictating to you.

Hill: I am trying to find out what the reason is behind it.

Yakel: They will live along together in a harmonious manner, not let this thing continue on.

Hill: What if they think they can live along in a satisfactory manner and they want to stay there?

Alderman: They will create friction between the majority of the members.

Hill: Who says they will?

Yakel: They have.

Hill: You will have to settle your own problems on getting your members and you are not going to have the Company step in and coerce people, in violation of your own Section 4, into joining the Union.

. . . .

Grimaldi: It doesn't conflict with Section 4.

Hill: It reads that way with me.

Chalaire: That in effect by requiring a man to join the union in order to keep his job that he is really being coerced into the union. That is Mr. Hill's point and that conflicts with what you asked the Company to agree to do and what you agreed to do in Section 4.

Grimaldi: I disagree when you say coerce.

Hill: When a Company asks a man not to join a union to keep his job it is coercion. Why isn't it coercion when you ask him to join a union?

Grimaldi: We are only asking the Company to protect itself so you don't have different organizations set up in the Company.

Hill: We don't need it.

Grimaldi: Everybody needs it. Everybody else accepts those points you are being stubborn on.

Hill: It is coercion.

Grimaldi: It is not.

Hill: I say it is.

Yakel: Let's proceed. It is no use bickering. It doesn't seem to get across to the management at all.[42]

On August 8, a formal impasse was declared and Harry P. Shulman, the Sterling Professor of Law at Yale University, was appointed arbitrator. Few imagined that his reputation alone would convince the parties.[43]

The parties continued to bicker in later sessions. Hill criticized Loren Hauser, regional director of the CIO, for using what he called "criminal language"—words like "stool pigeon" and "stooges"—to describe employees following the company rules in reporting violations. "I've been reading this literature that you pass out, and why do you have to get so abusive? Now this causes a lot of resentment." Hauser defended himself. Another man broke in by saying, "I don't want to get heated up. I want to get along in this thing." Hill's response was "We can negotiate on any basis—heated or otherwise." On wages Hill was consistent: the market was the test, not good intentions. "Anyone is perfectly at liberty if he feels he is not being paid what he should get to go over to Bendix or any other shop and get a job where he can make what he is worth. If he is competent he shouldn't have any trouble to get it."[44]

Hill could not understand what the union was giving up in this supposedly give-and-take negotiation. It seemed to him that there were only demands, at best an occasional lessening of a demand. The short answer by the union to his question of what the company was gaining was "men and protection." Hauser noted: "We're in a stage at this date that is somewhat different than it was three, four years ago in regards to organized labor. Three or four years ago they used to bump us around a lot. I think we are in a much better position to not be caused to wait the months and years to get satisfactory answers to our requests."[45]

Probably most divisive was a deep difference of opinion about production. The company repeatedly stated that it could guarantee 100 percent production if the union would not cause further violence and disorder, even though the strike might continue and an orderly picket line be maintained. The union and the board, on the other hand, made it plain that they felt the only way to get production back to normal would be to make an agreement that was satisfactory to the union.[46] That tie of a union contract to continued defense production and no third choice set up the situation that made the second strike at Air Associates different from the first and fatal to Hill's plan for the company.

The union call for a closed shop, a checkoff, and what Hill called a "Soviet formula for grievance procedure" were all issues that could not be solved in the negotiation sessions and were submitted to the arbitrator and fact finder, Dr. Shulman.

On September 19, the union voted to authorize another strike if the Shulman report did not side with its demands. On September 30, while the Yale professor was deliberating, a second unannounced picket line formed at the plant.[47] Hill's attitude was the same as before. "We dispute the right of the union to prevent people who want to work from entering our plant. We will not be intimidated." He denied the union claim that the company was moving equipment out of the plant, and he advertised for replacement workers. "Again," the ad said of the union, "their demands are unreasonable, impractical, and impossible of fulfillment."[48]

Charles Baird could not fathom why the union would act in this way. In his *Freeman* article, he stated that the Shulman and NLRB reports would doubtless have been mostly favorable to the union but that the union was determined to force an executive seizure. The reason was that in the seizures at North American Aviation and Federal Shipbuilding, the union did better than it had under the NDMB recommendations.[49]

The ads for replacement workers brought in thousands of applications "filling all places of strikers and terrified absentees," and Air Associates continued in production with these. This move created still another issue. While the company argued that it was within its rights under the 1938 Supreme Court decision in *NLRB* vs. *McKay Radio and Telegraphy Company*, which allowed hiring of permanent replacements for strikers in "economic strikes," there was disagreement on whether the company had committed illegal acts that caused the September 30 strike. Hill argued he was simply waiting for the NDMB decision, completely legally, and so had a right to hire other workers. But the National Defense Mediation Board, following the now available Shulman report, recommended not only that Air Associates give the union most of what it wanted, but that the company put all striking workers back in their jobs even if it meant firing replacement workers. Earl Harding, who wrote an article for the *Saturday Evening Post* on the strike that was never published, claimed that Hill and Chalaire were told that a contract acceptable to the union must be signed "whether the company agreed or not . . . and the Mediation Board proceeded to frame one itself." The worker replacement issue was another reason for company resistance to the contract, though the core reason was surely the contract itself. Of course, the existence of the replacement workers meant that no one could argue that seizure was justified at Air Associates due to interruption of war production: the plant was operating at nearly full capacity.[50]

There was little expectation that the standard processes would work the second time around. The Mediation Board accused Air Associates of noncooperation in the defense effort and threatened the company with federal seizure of its plant. "This company," wrote a representative of the board, "has not exhibited toward either this certified union or the National Defense Mediation Board that attitude of cooperation to which the public is entitled on the part of a company whose operations are essential to the defense of the nation." One incident in October, when Hill and Chalaire supposedly "walked out" of a meeting with officials in Washington, even after the board had rearranged a conflicting appointment with the army that supposedly made this necessary, was used as particular evidence of a poor attitude.[51]

On October 6–8 Hill and Chalaire met with a Mediation Board panel in Washington. On October 10 the Mediation Board, with the Shulman report in hand, recommended that all strikers be hired back to their old positions immediately. While Hill had earlier agreed to something like this, this time he refused to dismiss the replacements, whom he felt he was within his legal rights to hire since he defined the strike as an "economic" one. He promised to return all workers within thirty days, but that was not satisfactory to the board. The Mediation Board held that this offer was a rejection and said it had washed its hands of the matter, referring it to the executive branch.[52]

Hill was upset by renewed threats of a government takeover. He was unimpressed, too, by the work of the Mediation Board. "All of the members of the Mediation Board," he wrote, "and all of the other Government officials that give us advice, threaten us, make demands, warn us of consequences and pass out recommendations, decisions and new releases, have never been in our plant, talked to our employees, or made any effort to really get the facts. It seems pretty obvious that they are not the least bit interested in the facts." He issued a statement on October 19 saying, "Now it remains to be seen whether the Defense Mediation Board is out to get production or universal compulsory unionization." If the board pursued recent policies, the company would be forced eventually to capitulate to the "private army" of pickets that could be mobilized by the CIO. However, Hill thought the federal power should be used instead to protect the workers working in the plant. "If we are let alone and if our employees are protected in their right to work, our defense production will mount steadily and the strikers who want to work can be re-employed long before the thirty days expire." But events in the field were not promising for a peaceful settlement. On October 23, between 2,000 and 3,000 pickets closed Route 2 leading to the plant as workers from numerous CIO locals along the East Coast joined the line.[53]

There was, however, one more negotiation, which Hill thought was a critical one. On October 24, Hill, the Air Associates directors, and Chalaire, the company counsel, met in Washington at government request with Undersecretary of War Robert Patterson and William S. Knudson, director of the Office of Price Administration. Hill explained the difficulty and the actual danger of reinstating the strikers all at once: the nonunion employees and replacements were not pleased with the strike situation, and it was unclear whether the union represented a majority of the total workers as contrasted with the "bargaining unit." The two officials agreed, and also consented to a modification of the Mediation Board order to allow reinstatement of the strikers over time and to pay them in the meantime for not working. This last was a further compromise by Hill, who agreed to put all workers immediately back on the payroll, though waiting thirty days before replacing them in their original jobs.

A press release was issued thanking the company for its cooperation, and a *New York Times* front-page story declared the strike settled.[54]

That accommodation lasted only for a weekend. On Monday the union threatened to call a general strike in the eastern United States unless Hill agreed to immediately reinstate all strikers and fire replacements.[55] Sixty-five strikers reported for reinstatement, but balked when they were requested to sign slips to establish a payroll record. The union objected to the workers' signing anything, arguing that it was unjust that, though the strikers were to be paid full time at their normal wage rates while awaiting reinstatement, they did not get the overtime their replacements were earning. Justice demanded full reinstatement, not the Patterson-Knudson agreement. The strikers were marched back out of the plant by their organizers and the picket line was resumed. Edward F. McGrady, labor advisor to the War Department, telephoned Hill to tell him that the Patterson-Knudson agreement was unacceptable to the CIO. The next day CIO director Richard Frankensteen flew from Detroit to New York and held a press conference in which he announced he was not interested in any "back door" Washington agreements with the company. He promised to call a five-state strike, bring in large numbers of pickets, close down Air Associates entirely, and keep it closed until the army took over, enforced a contract, and changed the company management.[56]

October 30 was an extraordinary day. Frankensteen was at the White House that morning talking with the president about the Air Associates situation. Army officers Colonel Roy Jones and Major Peter Beasley, assigned to the plant to reinstate the workers by force under the original Mediation Board order, told Hill his help was not wanted. Hill left the plant that afternoon and was never permitted to return, not even to take his belongings from his desk. That evening when the officers tried to reinstate the strikers, the nonunion workers in the plant rebelled. There was fighting and a demonstration. The CIO ordered more pickets, threatening not to let the night shift of nonstrikers "get out alive" and intimating they would "take the plant to pieces brick by brick."[57]

Hill wrote Isabella that night that "this marks one phase of this case. However, we are still an open shop and we have no contract with the union." He predicted, however, that the next step might be for the War Department to force the company to sign a contract.[58]

Actually, he was more isolated than he thought. Late in October Hill got a letter from a labor relations advisor suggesting appeasement. The man had had many phone conversations with Hill and knew he was a fighter, but thought he needed to be realistic. "As for such moot considerations in the circumstances as fairness or unfairness, or principle or appeasement or face saving or the surrender of rights, etc., it appears to me that these might reasonably or, at least temporarily, be made subservient to the vital immediate needs of the defense program—and there is nothing appeasing about that . . . . I have faced situations similar to this with several employers—many of them stubborn as hell in their determination to hold out for what they regarded as principle—but, without really retreating one inch from their convictions, all of them came to see issues in this crisis which transcended temporary differences and they went along with government policy hoping that any inequalities and un-fairnesses would eventually be corrected . . . . This is a great country."[59] This view was typical of the attitude of the directors, whom Hill reported early in November felt "we are entirely licked." "They all feel that I have been reckless with the Stock Holders' interests, but since I own a pretty large block of stock myself, they cannot accuse me of bad faith."[60]

The next steps put Air Associates and Hill back on front pages nationwide, both in the news and editorial opinion columns. President Roosevelt, saying "our country is in danger," issued an executive order on October 30 specifying seizure of the plant by the army, which moved in 2,000 troops with machine guns and fixed bayonets on October 31. The branches were also seized a few days later.[61]

The other shoe dropped immediately. The War Department notified the corporation's board that it would not release the factory back to private operation until Hill and Vice-President Harold Crow were dismissed from the management. Hill was "alternately rueful and indignant" at a board meeting called to discuss this and said he would do the same things over again in the same situation. "I think this is the wrong way to win wars and get production. The record of the company speaks for itself, for the management it's had for the past fourteen years." He refused to resign voluntarily, and when, on November 19, the directors removed him, Hill insisted it be entered in the minutes that he had resigned under duress. A few days later Frederick Coburn was appointed president of Air Associates. On December 26 Coburn signed a contract with the UAW that included a union shop and the other demands, and the 250 of 800 employees that voted in the contract ratification election all voted yes. On December 29 the War Department turned Air Associates back over to its board of directors.[62]

"We've got a job and we're doing it!" announced the Air Associates ad in *Air Facts* magazine, run under a large picture of a worker in overalls on December 1, 1941. "To manufacture the hundreds of precision-built aircraft parts required by the aviation industry . . . to make them with the efficiency and reliability for which we are known . . . to man our machines to their full productive capacity . . . to constantly expand our production facilities . . . to maintain adequate stocks for immediate delivery of your orders—that is our part in national defense and that is the job we are continuing to do!"[63] Onward and upward!

Hill had to watch these last events from a distance, operating out of his apartment at 100 Prospect Avenue, Hackensack, New Jersey. He was not, however, at a loss for words. He wrote Acre on November 4 that "there seems to be much going back and forth to Washington and I don't know whether they intend to keep the plant for a month or turn it back it a few days." His analysis was bitter. "It is quite apparent that this action by the Army on Presidential proclamation is entirely vicious and punitive instead of protective. The New Deal, through this malicious, disruptive and damaging action, seeks to punish the Company for refusing to bribe the labor bosses to refrain from mob violence." Even Crow had lost sympathy with Hill's stand in the end and Hill was "getting a lot of recriminations from some of [the directors] who think we should have folded up and played ball with the New Deal." When Acre pointed out there were some divisions within the labor movement, Hill replied: "You don't understand the situation in Washington. Roosevelt's feelings towards Lewis amount to an intra-factional dispute, and does not affect the policy to destroy private enterprise." He felt that any new business he entered would have to be under an assumed name, as he would be blacklisted from government work. "You can see that the fight is basically political. That is a business that I know nothing about, and when you go into somebody else's business, you don't usually set the world on fire. However, I had no choice in this instance, and I am trying to stir up some political resistance. . . . There is a certain amount of satisfaction of taking a crack at it." Hill wrote Acre, "There are a lot of people who are indignant at this high-handed action by the Labor Government."[64]

To be sure, there were. There was coverage in *Time, Life,* and the *Saturday Evening Post.* The U.S. Chamber of Commerce wrote that any government official using his power to urge the owners of a private business to remove any of their management was violating a fundamental principle of the free enterprise system and the American way of life. It was wrong, it said, for the government to assist any group of citizens to force others to surrender their rights and freedoms. The *New York World Telegram* noted that Hill and Crow had built the company: "They worried over it and nursed it along at a time when the government's only interest in it was perhaps to collect taxes." Many newspapers pointed out the irony of John L. Lewis of the United Mine Workers ignoring Mediation Board orders in the November captive mines strike with seeming impunity, while a different standard was applied to management at Air Associates. The *Philadelphia Inquirer* spoke of "A Questionable Procedure," while the *New York Times* called the action "One Way Compulsion." "The conclusion is inescapable," wrote the *Times* reporter, "that the Government has deserted its true function as an impartial arbiter and become more and more frankly partial to 'labor.'" Commented the *New York Sun:* "If the action taken in this case represents settled Government policy, we have already passed the line between liberty and dictatorship." The *Trenton Times* was more succinct: "Can you blame Hitler for laughing?"[65]

Hill wrote to a few of these papers thanking them for support and understanding. To the *Trenton Times* editor he commented: "I don't deserve any sympathy because I really didn't have to lose my job. I could see the situation developing a month or six weeks ahead and I had plenty of time to say 'I give up.'" That he did not say it was an object of pride: "I got considerable satisfaction out of telling them to go to Hell."[66]

He received numerous letters from CEOs around the country expressing appreciation for his stand, but, of course, with a "better you than me" implication. He got many invitations and copies of speeches and position papers from conservative groups, and even a letter analyzing his character based on his physiognomy from a phrenologist who had seen his picture in *Life* magazine. The width, height, and development of Hill's forehead, the man said, indicated great reasoning power and vision, while the "Rooseveltians" pictured were "low-browed or retreating, commercial nosed and big-jowled."[67] Hill thanked the man briefly but did not comment on that one.

Some government officials also objected to the federal takeover. Hill thanked a New Jersey state legislator, saying his action "shows that there are still a few representatives of the people who are interested in just law enforcement and who are willing to openly resist the present trend toward dictatorial rule, regardless of political consequences . . . . Apparently the force of the local, state, and federal government is no longer available to protect law-abiding citizens, but has been given to support of organized law breaking, in return for political support."[68] Leland Ford, a member of the House from California, protested to the War Department, saying that "a tremendous wrong was done to the owners in . . . that the Constitution of the United States has been violated in respect to invasion of private property." There were 750 employees willing to work, Ford wrote, "but through a cowardly surrender to a group of high jacking, socialistic, communistic, subversive outlaws this plant was taken away from its rightful owners and the owners of the plant made to pay the penalty of the violation of American principles and law committed by those same outlaws."[69] Ford and others claimed in congressional debate that the administration's policy was "decidedly inconsistent as well as unfair" and that the general public was overwhelmingly opposed to the closed shop.[70]

After a time under army management 500 Air Associates employees petitioned to have Hill back as president.[71] In fact, Roosevelt had to keep the troops at the plant for several weeks because of threats of violence and a sit-down strike by a group of nonunion workers sympathetic to the Hill management, and he considered the formation of a government corporation to run Air Associates for the duration if compliance could not be gained. The government advanced credit to Air Associates only on the condition "that the company permanently replace its defiant president," fired the company's strikebreakers, and restored the union though management was still resisting recognition. This was as severe a combination of sanctions as was ever imposed in a similar case.[72] But there was not a chance of Hill's return. On December 7 the Japanese attacked Pearl Harbor and the whole Air Associates issue was buried on the back pages as a world cataclysm of unprecedented proportions unfolded.

The day he was dismissed from the management, Hill wrote his mother that he had "been leading a very hectic existence" and sent her some clippings. "Mr. Roosevelt and his labor partners have been out to get me and they are getting along pretty well. . . . The seizure of our plant is a very high-handed procedure, unconstitutional and with no basis in law, but the New Deal is in a position of power where they can shamelessly flaunt Congress, the laws and the Constitution . . . . I have been getting a lot of fun out of the fight, so don't worry about me."[73]

His family was as supportive as usual in their different styles. Nellie Hill wrote in January 1942 that she had no idea where his birth certificate was (Hill may have needed it in looking for a job) but explained all about the night he was born on July 16, 1894. She dutifully read the negotiation transcripts he sent. She made no specific comment but said "Hurrah for your side of the question."[74] Isabella and Beverly, who returned from China in the spring of 1941, kept track of the strike also and read transcripts of the July negotiations. "It certainly burns one up to read it," Isabella wrote. "I gave them to Uncle Fred to read last night and he kept getting madder and madder. It was quite funny. I call Mr. Yakel YAKEL to rhyme with jackal."[75] Beverly read the records too. "Those union guys sure have some crust," she wrote. "You sure are important," she said in November. "I keep reading about you in the paper & in *Time* & somebody said you were quoted & acted in the 'March of Time' program on the radio & also someone said they saw you in a newsreel." She asked her dad to call her someday at school and talk to her all by herself.[76] For Ellen, soon to be Hill's wife and his helpmate in a new life at Rockford, Illinois, the strike and his behavior in it were the key event in their relationship. She had thought Hill was far too old for her to consider a romantic interest, but when she observed at near range the courage and style he showed during those days of crisis, the age difference disappeared altogether from her consideration.[77]

For Hill himself the Air Associates strike was of course a landmark, an absolute life-forming series of events. The strike confirmed all that he had learned and influenced all he was later to do. It reached the core of his personality and belief and provided a vivid and personal twist to any theoretical discussion of human behavior and possibility. It did not eliminate or modify the engineer or manager in Hill: that was a given since boyhood. But it added a layer which was never again absent.

He did not become discouraged or defeatist. "It has been quite an interesting experience to buck the CIO and the New Deal," he wrote a friend, "and as you may have read in the papers, I am now without a job as a result. However, don't feel sorry for me as I knew it was coming and I don't think I am going to starve." Amid all his objections to the "class struggle" being engendered in the United States and to the threats to American freedom he saw illustrated in his personal situation, he did not lose his sense of humor or give up on the United States any more than he did on his personal career. "If this had been Russia," he quipped to a friend, "I would have been shot a month ago, and if it had been Germany, the pickets would have been shot. So, I guess we are better off in America."[78]

Rockford

*T*he move to Rockford, the move away from Air Associates, a second marriage, the startup of new companies, a new schedule, and new priorities were things which, combined, represented a big change in Leroy Hill's life. In many ways it was a return to himself after a narrow epoch of outlandish stress, excitement, and opportunity purchased at high personal cost. He took up his diary again after a hiatus of over twenty years. He focused his attention more on political and philosophical issues than before—and in a way that was both broader and more active than ever. He went back to some of the outdoor hunting and fishing activities he had loved as a youth, which had been largely abandoned during his thirties and forties because he did not have, or would not make, the time for them. Most significant, he was in love—deeply, however late—and was able, with a second family who remembered Daddy always as a white-haired man, to indulge his domestic instincts, so diverted and confused the first time around.

Ellen Mayo went to Roosevelt Field and Air Associates in 1939 to acquire solo air time. She ended up getting a job typing proposals for the army and navy business that was increasing then, and in about a year met the president of the company, Leroy Hill. Ellen saw little of Hill until the move of the company to New Jersey—a dinner now and then, a drive home—but events surrounding the strike not only brought the two together more but deepened their respect and affection for each other. In January 1942, just at the denouement, when Hill left Air Associates and his office was his apartment in Hackensack, they married.[1]

It was a quiet ceremony, but early kidding by his friends, when they learned of it, gave way to the recognition, once they met Ellen, that it was a good, if unlikely, match. "So you're beginning to recognize Ellen's prowess, eh," Walter Chalaire wrote the first spring of the Hills' marriage. "Still it's too bad you ever let her know you could cook."[2] From Mary Lougheed after talking to Acre came a comment too: "Ray tells me Ellen has an angelic disposition—he likes her very much. In fact—*how* did *you* get her? You must have deceived her—or gone back to your California self! When you never grumbled!"[3]

Ellen could have "black moods," Hill would sometimes report to his diary, but he related to her as an equal and respected her energy, take-charge attitude, and complete competence in shouldering responsibilities and adjusting to changes.[4] He took her with him on business trips right away. As the years passed and he insisted on getting up at 4:00 in the morning to depart on family vacations (documented down to exact fuel consumption and motel costs), she was right there with him.

Ellen quit her job at Air Associates in mid-January, and the two drove to Rockford, Illinois in Leroy's new Cadillac at the end of the month, with a stop to see Bill and Moya Lear. At first the newlyweds lived on a farm, where Ellen could enjoy horses, but in the fall of 1943 they moved to 1405 National Avenue and a year later to 2326 Clinton Place, two blocks from the Rockford Country Club, where they often had supper. In 1945 they moved again—to 841 North Main Street.[5]

It was, as one of their daughters put it, a "big square house . . . built around the turn of the century, at about the same time that my father was born. Like him, it was solid and sensible and big, with a grace characteristic of the Victorian period, and a unique charm all its own." With fuel rationing during the war, few could afford to heat such a large three-story house, so the Hills purchased it at a bargain price, though the heating costs in the cold midwestern winters were significant. The Hills kidded about the Main Street house. When the children visited their widowed mother there many years later, she pointed to the smoke coming from the chimney and said, "See that smoke from all the money being burned up in the furnace." Leroy in 1975 described the house, then seventy-five years old, as a fifteen-room "worn out mansion" surrounded by high-rise apartments and office buildings. "It's the last of the old slums on this street." But that third Rockford house truly filled the bill for the family: it was home.[6]

Five more children arrived—all girls. Ellen (Nellie) was born August 16, 1942; Marcia, June 8, 1944; Holly, December 24, 1945; Elizabeth, September 8, 1949, and Isabella, July 1, 1952.[7] "My five sisters and I all knew," Elizabeth later wrote, "that we were all to have been named Frank Leroy Hill if we had only turned out to be boys, but, second best though we were, seemed to us like well enough."[8]

One slight awkwardness was that shortly before Nellie was born, Leroy and Ellen went to Beverly's graduation from the Anna Head School in Berkeley. "Strangely," Ellen remembered, "no one had told her I was pregnant and it must have been quite a shock to a 17-year-old girl to meet a new mother in such a condition." However, Bev handled it with poise. "In all the years she lived with us she never showed resentment or anger. She had developed what Leroy called 'passive resistance.'"[9]

Ellen welcomed visits from Hill's mother, brought Bev to live with them for various periods, and encouraged her husband to go fishing, spend time at the lakeside property they shortly acquired in New Hampshire, or do anything at all but record in his diary "Worked at Shop" *every* day. Ellen and Leroy were an easy pair, sharing good and bad habits alike with considerable joie de vivre. They smoked and drank together (Ellen took up smoking that spring of 1942, maybe in self-defense), stopped smoking together (many times before it stuck), worked at the shop together, played backgammon, and shared in vigorous sports (skiing, tennis, scuba diving) right to the end of Leroy's life—despite their age difference. Hill, writing to a friend in 1952 about Ellen's activity in the Ninety-Niners (a group of women aviators), commented: "My wife is 22 years younger than I am but it doesn't seem to bother either of us very much. I made her promise to push my wheel chair when the time comes before I would consent to marry her."[10]

For a time Air Associates was much on his mind, an inevitable bitterness that lingered. "The rank stupidity and injustice of the punitive action of the War Department to force unionization of our company regardless of whether it was wanted by the majority of its employees or its effect on productive efficiency," he wrote early in 1942, "is just as damaging, in fact more so, now that war has been declared. Putting the interests of the unions ahead of national welfare does not seem to me a good way to carry on a successful war effort. . . . I feel very strongly that operation of any cooperative enterprise must be controlled by individuals qualified to direct the operation, whether it be a football team, a military organization, a factory or a government. The function of management is simply one of the necessary details in cooperative effort, and individuals engaged in such effort should not be considered as members of a separate caste whose interests are opposed to the others. . . . We now have a paradoxical situation in this country where the individuals naturally able to direct the effort of others will be opposed by all those who are not able to perform this function. In other words, it's a kind of an upside-down situation where the incompetent do the work of the competent and vice versa. If that is a way to win a war then I am crazy."[11]

He was galled when Air Associates objected to his competing with them with his Rockford ventures, Aero Screw and Aircraft Standard Parts, which made and marketed engine bolts, hose clamps, and other small aviation items. The diversity he had built into Air Associates made it inevitable that he would have to compete with it, but "after I started my venture, they seemed to feel that I had done something wrong and unethical. It seems to be overlooked that I didn't leave Air Associates— Air Associates left me." One would think, Hill wrote Haven Page, they would rather have Hill as a competitor than someone else. "But if they want to take such a silly attitude why I'll just have to struggle along without their friendship and good wishes. Certainly I am not going to lay on the shelf nor consult them for approval of any venture I wish to engage in." He held on to his 8,500 shares of Air Associates stock for a time and did not think ill of it as a business, only in its actions toward him.[12]

The crowning blow was the attitude and behavior of his old friend, Harold Crow, who, when the dust settled, not only got back into Air

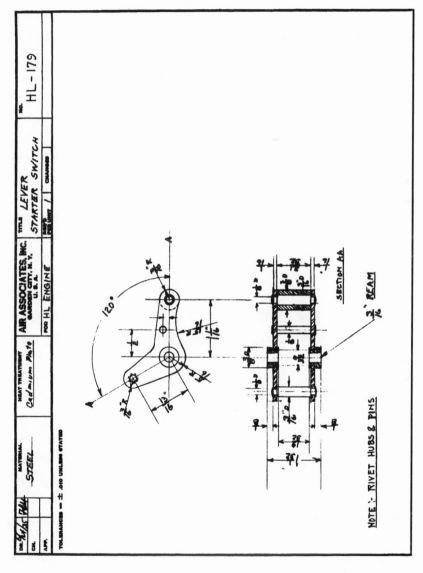

A typical drawing by Hill at Air Associates, one of hundreds in his papers.

Associates but became its president. Ray Acre, who was vice-president of Air Associates and still ran its western division, kept Hill closely informed not only about the company, but about Crow, whom Acre had also known intimately for many years.

At first both thought Crow would encourage Air Associates to subcontract with Hill's companies, as it was in everyone's interest. He had not been in agreement with Hill's stand on the union issue and was embarrassed to be in the middle of all the publicity, but, Acre noted, "there was no personal bitterness in this. He doesn't have many friends and doesn't want to lose any. Especially his oldest friend." When Coburn, described by Acre as "a flat tire," was still president (Crow took the job in April 1942), Acre and Hill thought Crow might even quit the company and "get some work with less headaches." But with his ascension they expected some cooperation. "You know," mused Hill, "come to think of it, this is the first time that I can think of that I ever was in a position to have a favor or act of friendship from HC. Heretofore it's always been the other way round."[13]

Given this expectation, the actual contact with Crow was a shock. In the summer of 1942 Hill's Rockford thread mill lost a bid for a screw-making job from Air Associates. "What a chump Harold is," Acre told Hill. "There is such a large margin of profit that AA wouldn't be permitted to take but a small part of it. Here was an opportunity where AA could have made its max profit, he could have made the handsome gesture of reciprocating to you a whole life time of friendship & sponsorship that you have given him. I presume he may have suspicioned that you would cut me in on the deal. Wouldn't that have been terrible—to see another old friend make some money. And his sensitive ethics. Balls! Did he refuse the handsome profit you handed him on his Aircraft Std Parts investment? He'd fire me, or any minor employee, who would set up an outside deal to sell goods back to AA, on the same conditions. His apparent reluctance, and unwillingness to do business with you mystifies me. I don't think he wants to quarrel with you. . . . If you were suing, or were about to sue AA, a most practical, common sense thing would be to adjust this by giving you the jack screw job. This would have cost AA nothing. He knows you are a large stockholder, and control other stock. Would it not be to AA's advantage to work with you in a friendly manner, to heal old wounds?"[14]

When Crow was harsh with Acre, Hill reacted in kind. "Harold is a hypocrite and like all hypocrites hates being exposed." He met in July with Crow, who later accused him to others of having called the new president vile names at that meeting. Hill denied that, but admitted that his repeated questions had annoyed Crow. "I didn't even call him a heel altho I believe I did say he lacked moral courage. I said that he probably was under the domination of Gibby Colgate (which he denied)." Hill described Crow's attitude at their first meeting since Hill's departure "practically insulting." Hill laid him out and proceeded to do the same with Gilbert Colgate "with no attempt to spare his feelings." Hill had a $15,000 claim against the company for salary related to his sudden departure. The directors had approved paying it, but Colgate and Crow hedged, and Hill collected only after there was considerable delay and he filed a lawsuit. He recorded in his diary that Crow called him "and discussed his general inimical attitude towards me and his refusal to represent my interest on collection of my $15,070 from Air Associates. He pretty well made himself out to be a complete heel. 25 years of friendship and favors to HC adds up worth exactly zero." Hill believed that Crow had put out the word not only not to subcontract with Hill's companies but to make no sales of materials to them. He found this stance painful and hard to understand, and commented that it seemed "far fetched." "Well," Hill concluded finally, "I think the guy is mentally unbalanced and is getting worse in his old age—so I can't waste any more time on him."[15]

However curt that may have sounded, there was no question Hill felt laconic about the loss of his friend, one of the main close male friends that he always took so seriously in his life. It was especially hard for him ("I probably have more pride than the ordinary man") to see Crow's smiling face with a line of union bosses in the union newspaper and to feel the attacks on his companies and hear of the rumors spread about him at Air Associates when that giant had so little to fear from its exiled ex-president. Acre wrote that, according to "some wise guy," as he put it, "ingratitude is the most infamous defect of the heart." In the case of Colgate, it might indeed have been a pleasure for Hill to "de-flate that ass," but any victory over Crow was a Pyhrric one.[16] One moment, it was "the guy is a psychopathic case" or "someone down there has gone nuts," but the next "I never expected him to turn on me. . . . I've been nursing and humoring him for years—adjusting my plans to his whims to keep him happy, and sacrificing anything to keep him from sulking. . . . Well—to hell with it."[17] The personal split was a wound, as deep as the split from the company the two had built together, and slower to heal.

However painful the personal rift, Hill was more and more satisfied with the changes in his life and often said in later years that his dismissal from Air Associates was the best thing that ever happened to him. In the summer of 1942 he was already thinking along these lines, as his Rockford companies took up war contracts and prospered. When a friend sent him a CIO circular, Hill's comment was: "I see they are still at it, and this sort of tomfoolery has become a routine part of operations. Our little enterprise is going along fairly well here and, thank the Lord, without any such nonsense, and I think everybody is pretty happy. However, don't tell anybody that because some of my 'friends' wouldn't rest until they had succeeded in disrupting things."[18]

Similarly indicative was his advice to Acre about the same time. Acre was having renewed health problems and had reported on his blood pressure. "I never used to take such things seriously," Hill wrote, "as I have always had a strong constitution. However, I'm just old enough now to feel a slowing down of my vitality and I'm realizing that I can hurt myself if I push too hard. I think it is making a better executive out of me and I'm getting enjoyment out of recreational activity like fishing. Now—when guys our age hurt themselves by pushing too hard, they don't recover fully, so for God's sake don't make an old broken down man out of yourself over that god dam flap operator. Anticipate your collapse by quitting before instead of after—and the only way to do it is to walk away leaving someone else in charge." Hill asked Acre to come and see the Hills in Rockford "until low pressure existence ceases to bore you." He had good fishing gear, he said, and had just bought two guns. "In short I am concentrating on making life enjoyable and it seems just as easy or easier to make money under such conditions."[19]

For the rest of his life, every time he heard about a major strike, Hill would write the chief executive expressing sympathy with the company, advising it to stand firm, and often sending along the history of the Air Associates strike written by Earl Harding. He joined organizations, pushed for Libertarian causes, and wrote letters and treatises on free enterprise (he was a tongue-tied speaker and froze on the platform). Otherwise, he put that world behind him like a bad dream.[20]

That did not mean he retired. In fact, much to his later chagrin, he never really retired. And with war contracts being negotiated daily with big numbers and with engineering and manufacturing know-how in short supply, he was not about to take a business back seat in 1942. He started his Rockford companies quickly, and, as was typical of war enterprises, they expanded at an unprecedented rate. The first Rockford company was Aircraft Standard Parts No. 1, a small joint venture with three others, including Acre, for a special screw-drilling operation. It was liquidated in February 1942, though the name survived in a subsequent company. In 1942 Hill expanded greatly. He bought into Cotta Transmission Company, a Rockford manufacturer of gears and transmissions since 1910. Hill owned 42.5 percent of it, his friend Andy Charles of National Lock Company (who had been Hill's major correspondent in Rockford in the 1930s) another 42.5 percent, and Emery Hall the remaining 15 percent. That same year he established Hill-Bartelt Machine Company in partnership with Harold Bartelt for the purpose of designing and building thread mills and selling them as machine tools to manufacturers.[21] The last two companies—and during the war the most profitable—were Aero Screw Company and Aircraft Standard Parts No. 2. Both were partnerships that included his sister Isabella

Perkins, his wife Ellen, his uncle Fred Potter, Ray Acre, Walter Chalaire, and apparently for a time Harold Crow. They were dominated by family members and were designed to exploit specific wartime opportunities.

Aero Screw, organized in April 1942, specialized in AN (Army-Navy) specification aircraft hardware, especially, as its name implied, bolts and screws. Its catalog included hexagon and drilled head bolts, clevis bolts and clevis pins, fillister head and washer head screws, washers, castellated nuts, and threaded taper pins. Aircraft Standard Parts No. 2 was formed in September 1942 to take advantage of the success of a single product developed first at Aero Screw, namely the Aero Seal hose clamp designed by Hill.[22]

A key player in these businesses was Howard Hansell, who, through thick and thin, remained a friend of the Hills. He was, according to Ellen, "a charming Philadelphia Quaker gentleman . . . who could sell *anything* because he believed in it himself." He was also a gambler who had lost a couple of fortunes and would involve the Hills in some very shaky deals.[23] Still, like Victor Lougheed, he was a mover and an exciting person.

In November of 1942 Hill reported that contracting with the military for the design and manufacture of hose clamps was particularly lucrative. The Aero Seal clamp was adopted as standard by the army, and imitators had a hard time duplicating it. At that date, which was prior to the beginning of full production of the clamp, he had a backlog of $5 million in orders (mostly engine bolts), had shipped $2.5 million already that year in his companies, and had a profit of about $800,000 (subject to arbitrary reduction by federal mediators in what was called at the time "renegotiation"). In December he got an army order for 1.1 million hose clamps at twenty cents each. In June 1943 his company was manufacturing 10,000 hose clamps a day and expected to make 100,000 a day by September. Estimated demand of 16 million clamps per month meant there was still room for expansion. Hill remarked that the combined bank balances of Aero Screw Company and Aircraft Standard Parts Company in

"Aero-Seal" WORM DRIVE HOSE CLAMPS

ORIGINALLY
DESIGNED FOR
ARMY and NAVY
AIRCRAFT

BY

Aircraft Standard Parts Co., Inc.

For Better, Faster, Tighter, Clamping...

The **WORM DRIVE PRINCIPLE**, as developed in "Aero-Seal" Hose Clamps, uses a special 10-pitch hardened steel worm which engages perforations in the band, thus producing a **TRUE TANGENTIAL PULL** to give a belt-like tightening action and **UNIFORM CLAMPING PRESSURE** all around the hose. Thus there is **NO DISTORTION OF THE HOSE**, no cramping, squeezing, or pinching that could produce leaks. Proof of the effectiveness of this principle is the test data (available on request) showing **NO LEAKAGE UNDER HIGH PRESSURES**. Also, uniform peripheral pressure means the clamp **WILL NOT DISTORT OR COLLAPSE THIN-WALL TUBING**.

The worm drive principle also permits the band to come *through* the worm housing and thus provides **EXTRA LONG TAKE-UP**. This is particularly useful on self-sealing hose and gives plenty of leeway on any type hose to cover variations in hose diameter, wall thickness, and the flow of rubber under repeated tightening of the clamps in service. The band may be backed completely *out* of the housing so the clamp can be sprung open and **INSTALLED OVER THE HOSE IN PLACE**. Severe vibration tests show that **NO LOCK WIRE** is required, though a lock wire hole can be optionally fur-

nished in the thumb grip for sealing purposes if desired. As can be seen from the illustrations, the housing is **VERY COMPACT**, so the clamp will fit in cramped locations and use a minimum of space. There are **NO LOOSE PARTS** to lose or fumble with, since the worm is fully retained at all times by the riveted-on housing. "Aero-Seal" uses a **NON-WELDED INTERLOCKED JOINT BETWEEN BAND AND SADDLE** which actually is stronger than the band itself as shown in destruction tests where the band failed in every case before this joint loosened in any way.

The band itself has **HIGH STRENGTH** with sufficient factor of safety to hold all pressures encountered in service. Proof of this is the fact that "Aero-Seal" Clamps meet *and on many points exceed* all the stringent requirements of Army-Navy Specification **AN-FF-C 406a** and drawing **AN-748**, and thus have been approved for the severest aircraft demands in the world today.

AUTOMOTIVE

"Aero-Seal" Hose Clamps are applicable throughout the automotive field — on passenger cars, , trailers, trucks, tractors, farm implements, earth movers, power shovels, cranes, road machinery, and many other places — wherever a high-quality, durable, dependable clamp is needed. The principal uses will, of course, be on radiator and heater hose connections and they will also be found to provide excellent service on water lines, coolant lines, air lines, oil lines, and any other places where pressures are within "Aero-Seal" range.

AIRCRAFT

The place of "Aero-Seal" in military aircraft service is well-established by an outstanding record under the most severe wartime conditions. The qualities that earned "Aero-Seal" the approval of Army and Navy authorities will also merit their acceptance by operators of commercial and private aircraft of all kinds. For hose connections on fuel, oil, air, and coolant lines of all types and sizes, "Aero-Seal" clamps will give dependable service, assuring the operator of tight and leak-proof joints with a minimum of maintenance trouble.

AIRCRAFT STANDARD PARTS CO., INC., 1711 NINETEENTH AVE., ROCKFORD, ILLINOIS

Hill's Aero-Seal business in Rockford dominated the P-51 hose clamp business during World War II and branched out to other applications.

1943 were nearly $1 million. "Renegotiation and taxes will take most of it, but its still a lot of money.[24]

By the end of the war Aircraft Standard Parts was producing two million hose clamps a month, and Hill planned to give it capacity to make as many as seven or eight million a month. He delighted in seeing pictures of the P-51 Mustang with Aero Seal clamps visible under the engine cowling, on the coolant lines, and on various other parts. "My God!" Acre wrote Hill, "That hose clamp thing is astonishing."[25]

The companies made significant money during the war, leaving Hill better off perhaps financially than he might have been had he stayed with Air Associates, and much better off physically and emotionally. In 1942 Hill drew a salary of $24,000 from Aero Screw alone, not far from the $36,000 salary he had received his last year at Air Associates, and far better than his $12,000 salary in 1939 before the war boom. In addition, he was paid a $20,000 bonus by that company, and Fred Potter was paid a salary of $1,800. In the renegotiation process Aero Screw was required to refund to the government $465,000, which was declared excess profit for fiscal year 1942 on sales of over $2.3 million.[26] Originally profit was 32 percent, reduced to 11 percent by the renegotiation committee. The next year, net profits for Aero Screw were over $1 million, and the distribution to the partners included a single payout of $94,000 to Ellen Hill, $95,000 to Acre, $98,000 to Potter, and $94,000 to Perkins.[27] By then Hill had about 700 employees between Aero Screw and Aircraft Standard Parts and had not, as he put it, "been tagged by a union. When we do I guess I will move on again."[28]

Of course, Cotta Transmission (which built from annual sales of $500,000 when Hill came on board $10 million in 1979), Hill Machine Company, and Aircraft Standard Parts contributed more profits. No wonder the Hill family began in the mid-1940s to distribute its wealth into a number of trusts, often for the benefit of the next generation, both to minimize taxation and simply to distribute the grain.[29] Hill's independence was indeed secure. By the time he took a swim at the Rockford Country Club on his fiftieth birthday, July 16, 1944, he knew, if he had ever doubted it, that, despite the crisis at Air Associates, his engineering talent and entrepreneurial instincts had retained for him large income and high-level business responsibilities—in New York as well as in Rockford.[30] "Both Ellen and I like it in Rockford," Hill wrote to a friend at Curtiss Wright in 1943, "and I think we will stay here for quite some time."[31]

That the end of the war eliminated much of his business mix was to Hill simply another challenge. He had never believed that much of this activity would outlast the war or that there was any long-range security in it. "People that try to get jobs that will have a post war future are wasting their time," he wrote in 1942. "There'll be a greater re-shuffle of ownerships, jobs, names, products etc. than we ever dreamed of. But the knowledge of how to do things will stay right where it was, and will continue to be a salable commodity. Right now, the country is such a mad house that luck is a large factor in determining the size of individual earnings—in spite of the fact that 'know how' is in extreme demand and can be sold at high prices. Making money in this period by constructive effort in no way hurts the war effort and has nothing to do with patriotism." When the crunch came in 1945, Hill adjusted. "Am slashing the overhead," he wrote Chalaire, "and tightening up all around to stay in business. In a way, I like it. Better to have to struggle again."[32]

The pattern of decline can be seen from the partnership tax returns for Aero Screw. Gross profit for calendar year 1942 was $967,000; for 1943, $1.5 million; for 1944, $442,000; and for 1945, $195,000.[33] In its record month Aircraft Standard Parts made 4.5 million clamps, while the figure early in 1945 was 900,000 a month, with its backlog "melting away" and a price war going on in the bolt business.[34] In November 1945 Hill wrote Fred Potter that VJ Day had caused a near 100 percent cancellation of orders. He elected to dissolve Aero Screw at the end of 1945. At the same time he changed Aircraft Standard Parts from a partnership to a corporation and sold it to the Breeze Company, a diversified firm based in Newark, New Jersey, relying for part of his payment on a profit-share arrangement. As though to make a clean sweep of it, he sold his Air Associates stock. He finished selling it in February 1946 at 11½, after which it promptly moved up to 22. "I don't worry about it," he mused, "but it makes me pretty mad at myself."[35]

He did not follow these withdrawals with an immediate jump into something comparably large. He said he was "up in the air." To a friend he wrote, "I have decided to make up my mind to nothing for the present and just plug along winding up these terminations and see what happens or turns up. My advice, therefore, is for you to do the same. If you made some money hang on to it—you might get a swell opportunity to use it after while."[36]

He had some misgivings based on philosophy and politics, as well as short-range economics. "'False premises lead to absurd conclusions.' But popular acceptance of absurd conclusions are not based on logical reasoning and cannot be broken down by reasoning. I think it will be a long time before we will again have sensible government and industrial management in the U.S." He wrote Earl Harding: "Every once in a while I get a few minutes of leisure coincident with an urge to tell somebody what's wrong. The result is a letter or two like the enclosed which I send to you because you have always been such a sympathetic listener to my gripes. Of course I know perfectly well that it is futile to buck a trend, but there is a certain satisfaction in being balky once in a while."[37]

This is not to say that Hill withdrew entirely from business, even temporarily. In 1945, after the combination with Bartelt had proved unsatisfactory, he created the Hill Machine Company (later renamed Hill-Rockford Machine Company), which was a major vehicle for him for the rest of his life. A machine shop, after all, was flexible in what it could do, and Leroy Hill and a machine shop where he could work, manage, and invent were a potent combination.[38]

A second major interest was less successful. The same year Hill became a one-third partner in the Rystrom Engineering Company, a firm organized to manufacture oil burner pumps in Polo, Illinois. He changed the name to Polo Pump Company in 1946 to please the locals, but could not change the product or its reputation fast enough. Charles Rystrom, who had started the company, priced the product too low, manufacturing capacity was short of orders, there were many returns of the poorly functioning pumps, and Hill quickly got tired of the eighty-mile round-trip commute to the factory. As early as the summer of 1946 Hill was calling it a "pretty sour project," and by the end of that year was actively trying to get rid of all or part of his interest. "Am desperately trying to improve the pump," he wrote in December, "before the customers quit buying them."[39]

In addition to these ventures, Hill in this period, as always, had a personal portfolio full of ideas, deals, and potential enterprises at various stages of development. In 1943, for example, he had begun seriously investigating washing machines. Initially this was Acre's idea. Acre was a great investigator of markets and new ideas and had great knowledge and experience. His main faults were excessive optimism and his some-times borderline sharp business practices, both of which Hill often had to correct. Acre's point about washing machines was that the postwar market would be big for automatic washers, which were still in their infancy. He was correct in spotting a trend toward the automation of everything in the laundry and kitchen, from dishwashing to garbage disposing to laundry handling. And these machines were increasingly fully automated.[40]

Bendix had a virtual monopoly on the field with its round-tub machine with the all-important feature of making the water extraction phase of washing completely free of manual work. Yet its machine was expensive and had numerous obvious weaknesses that made the field ripe for responsible competition. Don Scott, who had been in on the pioneering stages of the Bendix washing machine, was no longer with the company, understood the field well, and had a personal motive to beat his former employer at its game. Therefore Acre and Hill held a number of meetings with Scott to discuss the possibility of getting into that business. Acre was greatly enthused about combining a washing machine with a coal stoker that Hill had invented in his spare time, with maybe even the purchase of the Roper Stove Company in Rockford as the basis for a large home appliance business, which he proposed calling Home

Utilities Corporation of America. He thought that Rockford, with its diverse manufacturing activity, would be an ideal place to build the washer. "There are great possibilities in this particular field, because home utilities and kitchen equipment will be completely revolutionized after the war. The present modern equipment will be thrown out."[41]

Hill thought the idea had possibilities and went so far as to study establishing a home utility distribution network in the East. Scott visited Rockford, and, while he was not impressed with the size of Aero Screw or Aircraft Standard Parts, the group talked about using Cotta Transmission and maybe some of the manufacturing capability of National Lock for washing machine manufacturing. In 1943 Hill developed an iceball-making machine, which he argued would "be a great convenience and will require some Goldberg type designing and inventing." He was afraid Acre would laugh at the idea, but, on the contrary, Acre picked up on it immediately and suggested that the ice-making machine be combined with a refrigerator, and the whole endeavor added to the new proposed home utility company. He thought a refrigerator with a turntable would decrease the size of the opening and reduce cooling loss. In the spring of 1943 Hill started building a prototype washer, or "chip wringer," as these things were called in Rockford. He hired a man from Bendix at South Bend to help and put together a "haywire rig" for spinning the basket—all at a time when he was just tooling up for full hose clamp production. However, by the end of the summer, the washing machine project languished. Acre offered to work on it in California on speculation, but the enormous increases in other business, combined with difficulties in the engineering, moved Hill to back away from it. "We are getting spread too thin," he wrote in December 1943, "and a side project like this will take money and time." Maybe later.[42]

A multitude of smaller projects indicated the breadth of Hill's interests as well as his capabilities. Acre pitched the idea of a motorcycle in the spring of 1943. He bought a British Triumph and experimented with installing a simplified automatic transmission in it. He predicted that 100-octane gasoline would be as cheap as regular after the war and that

 A-N AIRCRAFT HARDWARE

STEEL DRILLED HEAD AIRCRAFT BOLTS

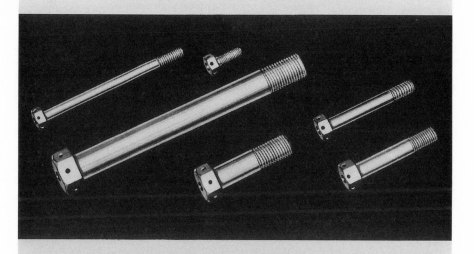

★ These steel Drilled Head Aircraft Bolts are manufactured in accordance with the latest Army-Navy Standard Drawings AN 73 to AN 81 covering diameters from 3/16 inch to 3/4 inch.

All sizes of Drilled Head Aircraft Bolts are made with either Fine Threads (N.F.3) or Coarse Threads (N.C.3). Part numbers of fine thread bolts are identified by plain dash numbers. (Example of part number: AN73-4 is 10-32 x 1/2 inch). The coarse thread series is designated by the letter "A" between the part number and the dash number. (Example of part number: AN73A-4, is 10-24 x 1/2 inch).

These bolts are cold-headed from steel wire that is especially drawn from electric furnace steel that undergoes a thorough inspection for cracks, pipes, and seams. The material conforms to Army-Navy Material Specifications AN-QQ-S-689 or AN-S-14.

The heads of these bolts are thicker than the standard hexagon head aircraft bolts and have holes drilled through each of the six faces and one hole from the top center for securing with lock wire. Bolts are heat-treated in atmospherically controlled electric furnaces to a minimum tensile strength of 125,000 pounds per square inch, and are plated in accordance with Army-Navy Specification AN-QQ-P-421A.

High quality is maintained by strict adherence to Manufacturing Specification AN-B-3.

Fine machine shopwork was a Hill specialty in Rockford. There is no fluff in this World War II era catalog copy.

there would be a big demand for a high-performance motorcycle.[43] Again Hill, understandably, pled that he was over committed. "I can't get much interested in it at the present time because of the number of irons in the fire. Until some of these other projects get under way I am going to confine my thoughts to them so as not to get my limited idea capacity spread way too thin." Acre persisted, but Hill refused to let him buy the Triumph on behalf of Aero Screw. He was having a similar problem paying Scott's expenses on the washing machine and calculating how to account for them and to what company to attach them.[44] Before the end of the war, Hill seriously investigated making spark plugs with a partner who had a new idea, worked on a hedge trimmer proposal, looked at a plan for a turbo power unit for a jet aircraft, and further developed his coal stoker, which he patented in 1944. There were niggling problems with all of them. On the hedge trimmer, for instance, Hill worried about the problems with a small engine. "Did you ever play with one of those model airplane engines?" he wrote the hedge trimmer inventor. "They are too tricky and inefficient and while a model airplane builder can handle them with no trouble, the average person who trims a hedge is too unmechanical." He couldn't visualize the expenses connected with the jet engine or imagine when the income might come it.[45] He considered briefly buying a resort hotel ("I can't imagine myself as even a part owner of a gadget like this"), and even went so far as to invest and lose a good deal of money with Victor Lougheed in the Magmatic Minerals Corporation.[46] Lougheed wrote him, in his inimitable style, in March 1943: "This will acknowledge your characteristically cantankerous communication of 1 January 1943. Consonant with our policy of extending the most meticulous consideration and fairness to even our smallest, most ignorant, and most irritating stockholders, your screed was placed on the table at our annual meeting . . . . In conclusion, I cannot refrain from commenting that your stupid greed for 'returns on investment,' in the face of the fact universally known (except, apparently, to yourself), that 'returns on investment' automatically are garnered by the administration in Washington, and not allowed to be given to stockholders, is of a piece with the rest of your silly complaints."[47] It is no wonder that Lougheed had an unlisted phone number.

Business, however, was far from all-consuming for Hill. His family and the nature of the time spent with them were equally important, and he used the money he had and the time he made to entertain himself while being with them. A key event in the private kingdom of the new Hill family was the purchase of a primitive lakeside farm property near Francestown, New Hampshire, in 1945. The prospect came in January through Oren P. (Dome) Harwood, who had been an eastern sales representative for Hill's wartime businesses. A World War I pilot, wing-walker and barnstormer, former head of the Civil Aeronautics Administration, and a fundamentally great salesman and a great wit besides, Harwood described the farm near the attractively named Pleasant Pond in such glowing terms (a hand-drawn map was included) that Hill, who was himself not very pleased with the idea of no electricity, confessed that his wife was so sold she wanted to buy it sight unseen. Harwood averred that the woman owner wanted to sell because she was old and that it was just as well for Leroy to spend his money on something like that than on war bonds or "glamour boying around in saloons." Maybe most telling to Hill was the political angle. "The more I see of this government and stuff," Harwood wrote them, "the better that 'Squatters Shack' in New Hampshire looks . . . . Under the new deal you dam well better get a place like this to hide in or to keep from starving to death when things get tough . . . which ain't so far off." It was the most beautiful country in the world, Harwood claimed, and the taxes were only $20 a year. The agent had asked $3,000 for the improvements and thirty acres: Hill offered $2,000.[48] By March, maybe after further negotiations, Hill had bought the property, sent $1,000 cash for a down payment, and asked Harwood to put the deed in the name of Ellen Mayo Hill. Harwood confirmed the deal with another of his maps, showing a trout stream running through the property and the old mill pond nearby (he promised good bass fishing) with a sandy shallow beach and the looming low mountains behind. The closest place of any consequence was

Bennington, and it was not very close. With Ellen especially that was just fine. That fall the family visited their "estate in New Hampshire" during a 3,000-mile trip in the 1941 Cadillac, despite Ellen's advanced pregnancy. They just could not wait.[49]

In fact, having a retreat in the summer was important to the Hills before they ever visited New Hampshire. In the spring of 1945 the family had rented a large house at Lake Geneva, Wisconsin, only thirty-five miles from Rockford, from June to September for $1,500; Ellen had quit her job at Aero Screw in order to take the children there for the summer. They bought a 22-foot ChrisCraft Runabout for $1,100 to operate on the lake. There they celebrated the Japanese surrender with "many drinks" at the dance hall in Lake Geneva City.[50] Hill commuted back and forth to fulfill his obligations in Rockford, as he was to do during the family's long stays at the "camp" in New Hampshire, but he spent a good deal of time at the lake and enjoyed it thoroughly. He was reading Henry Hazlitt's *Economics in One Lesson*, F. A. Hayek's *The Road to Serfdom*, and other like literature that reinforced the lessons of his experience. "It isn't the big business that will break me down," he wrote Harwood, "—its the social whirl around here. Tomorrow night Ellen is giving a dinner party for 16 people at which she is having a 47 pound pig roasted whole, then a large formal dance at the country club and the next day another dinner with two large turkeys. All accompanied by a commensurate amount of drinking. Guess I'll have to have more kids to slow her down and prolong my life."[51]

In Hill's life, 1947 might well be called "the year of Aldrich." Partly because he was trying to sell Polo Pump to the Breeze Corporation, which had done well with his Aircraft Standard Parts, Hill early that year became involved in an attempt to buy the Aldrich Company, a manufacturer of oil burners and boilers located in Wyoming, Illinois. Hill had the idea of selling it and Polo as a combination to Breeze, but as it happened he succeeded only in being the intermediary in the sale of Aldrich to Breeze and in the process got himself a job managing the company for nearly a year and attaching to his schedule a longer commute (115 miles one way from Rockford) than any previously.

Aldrich was a good deal on the surface. It was entirely a personal fiefdom managed by Lloyd Aldrich, a cantankerous and independent older man with an accounting system consisting entirely of one secretary who shared many of her boss's personal characteristics. "It is the most disorganized place I've ever seen," Hill recorded in his diary, "but lots of orders. All personnel seem cooperative and glad to see organization start." But even with no engineering, sales, purchasing, or production controls and financial statements consisting only of a monthly trial balance, the product was so outstanding that Aldrich had all the orders and income it could handle. In a field with over 200 manufacturers, the company sold half of all boilers of that type that were made in the United States. The asking price was $1.3 million, and the man from Chicago who was hired to evaluate the situation estimated that it had the potential of $1 million a year in profits.[52]

Hill's summary of the businesses with which he had been involved indicated that Aldrich was one of the businesses that returned him over $100,000 in profits, but it was not without some pain. He did succeed in his nine months as general manager in getting the books in order and revolutionizing the shop methods, but it was a strain. "I don't know anything about the heating business," he wrote in March. "I thought I did before I got into it building oil burner pumps but after a year of making them and attending the heating and ventilating show at Cleveland in January I have come to the conclusion that I know practically nothing. However, having learned that much I feel that I am making some progress."[53] The closing with Breeze was tough. Aldrich refused to go to Newark and constantly talked about having another cash offer. There was endless debate about wording, and Polo Pump was left out while continuing to lose money and requiring constant cash inputs from Hill. "I am sorry that Breeze has kicked this deal around so shamefully," Hill concluded, "but I think we did the best we could to give it to them."[54]

Hill worked very hard as general manager of Aldrich, though the deal as negotiated did not leave him with a piece of the company and did not relieve him of Polo Pump as planned, but only as a salaried manager and a fee-paid consultant with a few warrants in Breeze. He told Harwood that "this dam job that I have is very demanding and I never worked at one that I had less enthusiasm for." The company had a Bellanca Cruisaire aircraft, and Hill flew it on his commute for a time. However, he crash-landed it once in poor weather, and, in general, it was an unsatisfactory time-saver. "The private flying business hasn't changed much," he observed. "Either the airplane is laid up for a check, or bulletin alteration, or something has fallen off of it, or else the weather is bad when you want to go, so actually when I depend on the airplane, nobody can depend on me." "It's a dog's life," he wrote to Acre. "I am working harder than at any time during the war. It sure is a hectic enterprise."[55]

Before he resigned from Aldrich management at the end of 1947, however, Hill had accomplished a good deal there. He hired good employees for the key management positions, redesigned the boiler and the transformer that were key products, and revised pricing to be more competitive. Doing so had caused him to neglect his other businesses, however, and he felt "as though I had a bear by the tail but have tamed it a little bit." The Breeze management accepted his resignation in December with thanks for the job he had done. He bought Ellen a 1947 Cadillac convertible, trading in his old Graham-Paige, arranged to run electric wiring to the New Hampshire property, and turned his attention back closer to home.[56]

It was too late for Polo Pump. Hill recorded in January 1948, "I desperately try to get engineering done that should have been done a year ago." He tested pumps and found "all kinds of things wrong with them—too late I guess." By May the company was down to eight employees. While Hill Machine was doing well and there were some upward cycles at Polo over the next months, Hill was lucky to get enough for its assets and buildings in the summer of 1949 to pay off its current creditors. He wrote, "I don't have the ambition or energy to work it out of the mess it got into."[57]

There were regular chances to buy into bigger businesses. In 1948, for example, came the Super Electric deal. There were negotiations for Hill to buy that company, but at the last minute he backed out. "I'm sorry about running out on the Super Electric deal," he wrote Howard Hansell in Philadelphia, "but I decided that I had better play my own hunches, and I sure have a strong one against the deal as it finally turned out."[58]

He was doing well enough with Hill Machine and seemed for the moment to have more fun with Harwood's "Haywire Enterprises," which involved New Hampshire projects such as building new chicken houses and a dam, than he did with "real" big business. He wrote (Dome) Harwood that, according to the *Wall Street Journal,* there was a chicken and egg depression and the business was glutted. But he liked chickens "alive and [I] like them very much dead and fried by Leona (Harwood). Ellen also has some very good tricks with chickens . . . . I believe in depressions as they shake out the lazy, the inefficient and the ill-adapted and get them relocated in other activities for which they are better suited. I would assume that you would weather the chicken and egg depression and take advantage of the prosperous era which would follow." Ellen said Dome could build his chicken house on her property "provided your chickens are house broken and do not dirty and smell things all up."[59]

An offer from Fairchild Aviation in 1949 to be its president was a different matter from these miscellaneous negotiations. Fairchild was a major aircraft company, several times the size of Air Associates, Hill's largest association previously. In August Hill wrote to a friend at the company that it was more gratifying than any other offer he had ever received. "I don't know anyone I'd rather work with and the opportunity for achievement is a tempting challenge." He had a strong impulse to seize it. "I told you on the phone that I would expect you to fire me forthwith if I didn't perform, but I think I would be more critical than you and would be the one to relieve you of that unpleasant duty. When you bring an outsider into a responsible position in an organization as large as yours there is bound to be some criticizing and beefing. I'm not worried about that but you should have full information about me because some of the criticism will be directed at you. Dome thinks I'm a genius which is flattering even though I know it isn't so. As a matter of fact I am a slow thinker and maybe a little stupid but I have been able to make up for it in the past by working longer and harder than most other people. I have had an unusually wide variety of experience in manufacturing and know how to do a lot of things myself but have been a poor teacher. However I think I have improved considerably as a manager and organizer in the last ten years. I am not a good judge of men and cannot rate them correctly until I have worked with them for months." He was not sure what the Air Associates directors would say about him if asked, "except that I guess they would admit that I built it from nothing to where it was when I left it."[60]

Obviously, he considered the offer most seriously. However, early in September, he turned the job down. Even in his upbeat first response, one negative factor came immediately to his mind. If he took the job, his personal affairs would have to "undergo a painful reorganization." At first he dismissed this with "that's my problem," but the more he thought about it, the more he disliked pulling up roots in Rockford for a chance that would perhaps do more for his ego than for his real happiness or even financial security. He visited Fairchild and concluded that he could do the job and would like doing it. However, in addition to the personal lifestyle factor, he listed two other major negatives in his letter of refusal. First, the job would take him away from Hill Machine Company, in which he had a personal investment of over $100,000 and which was not organized in such a way that he could walk away from it. If he did, he would have another Polo Pump Company on his hands. A second factor was that Fairchild had a CIO union. "Your local boys may be O.K. and I might never have any trouble with them, but I know the national's policies and I think that sooner or later a situation would develop involving a sacrifice of principles. It would be unpleasant and I would get fired again." The situation, he confessed, was "almost irresistible," but he could not and did not take it.[61]

It was a momentous and courageous decision—coolly, consciously, and conscientiously made. Few who were not frightened by it could have resisted it, and it was a measure of Hill's maturity, not necessarily a given even in a man in his fifties with wide experience, that he could make it. The Fairchild job offer, he wrote his old associate Haven Page several years later, "tickled my vanity but I turned it down. I like my little show here. No unions, boards of directors or stockholders."[62]

Youth, it is said, is a gift of nature, age a work of art. And so it was in this case. Weeks after his decision, Elizabeth Puryear Hill, 7 pounds, 13 ounces, was born. Ellen wanted a boy. But Hill wrote, "I guess she is resigned to her fate now."[63] And so was he—not just resigned to but settled in it and as well adjusted as a genius-level bundle of energy could be.

It seemed the end of some things. Any career as a big-time executive was permanently behind Hill, but he had the comfort of knowing that it was wholly by his own choice. His 1941 Cadillac, which had served him for nine years and 106,000 miles, gave up the ghost in the spring of 1950 when the universal joint disintegrated and Hill walked out of a dinner party to find the drive shaft on the ground. He replaced it for $4,400 with a green Cadillac 60 Special—heavy, powerful, and ideal for the more and more frequent long drives east. His beloved mother, Nellie, ninety-two years old in 1950 and a regular visitor at Leroy and Ellen's house, died quietly in May of that year. It caused Hill to smoke four cigarettes after his last visit with her, but he averred that "am still quit." In October Ellen's mother died, and within two years the Hills had to take a sad trip to New York to move her father into a care facility and out of the apartment he could no longer care for.[64]

All these events marked another distinct stage in a life that was in a way several lives, but they marked change more than diminution. Since the war, Hill told a correspondent in 1950, he had shrunk his business activities down to a small machine shop employing twenty people, with $10,000 to $12,000 a month in sales—too small to take on "major" work. Sometimes he went to the shop only six hours a day, so he considered himself "semi-retired." But he was by no means tired or depressed, nor had he even quite yet given up, despite the odds, on having a son. "Ellen's cooking is still improving," he told another friend. "My health is pretty fair considering the amount of tobacco and alcohol I absorb."[65]

A Voice in the Wilderness

*I*n the 1950s, Hill kidded a lot about his relatively relaxed life. As early as 1946, when he was beginning to spend considerable time at Pleasant Pond, he added to a diary entry about shooting frogs with a rifle and making a weir dam—"Did nothing mostly—keeping very busy at it." In 1951, he was still worrying a bit about the long stays in New Hampshire. The family and their dogs were there that year from June until after Labor Day. "I have never taken such a long vacation," Hill commented to a friend, "but I guess I'm old enough to stand it." In 1954, noting that he was sixty years old, had a removable bridge, and stayed away religiously from unnatural exercise other than his daily doings, he was happy to add that "I love to eat, play with girls and have fun in both old and new ways. Am looking forward to the next decade as more enjoyable than anything I've had in the past."[1]

Hill had always been generous with his family, particularly in his long and nearly total support of his parents (they and his adult daughter Bev were listed for many years as dependents on Hill's tax return, and Uncle Fred was in effect a dependent also). And no matter how tough a negotiator he was in business, he was a soft sell (he sometimes went further in critical terminology about himself) in loaning money to friends despite the educational process that might have taken place with their constant defaults on these loans had his heart not been so much at the forefront.[2] Victor and Mary Lougheed were only early examples of a long string of friends to whom Hill regularly sent money, sometimes on the basis of a doubtful business investment scheme, but often from the purest concern only. With his postwar wealth, he was able to increase and add to these gestures and to make them a serious part of what he did with his life. In 1951, for example, he bought a $4,700 Jaguar for the Perkinses, his sister Isabella and her husband Jim, who were still assigned to Paramount Pictures and living in England. After sending his wife back to California, Jim Perkins got caught by the war in Asia, and became a Japanese prisoner of war, and Hill retained the image of him returning in a prisoner exchange haggard and weary.[3] He was similarly generous with his uncle Fred Potter, despite Potter's assurance that "after traveling the broad primrose path all these years it seems now to have degenerated into a bumpy squirrel track and I find I do not need very much money to keep up the reduced pace." In 1951 Hill financed a trip to Europe for Potter and received a heartfelt letter of gratitude: "You have carried me under your financial wing, always giving, giving, giving, and in a way that would almost make it appear that I was doing you a favor in accepting. And now comes this climax of your prodigal generosity and it leaves me without words to express what I feel. However, I know you must realize my very deep appreciation."[4] A laconic diary entry in 1948 concerned an incident in which Hill put Howard Hansell on a train to Oregon and "lent him $15,000 like a dope." On another occasion of a loan to Hansell fourteen years later, Hill wrote his sister that "I have told Ellen that she had better get me declared incompetent and get a conservator appointed while there is still time." He tried to help Victor and Mary Lougheed, and later Mary alone, and when his old friend Alice Blue needed a tape recorder or just a lift, Hill was ready.[5]

But while he was relaxed in a way, parochial in a way, and focused on his family, in another sense Hill in the 1950s and 1960s was more active and broader in his political and social concerns and action than ever before. For some time he had written to his congressman regularly, to the newspapers, and to others who might institute change upon the subject of the Wagner Act specifically and labor policy more generally. But after the war, he made, as he put it, a kind of "hobby" out of economics. He read widely on the subject, though particularly the works of the Austrian school of economists—Friedrich Hayek, Ludwig von

Alice Blue in her trademark pose at the organ.

Mises, and Henry Hazlitt especially—and wrote letters to his associates, journalists, friends, and heads of foundations and organizations to which he was a contributor outlining the logic of his positions and trying to influence policy. He did not write formal articles or give speeches, but his letters were sometimes printed in newspapers and newsletters.

He became a part of what was known as the New American Right or the Radical Right, an identifiable political strain that perhaps originated when corporations under the Taft-Hartley Act of 1947 were allowed to finance arguments against unionism, and therefore by implication, for traditional individualism, to their employees. Accessibly written books about the failings of socialism, like Hayek's *The Road to Serfdom* (1944), William F. Buckley's *God and Man at Yale* (1950), Russell Kirk's *The Conservative Mind* (1953), Leo Strauss's *Natural Right and History* (1953), and Ayn Rand's "objectivist" novel *Atlas Shrugged* (1958) gained some popularity. The career of Joseph McCarthy polarized people on the dangers of domestic communism. These events gave rise to magazines like *Human Events* and the *National Review* as well as such "think tanks" as the libertarian Foundation for Economic Education, founded by former head of the Los Angeles Chamber of Commerce Leonard Read.

Both von Mises and Hayek were early associated with the Foundation for Economic Education and contributed to its newsletters, publications, and seminars, often attended by upper-middle-class, well-educated business executives like Hill or William Grede, the Milwaukee foundry owner, who in turn supported the organization and the distribution of its publication *The Freeman*.[6]

In 1947 there was a ten-day conference at Mt. Pelerin, Switzerland, for the discussion of such ideas, and by 1949 the Mt. Pelerin Society, whose meetings the Hills attended regularly all over the world, was in full swing. The idea, put simply, was to educate and built a consensus among opinion leaders "about the moral and practical superiority of unrestrained capitalism" and of the desirability of an extremely limited role for government. Freedom was seen not as an end in itself, but as a means to securing a virtuous society. There was, or should be, these people thought, a natural social order, "something distinguishable from the kind of relativistic, even hedonistic, moral codes that shifted with the changing of the political guard." Often there was a harking back to ancient and Enlightenment philosophers, along with a reverence for the wisdom of the past. To educational organizations like the Foundation for Economic Education were shortly added activist organizations to push the same themes politically, most notably the John Birch Society, founded by retired candy manufacturer and intellectual prodigy Robert Welch in 1958 and headquartered in Belmont, Massachusetts.[7] Given what free enterprise had done for Leroy Hill, and what government had done to him, and given his propensity for action on his beliefs, it was no accident that this New Right movement in all its diversity attracted him.

Of course this "moral majority" was much analyzed and criticized, and it can be argued there has not yet been anything approaching a nonpolemical historical account of it. Seymour Lipset wrote about "the politics of unreason." Probably the most famous analysis of its people and attractions is historian Richard Hofstadter's essay "The Paranoid Style in American Politics." The New Right represented, Hofstadter argued, an elite group whose status in society was threatened—business managers threatened by unions and retired military officers afraid the military they knew was declining—responding emotionally to the political drama. It was, he thought, characterized by "heated exaggeration, suspiciousness and conspiratorial fantasy." Instead of viewing modern history as "a comedy of errors and a museum of incompetence," the New Right saw it as treason and immorality. The enemy became not the nebulous faults in all of us but "a perfect model of malice, a kind of amoral superman: sinister, ubiquitous, powerful, cruel."[8]

No doubt Hill could be viewed as suffering from "status disorientation" and his activism could thus be psychologized away. But he was far from alone. The John Birch Society had perhaps 100,000 members in the early 1960s, and the new religious right, led by Billy James Hargis and Fred C. Schwarz, was developing what by the 1980s and 1990s had become a significant political force. Maybe they were, in a way, fighting modernity, if modernity is defined as "the belief in rational assessment, rather than established custom, for the evaluation of social change," but they felt they were fighting for American values as they were meant to be and against drift. Social scientists surveying members of the New Right in the 1960s admitted that they did not seem to be "embittered misfits," but rather people like Leroy and Ellen Hill—"pleasant, considerate and law-abiding. They were comfortable and happy with their familial relations and very much in touch with the relationships and events in their interpersonal spheres."[9]

Hill was no fundamentalist Christian, but he fitted the profile otherwise. He certainly believed there had been a decline in values and in the application of principles to American life. He believed that character shaped events. He probably tended to oversimplify, as people who have had to make decisions in the real world and take risks based on limited information tend to do. He was an activist and a reader. And, as his Rockford years revealed, he was a family man. Dean Manion, whom Hill supported, put it this way: "The needed division is not between left and right but between right and wrong."[10] Like a number of other of the major financial supporters of the New Right in the 1950s and 1960s, Hill was far from ideologically pure about it—sometimes to the frustration of certain of the groups. As long as they were for freedom, he was for them, though his causes often did not get on well with each other over details.

Hill's letters on national and international issues are well reasoned, well written, filled with his acerbic sense of humor (paralleling his sense of the absurd in the modern situation), and always based on the view that principle is purely in everyone's long-range interest. Free trade was a regular concern, as, of course, was government economic intervention and planning in any forum. In 1948 he expressed his opposition to the Marshall Plan to his brother-in-law Jim Perkins, even though to be against the Marshall Plan during the Berlin airlift was akin to coming out against motherhood. "I am in favor of the elimination of restrictions on foreign trade," Hill wrote, "(except maybe tariff for revenue only or for protection of occasional strategic materials of industries which could not otherwise compete) with a return to export and import trading between individuals with 'exchange' finding the natural level resulting from the supply and demand relationship. From the charitable aspect, I am still opposed to it as I do not believe charity to be a proper function of our government. I am all for individuals contributing whatever they feel like . . . or buying European government bonds voluntarily. The only reason there is so much popular support in the country for the Marshall plan is that a large majority of the supporters are stupidly assuming that it isn't costing them anything—the government is paying for it." He added a postscript: "Its the wrong way to stop communism. People don't learn things if they are protected against the consequences of their mistakes. Let them all go communist and suffer—they'll learn."[11]

A typical Hill letter on free trade went to Dan Smoot of the *Dan Smoot Newsletter* in the summer of 1958. With free trade the rate of exchange adjusted automatically, Hill thought. The dollars that foreigners received for things we bought from them would be spent for things they bought from us, and the "lira" we got from them would be spent for things we buy from them. It did not matter whether the United States put a 100 percent social security tax on wages or passed a five-dollar-per-hour minimum wage law or did not allow any work over ten hours a week—free trade would still be valuable to the United States regardless of what any other government did. The actions of governments only restricted and harmed their own people by ignoring the fundamental economic principle that a trade always depends on a disagreement about the value of two things. Hill told Smoot that Smoot's own good grasp of economics was being corrupted by support he got from industrialists who grew up under the New Deal and "were taught that all corporations exploited and cheated their employees and it was only through the action of the great New Deal that these terrible conditions were corrected. They have learned that our great and good government is the source of all blessings and if an Italian or a Swiss or a German or a French adding machine, or sewing machine, or movie camera offers an attractive product to his customers at a lower price he says to hell with the good of the consumers or the general public, I gotta have protection from the government or I'm going to have to lay off 1,000 people and that will damage the economy something terrible, so let the customers pay a higher price for sewing machines and keep our 1,000 people at work—making sewing machines instead of making them go out and get jobs doing something else. Well, let's not antagonize these economic illiterates by trying to teach them something they don't want to know."[12]

Hill responded regularly to editorials and articles in the *Wall Street Journal* on economics, sometimes at length, and his letters were often published. In 1957, for instance, he wrote concerning an editorial arguing that the rate of industrial growth in the Soviet Union, though faster than that in the United States, should not be of concern since the economy there started from a smaller base. The United States, Hill noted, had also started from a small base and it was discovery and capital accumulation coming from excess earnings of individuals under the free enterprise system that made the miracle. Now accumulation was being slowed by a U.S. tax system "which siphons off excess earnings of individuals for redistribution by government bureaucracy to the less productive in this and other countries." Should we continue redistributing the products of past capital accumulation and the Soviets continue to aim at capital accumulation, albeit for the benefit of an elite group, their economy could catch up quickly.[13] Earl Harding wrote Hill in January 1958 concerning another letter to the *Journal,* saying that it was an "example of your extraordinary capacity for clear, concise thought so simply expressed that even 'the simplest mind on the Bowery' should understand." Hill was pleased at that. "For a person of your skill to respect my skill in expression," he replied, "gives me great satisfaction but makes me doubt your judgment. You know I bleed terribly when I try to write anything and I have to be pretty well worked up to make the attempt."[14]

A *Wall Street Journal* missive from Hill in the spring of 1958 concerned a defense of public housing from another correspondent and well illustrated his ability to illustrate general principles with a specific issue. "He is no doubt a very charitable person," he said of the letter writer, "and probably feels that it is only fair that the less charitable of our citizens should be made to share the cost of doing good. After all, the cost to each individual is small and the resulting good to the underprivileged is very great." But total cost meant higher taxes and inappropriate staff power. "The power put into the hands of the managers of these projects seems to create in their minds an illusion of superior intelligence . . . . This induces the authoritarian attitude in the bureaucracy. Thus has come about the metamorphosis of our federal government from a limited activity concerned only with duties enumerated and powers not prohibited by the constitution to the gigantic and all-powerful bureaucracy concerned with everyone's welfare, engaging in hundreds of activities formerly left to private enterprise and exercising greatly increased control over the lives of its citizens." The government created nothing, Hill said, and "some of us think that our welfare government marks the beginning of the decline of the great American Republic."[15]

Hill was doubtless one of the most regular of his congressman's and senator's correspondents. John Anderson, who represented his district for many years, agreed with Hill on many things and was willing, as was his Rockford constituent, to discuss others at length in letters. Other politicians had less of an interchange with Hill but might well hear from him if they took certain stands. Illinois senator Everett Dirkson heard in 1958: "This is just another weak cry of protest from one of the minority who cling to faith in constitutional government, states rights, individual freedom and responsibility as opposed to the welfare state." Dirkson had voted for the Area Redevelopment Act, whereby the government took responsibility for certain groups. This, Hill said, was socialism, and so was the Small Business Administration, and so was the graduated income tax. If foreign aid were ever put to a referendum vote, it would be defeated by a landslide. "But it seems as though the socialists (under various names), the economic illiterates and the average delinquents are in the majority and I suppose it behooves politicians to climb on the bandwagon. The decline and fall of the Roman Empire took over 400 years.

I think we can do it in another hundred. But I'll be dead long before that. However, I just can't bring myself around to joining the parade. I'll buck the trend until I'm liquidated. I thought I was bucking it when I originally voted for you."[16]

A similar independence of spirit and willingness to pursue issues was evident in Hill's pattern of never passively accepting a personal injustice, no matter how inconsequential. He no longer got into fistfights, as he often had in his youth, but he was not willing to collapse and take it because he was too busy or too tired to protest. In 1948, for example, he was arrested near his home for driving 33 mph in a 30 mph zone while passing another car. When he objected to being arrested and taken to police headquarters for such a minor offense, the officer threatened to jail him for disorderly conduct. Hill took it up with the Board of Police and Fire Commissioners in Belvidere, Illinois: "I do not dispute the legality of the arrest, although in my opinion the infraction of the traffic rule was of such a minor nature that it would ordinarily be overlooked or dismissed with a word of warning. What I object to and complain about is the ill-tempered, abusive, overbearing, and threatening manner of the arresting officer. I cannot see that any purpose is served—beyond gratifying a sadistic officer's sense of power and authority—in treating an otherwise law-abiding citizen caught in a traffic violation like a desperate criminal. I naturally resent such treatment."[17]

Another sample of the same was a 1951 letter to the Cadillac company over his troubles with Ellen's 1947 convertible, which "was and is a lemon," and the dealer who was supposed to service it. He said the car had always run hot, the paint had started chipping days after he bought it, and "the automatic windows have been a constant headache and godawful expense . . . . I am not a chronic kicker and I expect to pay much higher for Cadillac service than for my Ford Station Wagon. I am not wholly ignorant of automobile matters having designed in whole or in part a number of internal combustion engines and have been a member of the S.A.E. since 1916. However, I am too busy to supervise the repair and service of my automobiles or squabble with repair men about their diagnosis of engine and other troubles and the charges for bad guesses, etc. So I am going to try a Packard or a Lincoln and see if I am happier." He got satisfaction from Cadillac.[18]

But while Hill could be something other than mild-mannered, his letters on political and social issues were moderately phrased and appealed to rationality rather than spite. Earl Harding, a pro at this, commented to him once concerning a letter Hill had sent to Robert Taft and which he had worried did not "pack much wallop": "It discloses no venom such as he might expect from the victim of the most outrageous of all the seizures. The wallop is there, more effective with 8-ounce gloves than it would have been from bare knucks." Hill, he said, had an "inimitable way" of denouncing "monstrosities."[19]

Still, he minced no words, particularly when the subject was labor. To an executive facing a strike in 1949 he wrote: "To begin with, you have apparently accepted the idea that there is something sacred about 'collective bargaining'; that individuals have no right to deal with other individuals if they have been voted into a union; —that they have no right to protection from organized violence in the name of 'Labor'; that the picket line is a sacred thing instead of a coercive threat against individuals;—that strike breaking is wrong;—that to resist an unjust law is sinful;—that bloodshed must be avoided even if it means the surrender of liberty." The unions, he said, "have grown into monstrous political machines wielding more power than constituted authorities. . . . You've got a handful of communists, toughs and misguided fools walking all over you. Why don't you slap them down? Sure—somebody might get hurt. But what's the alternative?"[20]

A 1958 letter to a manager showed no mellowing. He had received the management newsletter from Republic Aviation, Hill wrote, and it was interesting. "In fact, it was kind of amusing, as it is so utterly damn ridiculous. It appears that the 'workers' are getting ready to take over Republic, you Warmongers and imperialistic Wall Street Capitalists. This will be about the next step after the finish of the 1958 negotiations. They have been working up to it for the past 20 years. It affords me considerable satisfaction to have faced up to the issue in 1941 and having settled on my operating principles once and for all at that time, I have never had to bother with labor relations. Of course I have to keep my business down to a modest size and maintain my financial position so that I can go out of business on a moment's notice, but I don't have to go through what you fellows do and I can keep my self respect."[21]

Sometimes it did not take long to deflate a government project, particularly when humor was employed. Hill wrote the *Wall Street Journal* in 1969, when he was seventy-five years old, in response to an article about an expensive study that proved Volkswagens (Hill liked them for their engineering, and Nader's Corvairs too) were more dangerous in an accident than larger U.S. cars. "Additional millions," he wrote, "and more bureaucrats may discover that in collisions, VW's are safer than motorcycles, that trucks are safer than 'standard' size cars and that bulldozers are safer than trucks. So what?" Commonly he reversed bromides with sharp wit. "I am a small business man," he wrote Senator Everett Dirkson. "I do not want any help from the government, please."[22]

The growing federal government was a threat everywhere, Hill thought. "I am pretty discouraged with the prospect of stopping the trend to socialism," he wrote Harding in 1951. "The big majority of voters won't read anything and I doubt if many people listen to broadcasts like yours. If you could only promise them something for nothing you might get somewhere. High taxes aren't felt by most people. Withholding taxes aren't noticed because the money doesn't come out of their pockets because it never gets into their pockets first. Most wage earners tear off the stubs from their checks and throw them away without even looking at them. . . . For my part, I don't want to defend the free peoples of the world—only the free people of the U.S.A. I don't want my government to give away anything or help anybody—I'll do my own giving and helping. And I don't want any help for my 'small business.' I guess I'm a nasty old isolationist and not even a little ashamed of myself."[23]

Hill participated in the political process, however discouraged he might get. In 1948 he wrote in his diary: "Truman elected—big surprise—the worst of 2 socialists." Later he said that one of Truman's speeches "sounds like a CIO organizer." But in 1950 he noted that the election that year "was somewhat gratifying" to him, though "we're a long ways from getting back to where we were headed before the lunatics got hold of the country in 1932."[24] He worked actively for candidates with long-shot chances but with kindred views—Robert Taft, Barry Goldwater, eventually even George Wallace.

Always and everywhere, whatever the subject, there was the quality in Hill of calm courage and peaceful surety that he had exhibited in the trenches at the Air Associates strike of 1941. Responding to the writer of an article in *Human Events* in 1953, he commented: "Privately many of these industrial leaders will say they would like to make a stand on principles if they could get support. 'You can't hold out alone—it's no use being a martyr' they say. My answer is that you can't get support if you don't hold out. A martyr is one who gets killed fighting for principles. Fighting always carries the risk of injury, defeat or death. The courageous accept the risk, the cowards evade it." For these reasons, and because he had great common sense and a perfect sense of himself, his isolation or the seeming unpopularity of his views never bothered him. "Mine is a voice in the wilderness," he said in 1957, "and there are millions like me who can hear each other but cannot get heard in Washington."[25]

Ellen Hill, who was active in the League of Women Voters, became the owner of a bookstore called Bookfinders, specializing in conservative literature. She was a regular poll watcher in these years and was as articulate as her husband on the subject of individual freedom. She was able and willing not only to write, but to speak in varied forums. In 1948 she responded to an editorial piece on WGN radio in Chicago thus: "I find that it is impossible to discuss the United Nations, the World Federalists or similar international organizations, with any view to criticism. The assumption that a third World War would surely consist of atomic warfare, and that this in turn would destroy or completely cripple civilization seems to many people sufficient ground for yielding on every other consideration for the sake of peace. The fact that people throughout history have risked death to defend their liberty, and that our armed forces continue to build up military power other than the atomic bomb has no value in such a hearer's mind." She asked for data on the possibility of surviving a military attack and demonstrated from start to finish that she was a true companion to Leroy Hill.[26]

Another occasion for Ellen to appear on a philosophical issue was a speech given in 1951 to a parents' meeting at the Keith School in Rockford, a private school which the Hill children attended. It was called "Development of Higher Regard for Cultural and Moral Values" and went to the heart of some of the things she and her husband thought threatened America. Children should be held responsible for their behavior, she said, but some of their shortcomings were doubtless due to "our own inner purposelessness and fear." Americans feared everything, she thought, including growing old and their own children, and many had less sense about parenting than a cat with her own kittens. It was necessary to decide whether Americans still believed in the precepts of the Constitution and the Bible and were willing to act upon these principals and to stand up and defend them. It was not enough to be lukewarm. One had to love freedom and hate everything that detracted from an individual's personal freedom. Children would learn self-respect if they were always treated with respect and if everyone in the family understood that moral choices mattered and were made every day. And being critical and pessimistic were two different things. The moral actor had to believe in the perfectibility of man, in the ability of people to grow intellectually and morally by trying challenges beyond themselves. Don't be afraid to read stories with morals to your children, she urged. Don't be afraid of making their lessons in living hard, and examine the priorities which put underpaid school teachers in luxurious buildings. Above all, she advised, learn the lesson from children of making the commonplace special and being happy in the world you are trying so hard to change. "We find these trifles everywhere when we are willing to move slowly, to walk instead of ride, to become closer acquainted with Nature and the out-of-doors in all seasons, and when we abandon the grim earnestness of educational fads for the humor to laugh at fables, the simplicity to learn from myths, the humility to believe in miracles. We can find these truths in the art and romance of cooking, or in such a product of creative energy as the high-speed printing press, of which Brooks Atkinson says, 'Its daring conception, its ingenious design, its perfect adaptation to its function express, as all art does, part of the human spirit.'" This approach would result not in raising a generation of "Mass men," but in creating "self-disciplined, articulate individuals, who depend on themselves for the prime satisfactions of life, and who have a moral security which no material uncertainty can shake."[27] That last phrase could have been a thumbnail description of her own husband.

Ellen was more oriented to local organizing that Leroy, and it was usually she who ramrodded the meetings in their home of local action units of various organizations, as contrasted with Hill's financial contribution and intellectual exchanges with the Leonard Reads, Dan Smoots, Dean Manions, William Buckleys, and Baldy Harpers of the world.

Hill became a considerable joiner of and contributor to organizations promoting a view of the world as he saw it, particularly those that advanced economic education from a market perspective. He read their publications thoroughly and attended workshops and seminars sponsored by many of them with Ellen to advance his own knowledge. Complacency bothered him, as did lack of the constant intellectual vigilance he thought was necessary to preserve freedom. The politicians, he said, were as economically illiterate as the voters, and so were lots of business people. "Charles E. Wilson," he wrote of the chairman of General Motors, "is undoubtedly a fine organizer in his own field but I doubt if he has ever given any more thought to the basis of the favorable economic climate in which he has operated than he has to that of the weather around Schenectady. It's too bad." Change, if it were to come, would come through education, and it would not be of the public school or regular commercial press type. Hill was not overly optimistic about the alternate information distribution system he found in the Foundation for Economic Education and other conservative think tanks that he began supporting or in the books he bought and distributed, but it was something. The writers on freedom, he said, "keep banging away with the truth and never reach hardly anybody that doesn't already understand it." But that could change. He added that he had "a forlorn hope" for a presidential candidate who combined public appeal, intelligence, education, and courage.[28]

A partial list of organizations to which Hill was a contributor in the 1950s and 1960s reads like a litany of conservative power, but illustrates in its relative diversity the catholicity of his fundamental interests. Examples were the American Taxpayer's Association; America's Future, Inc.; Intercollegiate Society of Individualists; Illinois Committee for Constitutional Revision; National Economic Council, Inc.; Republican Educational Foundation; Foundation for Economic Education; American Economic Foundation; Freedom School; Institute for Fiscal and Political Education; We the People; Americans United for Patriotic Action; Americans for Tax Reduction; Manion Forum; National Review; National Right to Work Committee; National Committee for Economic Freedom; American Progress Foundation; American Economic Foundation; Christian Crusade; John Birch Society; Mt. Pelerin Society; Institute for Humane Studies; and Liberty Lobby.

This list represents substantial variety. Hill himself was an agnostic. He never went to church and once declared that Christmas was "a pain in the ass." But Billy James Hargis of the Christian Crusade was Hill's houseguest when Hargis spoke in Rockford in the 1960s.[29] Certainly, Read of the Foundation for Economic Education or Buckley of the *National Review* were quite in contrast in personality and style to Hargis, who was in turn vastly different from Robert Welch of the Birch Society, or Robert LeFevre, the no-compromise libertarian of the Freedom School, or the Republican Party. The high-toned Mt. Pelerin Society, whose meetings the Hills attended regularly in Europe, was a different social stratum than some of the grassroots petitioners. But they had something in common. They advanced and protected individual freedom and choice, and so to Hill they were appropriate bedfellows in receiving his largess and occasional prompting.

Being stereotyped annoyed him. When a friend, writing in 1954, characterized Joseph McCarthy, about then ruining his reputation in the army hearings, as Hill's "hero," Hill snapped back that the simplification "irks me somewhat." He admired McCarthy as "a strong man with the guts to stand up against the terrific battering he is getting," but disagreed with him on many things, including the farm subsidy. He admired Eisenhower but did not worship him, and though he "despised Roosevelt with increasing vigor starting from a few months after he took office in 1933," he had voted for FDR in 1932 based on his official platform, which included balancing the federal budget. He was disturbed by the slanted press McCarthy was getting and recommended Buckley's book *McCarthy and His Enemies* as a corrective.[30] Never one to demand ideological purity, Hill once said of his friend Edson Gaylord, president of Ingersoll Milling Machine Company: "He is fundamentally or basically a Libertarian, although he doesn't always know why."[31] Hill himself did not bother to become a member of the Illinois Libertarian Party until the middle 1970s.

Hill's letters to organizations, like his letters to newspapers and to friends, were seldom perfunctory and often addressed fundamental issues at length. He read the organizations' publications in detail and was never loath to "take it up with them" when there was a point made at variance with his views. He bought multiple copies of their books and offprints of articles he liked and distributed them to people whom he then encouraged to become supporters also. He wrote Walter Selck in 1958: "The breakdown of our Constitutional Government and the trend to Socialism in our country is a disease which is spreading due to the lack of the preventative of fundamental economic education in the schools. A whole generation of economic illiterates has grown up. To fight this disease we need organizations like FEE just as we need the heart fund, the polio fund, etc. etc. etc., to fight other diseases. You probably are a pretty generous fellow with your contributions to these various disease funds

which are designed to lengthen life but what is LIFE without LIBERTY?"
He thanked R. S. Rimanoczy of the American Economic Foundation
in 1959 for a detailed response to one of his letters with the comment
that open minds were always useful and that "one or the other of us
should learn something from the exchange of ideas." He had distributed
copies of that organization's pamphlets "The Economic Facts of Life,"
"Things We Know That Are Not So," and others to "a private mailing
list which I maintain as a hobby."[32]

With some heads of nonprofits, like Leonard Read of the Foundation
for Economic Education or Dan Smoot of the *Dan Smoot Report,* Hill
maintained a frequent exchange customized to the style of the recipient.
Hill appreciated both Read's educational, intellectual focus and Smoot's
more slashing grassroots attacks. He complimented Smoot in 1960 on
a newsletter article entitled "Gestapo on Long Beach," which was about
arrogant bureaucracy. The case outlined was, Hill wrote, "a typical example
of countless unjust, arbitrary actions of the powerful bureaucracy—but
a very rare example of publicizing one." Unfortunately, Smoot's report
went to 15,000 people, and there were 2.5 million indirectly dependent
upon the bureaucracy for a paycheck. The enormous number of govern-
ing units with powers of decision were beyond the grasp of the human
mind. "No one person or agency, public or private, can grasp or understand
what is going on. No branch of the bureaucracy itself can attain any
breadth of understanding of the policies, whims and activities of the thousands of individuals, branches and agencies which now constitute the
Federal Government. This is planned chaos." The independent, bright,
and creative people who were now opposing the bureaucracy increasingly
in the future would join it, thus creating a ruling aristocracy. However,
it was possible they would be "careless" and have a rebellion. For instance,
control of the educational system might be relaxed just a little, allowing
the literature Hill supported to filter in and teach that free enterprise
would produce more for workers. That was hope enough to fight for.[33]

In the 1960s Hill's political activity increased a notch. For one thing,
the increased strength of the conservative wing of the Republican Party

and the publication of Goldwater's book *Conscience of a Conservative* encouraged him.[34] For another, not only did the educational and lobby organizations he had long supported seem to thrive in the decade, but new ones emerged that did not fear stronger language and tighter organization. In 1961 the Hills joined the John Birch Society. Ellen started a Birch chapter in Rockford and was the chapter leader or captain. "I got interested in it," Hill said, "when the smear publicity broke and I decided it was doing a good educational job and that Welch is a patriot."[35]

The Birch Society was more controversial than any other organization Hill associated himself with, partly due to some of the statements of its head Robert Welch as well as his general persona and partly, no doubt, because its relatively large following, mass media techniques, and substantial financial backing from business people of Hill's caliber made it a threat to which the established powers felt compelled to respond vigorously. Thus came what was known as the "smear"—a media attempt to discredit the Birch Society and its anti-communist, free-enterprise message as a wildly extreme and dangerous cult comparable to neo-fascism. Welch, while remarkably well read and intelligent, did have a strain of paranoia, and some of his suspicions, such as the one that President Eisenhower might be a witting or unwitting tool of the international communist conspiracy, were too much for middle America to swallow gracefully. Hill, however, well understood from personal experience what the press could do to its targets and how unfairly it might stereotype groups or individuals it disagreed with in the public mind. Concerning a *New Yorker* columnist, Hill once wrote: "Mr. Libling could make a damn fool out of Jesus Christ. I never read the *New Yorker* to avoid wasting time on the clever drivel of educated boobs like him."[36] Hill did not have to agree with everything Welch said to know that, as far as he was concerned, the Birch Society was on the right track and needed backers with the courage to say so.

Naturally, far from everyone understood, even among his own family members. "Am still brooding about the Birch society," daughter Bev wrote, "clippings like the enclosed are sort of off-putting. Does he really think these things, and/or are they really true???"[37] The challenges diverted Hill not a bit, though his good sense and sense of humor allowed him to put it all in humanistic perspective and to understand fully how his stand must look to some people. "Ellen is the moving spirit of the Birch society doings here," he wrote Alice Blue in 1963. "I go along with the main idea, but I sometimes think that Robert Welch goes out of his way to antagonize people who would otherwise be enthusiastic supporters." But he was at home with the image his political activity was bound to bring. He clipped a cartoon and put it in his file, which pictured a wife saying to her morose husband: "Clyde, you're dissipating all your hate. Why don't you join the John Birch Society and channel it destructively." Hill wrote: "I am known in Rockford as a dedicated Reactionary."[38]

The increasing verve with which Hill advanced his political views even as he aged can be seen in his extensive correspondence with John Anderson, who was through the 1960s the representative in Congress from Hill's sixteenth congressional district. In the summer of 1962 he wrote him from New Hampshire about the Constitution. Hill had just finished reading a book called *America's Unelected Rulers* and wanted to make a point about less government restriction. "All progress comes through the competitive struggles of individuals to be better off than others. Success or achievement can only be measured by comparison with the results of others' efforts." In any one world governed by an elite, "people will survive and live . . . but they will never realize what might have been. There is no basis for comparison." Hill sent along with that letter a subscription to the *Dan Smoot Report* for Anderson's reading.[39]

Sometimes Hill went too far, and he was willing to admit it. "I'll admit that I was a bit violent," he wrote Anderson in 1963 after Anderson chided him for dividing the population into two groups and shoving his congressman into one of them, "and that things aren't that simple. I apologize." But he still debated with Anderson on Anderson's interpretation of the Constitution as a "plumb line and measuring rod" which had to be elastic as society industrialized. "Good Lord, man," wrote Hill the engineer, "we could never have developed an industrialized society with an elastic measuring rod. Industrial production is completely dependent on a rigid and inflexible measuring standard and the more complex the society the more important it is to have rigid and exact standards—not only of length and weight but also of law and government and human behavior. The wealth that our industry has produced is the result of planning of millions of free men under a set of dependable standards, and the more complex industry becomes, the more important that the standards be dependable because the planning becomes longer range. . . . Principles don't change no matter how complex our industry becomes. The Constitution is a document full of simple understandable concise language that anybody can understand. There are few ambiguities in it. There is provision in it for amendment of its rules. There is no need for elastic interpretation, in fact that is what has pretty well destroyed it."[40]

The Anderson letters show Hill's views on the most controversial issues of the 1960s and indicate his entire independent mode of thought. Against the official grain of the Birch Society, he was against the Vietnam War, particularly because it had not been declared in the manner dictated by the Constitution. Why doesn't Congress declare war, he wrote Anderson in 1966, and make an honest man of Lyndon Johnson? He doubted whether the war was furthering U.S. interests.[41] He also opposed several civil rights bills, and there he split fundamentally with Anderson, though the two remained on good writing terms. Of a 1966 civil rights bill, Hill wrote, "This is the damndest, most unbelievable proposal yet to be spewed out by this gigantic socialistic bureaucracy that we call our government. This simply gags me. It will fire up interracial resentment and antagonism more than ever and the poor Negroes will get the worst of it." He denied that Dan Smoot was a racist, as Anderson had bluntly suggested. The problem with Civil Rights for Hill paralleled his problem with unionism—it identified people as parts of groups rather than as individuals and it provided unequal treatment for these groups, supposedly in the name of equality. Hill wrote Anderson that he had three black men working in his shop "and I never gave a thought as to how they were treated by me or any of the rest of the organization—and I'm sure they didn't either. But now I'm beginning to feel a little uncomfortable and I wonder if they don't too."[42]

Of all Hill's audiences for his political, social, and moral views, none was more important, and none taken more seriously, than his growing family and intimate friends. He could kid with Dome Harwood with a serious undercurrent, saying, "You are a man of high principle, of sterling character, as my Ellen has always maintained. You perform far beyond the call of duty and I admire you in spite of your lousy, nasty, disagreeable personality."[43] But the easy camaraderie with Harwood was important to him, as were occasional contacts with friends from the old days like Haven Page. But most significant were talks, usually not recorded in letters, of course, with Ellen and his large and multi-aged family.

One of these exchanges became a major Hill publication. In 1960 his fifteen-year-old daughter Marcia wrote him a letter from the private school Abbott Academy in Andover, Massachusetts, where she was enrolled, that in English class they had had an economics discussion. The teacher said that during the Civil War, American farmers produced an abnormal crop supply because of the army's necessities. Then after the war the smaller farmers went out of business. Marcia asked if the farmers wouldn't eventually find that they should produce less because of the smaller market. The teacher responded that the farmers of that period went at their problem from the individual viewpoint, and when they found they got less for their grain, instead of producing less they thought they'd have to produce twice as much in order to get enough money. Marcia's question to her father, therefore, was "Then what becomes of the farmers?"

The answer was a long letter from Hill to his daughter concerning how "under our free market system, production and consumption of millions of things, ideas and services are automatically kept in balance to provide the greatest good for the greatest number." Every day people, by buying or not buying millions of things, were "voting how much of each shall be produced." The scenario he sketched of free competition, and of the price system adding or subtracting from the supply until equilibrium was reached was straight Adam Smith. The answer to the question of surplus was for some makers, in the face of changing tastes and technology, to go into other businesses. Were this not so, the harness makers would now have a considerable surplus and the price for their product would have fallen to near nothing. What if, Hill asked, all the hand weavers had continued to be employed after power loom machinery was invented? A great surplus of cloth would have accumulated. "And I suppose, if some of our modern politicians were in control, the government would have bought the surplus cloth at 'parity' prices and stored it, or given it to the Africans." Instead, Hill wrote, "the wonderful free market system" took care of the surplus and the weavers found something else to do.

The same was true of the farmers, except insofar as political influence from farm states had been brought to bear to hamper the process of transition to more food production from fewer persons in that industry. Should the market be allowed to operate freely, the number of farmers would be reduced by a third and food would be considerably cheaper, leaving people with more money to spend on other things.

Hill concluded his letter by saying: "A great many people today believe that a few men with the power of government can plan and control production, distribution, and consumption better than all of the people using the free market system. I think they are wrong. My study of economics and a little history convinces me that their efforts, no matter how sincere and well meaning, can never match the results to be attained by the wonderful free market system. . . . ALWAYS REMEMBER: The Government has no money except that which it first takes away from people who would, if left to make their own decisions, spend their money for things they want."[44]

Though it was not written for publication, the letter was reprinted by the National Economic Council, giving Hill wider recognition as an author than ever before. His own comment on it was this: "I have watched the spread of the fallacy of Socialism for fifty years, since I was a school boy, and my understanding of the principles of economics have not changed appreciably—although perhaps I am better able to express them."[45] It was fun for him, however, to see this piece in print and to have it reprinted as an editorial in the *New Tribune* of LaSalle, Illinois. Other than his letters to the *Wall Street Journal,* it was the first time he had had anything published, and he admitted that he took "a childish satisfaction" in it at the age of sixty-six.

In a way, though, it was no surprise. While most of Hill's letters to his children, which became more frequent as they went away to college and then married in the 1960s, were not quite as theoretical as that famous one to Marcia, his approach to child rearing, more than any other aspect, reflected his whole personality, and in it he used all the fruits of his wisdom and experience in life thus far. Ellen recognized this and advised that he write a book for teenagers, using as raw material his advice to his six daughters. He actually drafted a chapter one summer at Pleasant Pond. But the real product was not books or articles, but the daughters themselves, and there was no doubt in his mind about the object of his late-life craft.

For many reasons Hill especially appreciated the privileges and the responsibilities of parenthood, and it was not only his economic views that he had to convey, nor only his daughters who did the learning and the growing from the exchanges with Dad. Fortunately, Hill's habit of saving everything, along with his sure sense of the importance of the personal, insured that full documentation of that parenting process remains and that, unusually, even in a biography, family matters can form part of the fabric, not just a footnote, of a life written as well as lived.

A Harem of Curls

The Hill family definitely was privileged by the 1950s. It had live-in help, traveled a great deal together, and wealth provided an opportunity for Ellen and Leroy to get away to exotic places by themselves now and then to recharge. The girls always, from elementary school to college, could attend any institution they chose, with the slight exception, as shall be seen, of Leroy's objection to his own alma mater at Berkeley as a fit place for his daughter Marcia in the 1960s. Hill could afford Rolex watches, fine cars, and rental of 16 mm movies for the kids. His house had six baths, eight fireplaces, nine bedrooms, and a stereo and tape player retailing for $3,000; made by his friend Bill Lear, it made the Hills the envy of Rockford after its purchase in 1949. Ellen and Leroy went to Europe in 1953 on the *Queen Elizabeth* and lunched at Maxim's in Paris. They visited Jamaica's Montego Bay yearly and sometimes chartered a sailing yacht for cruises, complete with crew and lobster dinners. They stayed at the El Mirador in Acapulco and went sailfishing. They had an ice boat in the 1950s to run on Lake Geneva, Wisconsin, as well as a Chris Craft and a dinghy for Pleasant Pond. Hill could fund his own inventions, including a "freezometer" and a portable compressor for filling the newfangled Aqua-Lung that he used often in New Hampshire and Jamaica and had trouble getting refilled.[1] "Life in Rockford is quite pleasant," he wrote Alice Blue. "We have lots of friends and go to lots of parties and do a lot of drinking of alcoholic beverages although we have not become alcoholics."[2]

In October 1961 Hill sat in his home office, "trying to avoid paying bills," and reflected on his situation. "I suppose a sign of advancing age is recalling memories of the past. I have trouble remembering recent events, names, faces, but the past seems to become increasingly clear to me. I squirm with regrets and remorse over past blunders and review my triumphs and successes and good decisions with smug satisfaction. Thinking about what might have been is pointless and frustrating and I try to avoid such postulating. Old friendships become more precious."[3]

He was sixty-seven years old that year and had been in Rockford nearly two decades. He had "done alright," he mused, having spent $14,000 on a trip to Austria and Germany with his kids, and he still had "enough left to keep going on." He could toy with the idea of buying an airplane and hiring a driver, but passed these up because he "never got around to it what with my machine shop and my messing around with deals, most of which turn out bad," not because he could not afford it. He was glad to hear of Bill Lear's success. It confirmed Hill's opinion of "his innate brilliance," but "I congratulate myself for repeatedly refusing to join up with him. I think I'm much better off than I would have been, although maybe not so rich." Phil Stephenson, who ran Hill's Aircraft Standard Parts from 1943 to 1947 and was in 1961 vice-president of Breeze, Inc., had visited recently. "I always enjoy talking with him but he still has a tendency to collapse after the 5th or 6th drink."[4]

Hill had always had a package of "deals" in addition to his major businesses. Sometimes these involved inventions, sometimes they were fliers with friends, and sometimes they were tests of a new field. Listing them is as ponderous as the list of the think tanks to which he belonged and similarly illustrates his capacities and breadth of interest and knowledge.

In a compilation in June 1974 Hill listed sixty-eight business activities in which he had been seriously involved in his life, as best he could remember. During the war he set up a number of companies purely to share sales of Aero Screw and Aircraft Standard Parts. These included Econo Manufacturing Company of Chicago and several companies in Rockford (Ferra Manufacturing, Midland Manufacturing, Drill Manufacturing, and Pinion Gear). He had a firm called Machine Salvage Company in Rockford during the war that was formed to buy and sell used machinery. Other minor companies of the war or immediate postwar years were Threaded Products, Rock River Screw Machine Products (a partnership to manufacture hose clamp screws), Standard Carburetors, Inc. (a deal with Harold Timian, a carburetor engineer, which closed when Timian had a heart attack), and Texarkana Supply (a partnership in Dallas in the jobbing supply business). From 1944 to 1950 Hill controlled these through F. L. Hill Manufacturing Corporation, Inc., a personal holding company for investment and management of his various projects.

That was just the beginning. There was the Super Electric negotiation, which fell through in 1948. In 1951 Hill purchased a building at 610 East State Street in Rockford, which he owned until 1968 when he sold it at a profit to Manpower, Inc. He owned a duplex in Rockford from 1954 on and leased it to Rockford Memorial Hospital. Between 1953 and 1956 he was an investor in Lanolin Plus, Inc., in Chicago. Hill was part of a group that bought the company from the owner, and his laconic comment in his summary of activities was "I was instigator but everyone but me made much money." He, however, made something over $100,000 on the Lanolin deal. In 1954 and 1955 he was a director and member of the organizing group of Neotronics, Inc., in Chicago, an operation based on a patented chrome process. "I decided it was impractical and sold out." In the same years he was involved in Camdale, Inc., of Detroit, a precision cam and gear manufacturing company. There he represented purchasers from previous owners and was board chairman on a salary and received 10,000 shares of stock for his trouble. Also between 1954 and 1956 he was a substantial investor in Bellanca Aircraft Company, headquartered in Newcastle, Delaware. He was a director and group member until he sold his interest and resigned. In 1954 he became a director and part of an ownership group of Walter E. Selck & Company, Chicago, which made floor covering and sink frames. He negotiated the resale of this company to Giffen Industries in 1968. Selck was a good friend. Other profitable deals in the 1950s and 1960s were State Pharmacal Company, Chicago; McAlear Manufacturing Company, Chicago (valves and fittings); North Towne Plaza,

Nellie, Marcia, Holly, and
Lizzie Hill about 1950.

Hill's mother Nellie in her
later years.

One of the family's
Hawaian trips circa
1960. Top row: Nellie,
Marcia, Ellen, Holly,
Thurston Twigg-Smith.
Bottom row: Leroy Hill,
Nanny Mae Stout,
Uncle Fred Potter.
On Steps: Lizzie
(above) and Isabella.

A caricature of Hill at about
age 60. Artist unknown.

Rockford (shopping center); Vance Industries, Inc., Chicago (a competitor of Selck); Graphic Arts Trust, Chicago (a Detroit building bought by a group including Hill and resold to the Church of Religious Science in Los Angeles after considerable tax litigation burdensome to Hill); Lamb Industries, Inc., Toledo (water heaters); Ponder Oils Ltd., Calgary, Canada (petroleum exploration and production); Assets Equipment Company, Inc., Rockford (machinery leasing); Tollway Properties, Chicago (land near the New York Tollway); Harwood & Company, Francestown, New Hampshire (a small contracting company with a lot of work on Hill's own farm supported by some work for others). These came and went. As Hill wrote Andy Charles when there was a feeler in 1966 about buying his interest in Cotta Transmission: "I will sell anything if the price is high enough."[5]

The above list represented successes, but there were failures. Lougheed's Magmatic Minerals was one, his loans to Hansell another. He lost money on the Spencer-Larson Aircraft Company in Garden City in 1937, where some friends were developing an amphibious aircraft. He lost on the Carlin Development Company, Garden City, in 1938—"a no good idea for an aircraft instrument." He lost on Polo Pump; Chicago Leasing Service; Skillman Hardware Company, Trenton, New Jersey; Laurel Bloomery Mines, Bristol, Tennessee; Commercial Trades Institute (a correspondence school for television and air conditioning trades in Chicago); and Syncronous Flame, Inc., in Walworth and Delavan, Wisconsin.[6]

Syncro Flame was a major worry of Hill's in the late 1950s and early 1960s. It was an oil and gas burner enterprise which, Hill said, took "plenty of my time" and experienced "steady losses." Hill became involved in 1954 because the firm had a patent on a clever burner and he wanted to install the new firm in extra space at the Aldrich plant. Perhaps he was still frustrated over not getting in much on the profits of the Aldrich company and wanted to take advantage of the product knowledge he had gained there in 1949. But also, he admitted, he had been "promoted" by Charles Stevens, the president of Syncro.[7] That investment fell into the category of companies that lost Hill over $100,000—he did not specify how much over.

Hill did not kid himself about it. "I was some boob to get into this," he wrote in his diary about Syncro Flame as early as 1954, "—will cost me 10 grand at least." But he held out some hope. In 1957 he wrote: "Syncronous Flame is in desperate condition. Stevens apparently sells consistently below cost."[8] By 1959 he knew for sure it had been a mistake. "I still cannot understand," he wrote at that time, "my stupidity in allowing the business to go as far into the red, but I finally came to my senses." In 1959 he joined with a group of other stockholders, fired Stevens, and became president himself. He made an agreement with creditors to try to raise additional capital, designed new patterns and tools himself, raised prices, and, for a short time, operated the company in the black. But his effort only prolonged the agony. The company went through a Chapter 11 bankruptcy in 1961, unable to "live down a bad reputation." In 1963 his comment was "Awful worry." In 1964 Hill sold the assets of Syncro Flame for $57,500 after trying unsuccessfully to sell the whole to another company "so that I will recover a small part of my losses on the god-dam thing." While this was going on, he had a car wreck in the Hills' new DeSoto station wagon and cracked a couple of ribs—an intimation of advancing age partly.[9]

To add to these cares, the fortunes of Hill Machine Company (the name became Hill-Rockford Company in 1962) went through up and down cycles in the 1960s and 1970s. The shop had expanded its building in the late 1950s and did quite well. But in the next decade performance became more erratic. The shop had a good year in 1965 "for a change," and he wrote Leonard Read that "the word has gotten around and the competition for my spare money has gotten pretty strong."[10] But he commented in 1962 that "my machine shop makes nothing but unusual queer machines so nothing is routine."[11] He enjoyed working at the shop, as he had since he visited the aluminum company with his dad as a small boy. Day after day, entries in his diary read "Shop all Day." But at his age he felt that he should not be its sole support and

Hill machine shop,
Rockford, 1960s.

Resistor Cap
Assembly
Machine, 1967.

made a number of only partially successful attempts to get a satisfactory manager. The succession of shop managers did allow him to leave Rockford for long periods of time, but he found, first, that profitability seemed to depended on his presence and, second, that eventually he had lost his touch and was personally not able to run it adequately either (Hill did not admit this until 1970 when he was seventy-six years old). By then it was losing money and he could not get a good offer for it. [12]

This was remarkable business activity for a man in his sixties and seventies who considered himself partly retired and spent lots of quality time with his family. Sometimes Hill thought it was too much. In 1963 he went to New York to see a friend, Jim Guthrie, who had had a stroke and just sat in his apartment watching television. It got Hill thinking and made him appreciate how lucky he was. "I can still hold my likker, play a passable game of tennis, water ski, skin dive and hoof my way around a dance floor if the music is good, although I can't sit up all night like I used to do." But, he admitted, he was slowing down and needed a good manager for the machine company business that he was "trapped in." It was time to devote himself to the Birch Society, the Liberty Amendment resolution, the National Committee for Economic Freedom, and the renewal of old friendships. "We are Super-Patriots and Right Wing Extremists!" [13]

Ellen was significant, of course, but she seldom traveled apart from Hill and so there are no exchanges of letters with her. However, fragments from Hill's letters to others about her give a hint of the nature of the relationship. Clearly, she was a stem-winder in all ways. A sturdy though not obese woman (Hill noted in 1967 that she weighed 146 and he weighed 202 and they were both going on diets), she was a competitive athlete, almost always winning the New Hampshire tennis tournament, and good at everything from surfboarding in Hawaii to scuba diving in Jamaica. She was a nature lover and a horsewoman par excellence. She drove a Jeep CJ2A in the 1950s, long before off-road vehicles were either luxuriously outfitted or trendy among wealthy suburbanites who never left the pavement. "Ellen is the outdoors type," Hill wrote, "and just loves hardships so I go along."[14] That "going along" included taking a raft trip through the Grand Canyon when Leroy was seventy-three years old.[15] She was the pusher on the New Hampshire property, though she was against even a bathroom being installed, and therefore most of the amenities that eventually appeared there were Leroy's doing. Various comments from her husband indicate, too, if her documented achievements were not enough, what a powerful presence and dominant worker she was at everything from child-rearing to politics. Hill wrote Harwood in New Hampshire in 1964 that Ellen was working everyday at phone banks at Goldwater headquarters in the center of Rockford. "We can't come to New Hampshire," he joked, "until Ellen has got Goldwater elected."[16]

But Ellen's powerful personality did not mean she was narrow or spiteful. She was tolerant as only a person with true confidence and a sense of humor can be, and that confidence went back generations. She wrote to her daughter Marcia during a troubled time in her relationship with her parents in 1965 that her Grandmother Mayo (Ellen's mother) was the eldest of six, worked her way through Hollins, and got a master's degree at Radcliffe in the first class of women to do so. She had medals in Greek, French, and German and married Grandpa Mayo only late in life. "She always said," Ellen commented, "it was too late for them to have children whom they could understand. Do you think she wasted her life?" The same story, she said, could be told of Grandma Hill and countless other women in American history. "In fact, the true movers of the world have always been those who understood something of the eternal nature of certain verities, whether derived from religion or simply an informed morality which sometimes sees beyond intellect."[17] She was sensible enough that Alice Blue wrote secret letters to Leroy about her problems, not wanting to "bore Ellen with my senseless despair," and yet tender enough that her daughters would try (unsuccessfully) to send secret letters to her to avoid the immediate and predictable reaction of their sometime irascible father. When Leroy had a stroke in 1975 that paralyzed his right hand, Ellen took over writing both his letters and his diaries from his dictation, and neither missed a beat.[18]

She was tolerant of Hill's past interests in women and present bouts with alcohol and tobacco, though their solid and rather traditional marriage shows no evidence of her having to put up with current or continued womanizing in the way some executives' wives did. Alice Blue would sometimes tease Leroy about being one of his old flames and making Ellen jealous, and Leroy sometimes liked to pretend Ellen might be. But Ellen's relationship to Alice, and even to Hill's former wife Melba and stepdaughter Bev, were always more than cordial. At a party she would occasionally get out one of Blue's "this one's for you" tape recordings for Leroy and pretend to be jealous, but it was an act. In an "epic" poem submitted to her dad on his birthday in 1967, daughter Lizzie wrote: "That dirty stinking slob—F.D.R. / and his unions drafted from the local bar / for personal power tried to kick Leroy out. / But F. L. Hill didn't stop to pout . . . . It was a heavy load for Dad to bear / But he had met Ellen, a girl wonderful and rare / So he moved from N.J. to Rockford, Ill. / And started a plant which fattened the till / and also a harem of five noisy girls. / He wanted boys but all he got were curls."[19] The chief of the "harem of curls" was Ellen Hill, and what Leroy got in it was more than a little.

Leroy knew Ellen's loyalty and trust and appreciated it as much as he did her intelligence and energy. She attended endless meetings and receptions for conservative groups (which she called "think and drink" parties) with her husband with few complaints, and the couple's occasional fallings-out arose when Ellen's behavior was wilder than that on which Leroy supposedly had a patent, as when she was arrested for drunken driving.[20] When he was fired from Air Associates for not obeying New Deal orders, he wrote Blue, "Ellen, who was working in the sales department of Air Associates, felt sorry for me and decided to marry me, which she did. . . . I guess I've had a pretty easy time of it since then. Certainly I have never worked the long hours and with the intensity of effort that I put into Air Associates. I guess that getting fired was the luckiest thing that ever happened to me."[21] They had a little rift when their friend, artist Mark Coomer of Scottsdale, did a portrait of Ellen in 1962 and Leroy had the nerve to tell him it didn't quite do her justice.[22] In his mind, nothing could.

Hill was a caring but stern father. His opinions, of course, were unbendable, so with girls growing up in the Age of Aquarius there were some trials. But he was kind. As much as he hated the Internal Revenue Service, he did as many as sixteen tax returns for friends, especially for his daughter Bev, with whom he was free with financial advice. He was generous to a fault with money for his girls, but was insistent that they account for it and send him written monthly budgets from an early age. The childish scrawls attempting double-entry bookkeeping are perhaps unique among personal family archives. And he was open to discussion with his daughters, in fact delighted in the debate that developed a mental sharpness and considerable literary style in all of them. He could even correspond and debate with his daughters' husbands (most of them temporary), who ranged from an economics professor, to a sculptor, to a coordinator for an Outward Bound wilderness school. He read the books they recommended, even the New Age poetry that came from Nellie, and he sent them "his" books to read. They were frank with him, as he was with them, on subjects ranging from homosexuality to self-support to dance styles. They surfboarded with him, ran rapids on float trips with him, played tennis with him, and picked berries with him in New Hampshire (he regarded this as business, not just fun), and they marched to his strict tune on the regimented car trips.

Yes, he was a man among a bunch of women. In 1953 there was Nellie, ten; Marcia, eight; Holly, seven; Lizzie, three; and Isabella, six months—as well as two dogs. They all danced on his toes, and when they played in the front hall near the door of his office, they heard his sonorous voice call out, "Why do you kids have to play right next to the office? What do you think I spent all that money on the nursery upstairs for?"[23] He was a conservative in a liberal age and a bit gruff (sometimes mockingly), but his daughters admired him, sometimes through their tears, and recognized always that he was, at very least, unique.

Sociologists and psychologists have written a good deal about generational theory as historical explanation. The clash of generations, it has been noted, is in all dynamic societies "an unavoidable bane and essential catalyst." In the family, "parents and children, readiest targets of one another's varied ambivalent emotions, both love and hate each other— are natural allies and natural enemies, mutual sources of satisfaction and frustration, pride and guilt."[24] The idea has been advanced that one's generation is more important to one's political views than anything else and that influences brought to bear between the ages of seventeen and twenty-five, when Hill was working so hard to have an influence on his girls, are more significant to one's future causes and political views than anything learned or experienced thereafter. This may be particularly true if the young person is caught up in some especially intense social milieu at that age, as was the generation of World War I, or the next one of missed youth in the Depression and World War II era, or the one of the 1960s youth rebellion, in which Hill's second family was centered and which engendered particularly voluminous analysis. Such intense generational experiences can create anomalous generation gaps, more severe than usual. "Rather than leading to a renunciation of youthful dreams," one author comments, "the passage of years solidifies them and surrounds them with a romantic glow."[25]

Leroy and Ellen Hill, of course, represented, in effect, two generations. Leroy's parents definitely were nineteenth-century types, and his formative years were in the World War I and 1920s cycle of idealism followed by frivolity. But Ellen's were in the 1930s and 1940s, and in a way, through his second marriage and his searing experience in that era, Leroy might be said to have had a sort of rebirth and secondary identification with those formative experiences. Their girls were a stairstep range of ages—Bev, born of a youthful marriage, was perhaps more the standard distance from Leroy, but his youngest was in late adolescence when he was in his eighties and had to try to deal with "times that were a'changin'" at an unusually rapid rate.

To attempt to apply the academic paradigms about generation gaps directly to the Hills would represent the kind of oversimplification that biography is designed to counteract. They were anything but typical middle-class people, and certainly that helped them to be flexible. But they could hardly have escaped some of the pains of the common lot of generational conflict. And in their case, the specific dynamics of inter-generational stresses were especially well documented.

The elder Hills' generation has been called "Promethean." It subscribed to an earnest, achievement-oriented life model that often was not fully shared by their children. These children in turn saw their parents as representatives of the "establishment" or "system," some of whose mistakes they could readily see. Sigmund Freud, when asked once what he thought a normal person should be able to do well, replied, "To love and to work." But to maintain these in balance is difficult, especially for adolescents. In some ways ideas of the "good life" remained rooted in the past, while the future came in the flesh.[26]

The post–World War II middle-class young, scholars claim, were raised in an affluent environment, almost a paradise. They were also raised in a permissive environment influenced by Dr. Spock, with tremendous focus on them and dedication to them by parents—ironically, almost more devotion than an individual could readily stand. Perhaps the more that industrial Protestant culture was threatened, the more the "establishment" generation had to believe in it through their children. Yet, as Henry Malcolm puts it in his *Generation of Narcissus*, "One cannot apply the value assumptions of the fallen Adam and the struggling Prometheus to a youngster who is living the life of an Orphic saint." The rules that the radicals among the young generation of the 1960s accepted were taught by the experience of freedom, informed by the independence and security that the parents had tried so hard to give them, rather than by the fear of chaos. They had a kind of Freudian connection to direct and present pleasure—narcissism—and a comfort with the irrational that could be profoundly disturbing to their elders. They seemed to have taken Freud at face value and rejected the price the discipline of civilization takes from the world as Eros. This was quite in contrast to the world of parents, who had grown up within the reality of practical and rational demands and whose own feelings of narcissism "are usually experienced as flights of fantasy and attempts to escape reality."[27]

Hill, more than many, had not accepted elements of the new world in which the "old-fashioned" entrepreneur, for example, had disappeared, to be replaced by faceless corporate directors and bureaucrats, or the world in which "feel good" replaced the work ethic. He was hardly a passive personality, watching for trends. And he was the man who, when feelings—grief, love, fear—overwhelmed him, took apart his car or invented something in the machine shop. The track to which he returned was always the one of service, practicality, and focus on controllable matters outside the pit of the self. The new world of his daughters was different—perhaps they were too, subtly different at least, maybe profoundly different.

The relationship between parents and children was particularly crucial in those times. "Strangely enough," writes Henry Malcolm, "we have long praised those adults who seek to instill and nurture self-expression in the young. At the same time, however, we have relied upon the assumption that everyone will remain repressed enough for those authority figures within society to be able to mold and manage the energies of the masses for the purposes of social order."[28] Hill's daughters in the 1960s, being readers and sharers of their thoughts, caused him pain when they read Wendell Berry, who questioned capitalism, or Norman O. Brown, the neo-Freudian, or Herbert Marcuse's *Eros and Civilization.*

The Hills surely would not have had some of the typical problems communicating with their girls about sex, or religion, or drugs. But they did not escape the standard predicament totally. It is always hard to accept the diversity in one's own. The girls' divorces were doubtless to some degree failures of the dream of marriage itself, and probably to some degree due to husbands being unable, despite generally good direct relations with their wife's father, to contend with what his girls became under his tutelage. They had formidable independence, a much-developed sense of self, and a congenital hatred of submission, dependence, or compromise, however important those may be sometimes in marriage.

The effects of parental love and a rational approach to child-rearing in a nuclear family were present. Scholars believe that children in this generation tended to incorporate parental values as their own to avoid losing parental love and affection, rather than following the earlier mode of adjusting trivially merely to avoid punishment. They wanted to please the parents, not just to placate them, and their feelings of self-worth were somewhat bound up in that desire, as were those same feelings in their parents. Stress in this intense relationship tended to be directed inward as guilt. And value internalization was a mixed blessing. "It may enable one to get his head smashed in a good cause," writes Philip Slater, "but the capacity to give oneself up completely to an emotion is almost altogether lost in the process. . . . Life is muted, experience filtered, emotion anesthetized, affective discharge incomplete." The parent, Slater claims, may become a sort of vampire from whose close influence the child must escape, perhaps through exaggerated rebellion.[29]

For their part, parents may tend to trivialize problems. When children cried for peace and justice in the 1960s, parents said, "Don't talk dirty" or "Get a haircut." It was a way of saying that this was not ultimately important, that it was a phase, that it represented a child who was mischievous or careless, and that it was just a family affair. There are signs of that pattern in the Hill letters—both in Leroy's reactions to some things as merely "silly" or "adolescent" and in his daughters' impassioned response that he wasn't respecting them fully as individuals who were more than an extension of himself. The literature indicates that parents of this era tended to think of children in a way as products—the ultimate product, the great achievement of their lives. And they believed in their capacity to rear a genius, a perfect child, and send that being into the world to continue the impossible—the fundamental and vitalizing rational, civilized human struggle that they in their own lives had pursued.[30]

Were it otherwise, it meant (and parents knew it meant) the end of a culture that they found deeply meaningful and to which they had committed their own lives. It manifested itself as a matter of "good taste" or "family quarrels," but it was more. One observer has gone so far as to say some youth of the 1960s became "mutants" in that they were "non-participants in the past . . . drop-outs from history." Youth protest might be seen as protest against "the very notion of man which the universities sought to impose upon them: that bourgeois-Protestant version of Humanism, with its view of man as justified by rationality, work, duty, vocation, maturity, success."[31] Anne Kriegel has summarized the new attitude as the view that "Nothing is ever said once and for all. Nothing is ever learned beyond the need for relearning. Experience is not transmissible, and the worst consequence of death is that it annihilates in one blow this form of primitive accumulation—acquired culture."[32] That attitude could lead to a "post-humanistic," "post-Faustian" casting off of adulthood completely.[33] It was against that extreme, not really so much against the actual aspirations of their daughters, that the Hills fought. They could not do otherwise.

Because she was older and because her single status and lackadaisical attitude toward advancing a career was a concern, Hill's most intense family focus in the 1950s was Bev. She had run away from his mother's house in 1943, partly because of disagreements with Hill's sister Isabella, and gotten a job at Douglas Aircraft Company in Los Angeles. In 1943 she came to live with the Hills in Rockford and applied her considerable talent as a writer to doing society and women's news for a newspaper there.[34]

Ellen's recall of that time was perfect fifty years later. "By now we had left the farm due to wartime complexities. I can't tell you how much help Beverly was to me. Marcia was born while we had the big rented house and we had to move to another one with Mom, the baby, and a two year old. Nothing was too much for Beverly." John Grimes, the newspaper editor, recognized that Bev had real literary talent and soon assigned her the whole local section. "She was popular," Ellen remembered, "with

Leroy's friends, friends my age, as well as her own. We kept open house in those days and Beverly seemed perfectly happy with the situation. But her father thought she wasn't getting anywhere and said she ought to seek her fortune somewhere else."[35]

In 1947 Bev went to England and the continent (the style of her tour is indicated by her base at Claridge's in London), and the Hills became genuinely concerned that she did not intend to return. In fact, when she did return, as Ellen later said, "her perceptions had changed and the young reporter was history."[36]

Typically, from the first of this European adventure, Hill was stern with her and about her. "Beverly is so used to having people worry for her that she is pretty helpless when it comes to planning a trip like this," he wrote. "I suppose it's her glands that makes her so sloppy and irresponsible. That excuse has served very well for years."[37] It was not the last time he would blame "glands" or "acne" for the "silliness" of his daughters. But while they found it inappropriately condescending, perhaps it was better giving up permanently on their outgrowing their opinions.

Bev, for her part, was warmhearted, though a little hesitant. She wrote Ellen and Leroy in November of 1942 from California that she imagined their good time on the farm and envied them when it started snowing back there. Wouldn't it be nice to have their fourteen-foot Christmas tree! "Daddy, I think you ought to get some horses and a dog. You could have so much fun with them." She wondered what to get the baby for Christmas.[38]

When she left for the Douglas job it was a major step toward independence, and one which, in general, her father supported. Typically, she was hard on herself. She hated to hurt Isabella, she wrote, or her Dad because they had done so much for her "but I feel I have to get out where I can be myself and make a trial of living by myself for awhile. Isabella can make me so miserable so much of the time. Maybe I deserve it but however much I do I don't think its right for anyone to be afraid of someone of Isabella's relationship. I feel inferior and I have absolutely no confidence with other people because I know I have always done something wrong and I will hear about it later and it keeps me from being natural." Later that year she considered going to Stephens College. "I know what the impression is a lot of people have about it—that it's a high class dump for girls where they don't have to work but it's really a very good place." Bev thought she might attend there for two years and then, if the war was still going on, take a basic training course in flying for the women's auxiliary ferry squadron. She had gotten up the nerve to write aviatrix Jackie Cochran about that possibility. She thought Ellen might be familiar with a French novel she was reading in translation, getting "a hang over from his flowing & flossy style," and vowed she would try not to be the cause of family friction again.[39]

Her dad oscillated between pride and disgust. He was disappointed that she "can't seem to get married." But after he had "shooed her off" to New York City, where she worked for several magazines, including *Time,* and had an apartment of her own, he commented in 1953 that Bev "seems to like living her own life which I was afraid she'd never get around to."[40] Ellen thought the New York publisher she worked for helped her with her self-esteem and posture (at 5 feet and 11 inches, she tended to stoop).[41] Her dad was more critical. He kept Bev informed on the "union goons" moving in at the Rockford newspaper where she used to work and advised her on claiming all deductible expenses on her income tax return. Still, he could write in 1952 that "frankly, the kid is a problem to me. She is 28 years old and I feel that she ought to develop some sort of independent life of her own—marriage or career—instead of being just another dependent child." She made $450 a month at the Rockford newspaper and was always broke. "She is bright enough etc. but she is shy and timid and tends to retreat into any safe haven. She would have stayed on the Rockford newspaper and here at home until she died if I hadn't booted her out. . . . I dunno. I guess I'll tell her to come on home and grow old here."[42]

He advised Bev to be patient with her aunt. "I hope you are now mature enough so that you can accept your Aunt Isabella for the loving relative that she is, with understanding and tolerance for the peculiarities which make her different from you." He expressed, too, appreciation for

Bev's expressed gratitude to him. "You have to wait until they grow up for the gratitude of children for the things you do for them. But after such a long wait it's doubly pleasant."[43]

Love, acceptance, and tolerance did not mean the end of chiding, of course. Hill wrote Bev in 1954 telling her not to beef about the salary on her new job (with a publisher of medical journals) and to put herself in her boss's place. "Get rid of that 'hate the boss' creed preached by the newspaper guild." He advised too that she should cut down on whiskey, which her budget showed way too much of. At the same time he blamed himself for being "so free with whiskey around the house."[44]

In 1957 he wrote her in Europe: "You appear to be striving desperately to avoid returning to this country. Just what is it that you want to do? If you have a definite aim perhaps you could work toward accomplishment." A few days later he returned to the topic: "Beverly, I think you have bummed around long enough. You are living a perfectly aimless, purposeless and unsatisfactory existence. Let's call a halt on this. You come home now and get acquainted with your family. Then make some kind of a plan or program and start off to carry it out, whether it involves living with your family, becoming an adventuress or whatever. At least you will have some purpose." When she returned in 1958 and went to work in Washington, D.C., as a copy editor for *American Heritage*, he took out a subscription for her to *The Freeman*, the Foundation for Economic Education publication, perhaps to give a philosophical boost to the virtue of discipline. "She is still not married," he wrote, "which irritates me."[45]

There was some change in the relationship in the 1960s. In 1966 Bev left *American Heritage* and moved to Antigua British West Indies and became a partner with Nicholas Fuller in an aluminum window and Alcoa franchise there as well as a tourist inn and condominium.[46] She visited the Hills regularly and kept up a lively correspondence with them that illustrated her talent as a writer as well as a social observer.

In 1969, for instance, Bev wrote about the Frosts, who were visitors. They were, she said, "two of nature's yokels, despite the fact that he works for a slick New York ad agency as account executive for the Mercedes Benz advertising. His wife has a truly remarkable pair of knockers, unfortunately topped by a phiz that would stop traffic." But they were a great pair—"so perfectly matched in unattractiveness— actually quite amiable cornballs." In 1972 Leroy wrote resignedly but not bitterly to Alice Blue: "Beverly is 47 now and I have given up hope of a son in law by her. She seems to lead a very relaxed and satisfactory existence." Two years later father and eldest daughter went on a cruise together of the Greek Islands.[47]

Bev spent more time with the Hills after Leroy's stroke in 1975. But shortly after promising that she would come home for six months out of every year and helping Ellen pick out a villa in the south of France that Bev would decorate and manage, Bev developed cancer. She was quite feeble on her visit to France in 1984 and died in 1985.[48]

Ellen Hill remembered that, while Bev was "sort of alienated" from her mother, Ellen and all the other Hill children were very fond of her.[49] Bev had corresponded with her dad all her life while usually in a form of semi-exile from him physically. She developed from a shy and overweight teenager into a confident, glib adult, as sure of her ground and as clever, in a way, as her dad.

Nellie, born in August of 1942, was next. Her real name was Ellen Wise Hill, shortened to Nellie doubtless because of the difficulty of having two Ellens in the house. She went through a period at St. Anne School in Charlottesville, Virginia, about 1956 when she tried using the name Ellen. "Everyone likes Ellen," she wrote her parents. "If you don't like it tell me." It wasn't that they did not like it: it just didn't stick. Typically, Nellie went with the family to New Hampshire—a 3,000-mile auto trip—almost from infancy and was the lead child (coming nearly twenty years after Bev) of the second Hill family. Once, when Leroy did not come home on time from a Christmas eve party at the University Club, seven-year-old Nellie was sent at the head of a delegation of Hill girls to inform him that his family time had officially begun. He laughed, but did not forget. He would give Nellie a dollar to go fetch a Sunday paper at the store or maybe five dollars for something else. When she returned with the change, he'd act surprised and with a little falsetto laugh say: "Oh, why thank you. Did I have change? I didn't know I had change."[50]

Hill began his correspondence with Nellie when he and Ellen delivered her to St. Anne's School in 1956. As with all his daughters, he started a special folder for her in his alphabetical correspondence file and kept her utterances in their entirety.[51] She sent her accounts every month, all in businesslike form, and got advice from her dad in return. He wrote in the spring of 1959 that he had gone over her school reports and found that the only A was in French and that her worst mark was in Practical Art. "If it really is what its name indicates—how to draw pictures in correct perspective—it should be a very useful course. If it is the usual random smearing of color to promote 'self-expression,' I suggest you choose another elective next year." A year later, by which time she was at the Milwaukee-Downer Seminary (founded in 1848), he wrote that he was pleased with Nellie's interest in economics. Again, however, he qualified what he meant by the term. "I mean basic, fundamental, true economics as opposed to the crackpot welfare state economics currently in the ascendancy." He encouraged her to attend summer school at Grove City College where she could hear such conservative luminaries as Russell Kirk and Hans Sennholz—and she did that.[52] She graduated from Downer in the class of 1960, where, Hill said, she was "notorious" for her successful arguments with her history teacher. She enrolled that fall at Washington University in St. Louis, taking with her a gift subscription to *Human Events* from her dad as a defense against academic socialism.[53]

Her semester started out with an auto accident, which occasioned an exchange with her father about basic honesty. She was hurt that he called her a liar, but her description of the accident to a car that she had taken to Milwaukee without permission did not jibe with engineer Hill's analysis of the physical damage. He hoped, Hill wrote Nellie, that she would gain a position with her father so that he could put her word against anyone's, but he honestly could not say that time had come in the year 1960. "I have always noticed that the indignation of a liar whose truthful word is doubted always surpasses that of a truthful person whose word is doubted. I ask that you now start to live down the reputation that you have earned by henceforth being fearlessly forthright not only with me but with everyone else." Others would like her better, he said, and she would like herself better. That said, he congratulated her on making the Delta Gamma sorority (she shortly broke her pledge), but got in one last dig: "Your spelling is pretty bad. The man's name is spelled Keynes and his false tenets are referred to as Keynesian—pronounced Keen-sian."[54] (Actually, the name Keynes rhymes with "rain," so Hill wasn't perfect, either.)

The straight and narrow path thereafter became increasingly crooked, from Hill's perspective, for his second daughter. By 1962 Nellie was in New York City attending NYU part time. In 1966 she married a sculptor, Bill Sildar, to whom her father took a considerable liking. "He seems like a decent fellow," he wrote Alice Blue. But by 1969 that marriage was on the rocks, and Nellie wrote that they would be better off without each other. She resented Sildar's seeming dependence on her: "It's not an equal deal." In addition, she said she needed to know herself better and what she wanted to do. First came separation and shortly divorce. Nellie lived at the family's New Hampshire place for a time and hunted, then, at twenty-eight, moved on to San Francisco where she wrote poetry and expressed a liking for hippies, who still proliferated there.[55]

Nellie had some success as a poet. She published in the little magazines of San Francisco and in several national and regional special-ized and popular magazines. She discovered environmentalist poet Wendell Berry and wrote her folks about her impressions of *The White Goddess* by Robert Graves and *The Seven Story Mountain* by Thomas Merton. Her own book *Astrolobes* was published by the Peace and Pieces Foundation, San Francisco, in 1975.[56]

But her dad was not satisfied with this course. At the top of a letter sending reviews of her own work and an article and poem by Berry, Hill

penciled in at the top "What awful drivel" and initialed the comment.
To him, his daughter's poetry was "a random collection of words with
no rhyme or meter of sense," published only by "off beat magazines."
To Blue he commented that Nellie was divorced from her sculptor "and
he is getting along fine without her." He wrote his daughter in the fall
of 1971 suggesting she pursue poetry as an avocation "until such time
as you can afford it as an unprofitable vocation. I think your writing will
improve under that plan." He enclosed $1,500 with his letter and
advised her that she should complete her divorce as soon as possible and
pay for it herself. More than a little disappointment showed through.
"We have spent considerable current effort and savings attempting to
bring our children up with some understanding of 'Economics,' and
training in activities which will make them self supporting." The message
was clearly that Nellie should be about it.[57]

Doubtless it did not please Nellie either that her dad continued to
correspond with and to some degree sympathize with her former husband. But when Bill Sildar expressed the thought of giving up art and
"involving myself in something more consistent with today's life-style such
as booze, drugs or welfare," he got the same kind of sharp answer Nellie
was used to. "You just have to apply your energy to the production of
things that are salable," his father-in-law wrote. "The main idea is to get
productive as soon as possible—don't wait for breaks." Sildar's response
was that he had gotten a job as a part-time bartender.[58]

From the time in 1956 that Hill wrote in his diary "Nellie giving us
lots of trouble—seems to be off her rocker," his love was a little blunt.
"Of course I don't expect Daddy to change," Nellie wrote Ellen, "and
no, I wouldn't want him to." But it was hard, she wrote, to laugh at his
poking fun at what she was living for.[59] He was a blessing, but a mixed
one sometimes, and there were tears as well as appreciation.

Marcia, born in 1944 and the recipient of that famous letter on the
surplus, had a stormier relationship yet with her father. She, like the
others, had her trust funds and her subscriptions to conservative publications from Dad. Like her siblings, she was smart and sometime a

smart-aleck, which, when applied to embarrassing her liberal teachers, was a delight to Leroy. But like Nellie, who early said she wanted to be an economist and had once been invited to speak about conservatism on the Washington University campus, Marcia's interests changed and, as she reached college age, some of her cleverness and independence became rebellion against the official Hill family philosophy.[60]

For a time there was a balance. In 1961, Hill offered to supply Frederick Bastiat's *The Law* and other books for sixteen-year-old Marcia's conservative club at Abbott Academy in Andover, Massachusetts, while chiding her for her spending habits and commenting that "your recent post card sounds goofy." Still, she was in the mold. "It's a laugh," Hill wrote her, "for those old women to try to teach a subject they know absolutely nothing about and furthermore have absolutely no interest in and which they no doubt feel is quite unladylike. I'm glad that your interest in life and nature is not as superficial as your teachers think is normal. Keep on being a problem. I'm proud of you."[61]

The crisis seems to have come in 1962 when Marcia went to the University of California at Berkeley, her dad's alma mater. As usual, Hill had given Marcia free choice of any and the best schools. She considered MIT and Stanford, but ended up at Berkeley. At first Hill was favorable enough, a little nostalgic, and only mildly apprehensive. "It is so big," he wrote, "that it has a disorganized fringe of activity around it in which the beatniks and queers of Operation Abolition circulate." However, he did not like the changes of the next year or so and blamed them on the school. "Your unsolicited suggestions," he wrote in September 1963, "as to my advice to your sisters is not appreciated as I take it as it is intended as sarcastic and nasty and I will appreciate your omitting such from your future letters as well as expressions of your feeling of superiority over ordinary mortals." That letter was signed "Your Father, Leroy Hill."[62]

Of course, in the early 1960s the Berkeley campus under Chancellor Clark Kerr was the quintessential radicalized multi-university. From the free speech movement to the Peoples' Park crusade, with Vietnam

teach-ins between, at the university "a counterculture of major proportions blossomed" amid what hitherto had been a rather conservative city
politically. In 1964, no other university had such close ties to the
government and government-sponsored research or such a neglect of
undergraduate students. More and more students lived in apartments
and moved away from the *in loco parentis* living and relating culture of
the traditional university community. Of course, it was also the middle
of the sexual revolution and a time of LSD and acid rock. Berkeley was
a place ripe for revolt, and it was a sort of revolt that Leroy Hill, as an
individualist, might theoretically have been in sympathy with had it not
been for its leftist sloganeering, destructive tactics, and "dropout" attitude
toward progress. The Hearst Greek theater was a place for rallies now,
not Sophocles. Joan Baez lived near the campus for most of the decade
and sang many an earnest folk protest song there. LSD was legal in
California until 1966, and Ken Kesey was promoting it as a positive
force. All was "spontaneity and theatricality," neither of which adolescent trait was precisely Leroy Hill's cup of tea. Still, a local newspaper
commented accurately: "There is no place in the United States more
exciting than this campus. There is no place or institution offering more
varied experiences; there is nothing like Berkeley."[63]

Things with Marcia got more serious. As late as 1964, Hill wrote a
friend that "one of my daughters, Marcia, is a freshman at California,
but she seems to be impervious to the kind of economics they teach. I
can't remember that we got any of that stuff when we were there. Do
you?" Soon he was not so sure how "impervious" she was. He forbade
her from returning to Berkeley for the spring semester of 1965, and she
defied him by leaving the house in Rockford and returning to California
against Hill's express orders. He wrote to Nellie that while Marcia was
home for the holidays, the tension had been high. She avoided mealtimes
and "generally acts like an occupant of a rooming house except that she
doesn't pay any board and uses a car now and then. I don't think I have
ever experienced such a complete brush-off and I have met some pretty

snobbish people in my time." He concluded Marcia must "have come under strong influences" in California.[64]

There was no give on either side. Marcia sent her parents (actually it was intended for her mother only) a remarkable letter on April 17, 1965. More her father's child than she might have wanted to realize right then, she had been reading a great deal—Martin Heidigger's *Being and Time* and Flaubert's *Madame Bovary*. She claimed that her parents thought she had resentment "if not hatred" for her family, and she admitted that she had a "dual side" to her nature in this regard but that the word "hatred" misrepresented her feelings. "Mother, I hope you will take this letter for what it is: a plea as one being to another, all family relationships, duties and political beliefs aside, for understanding." But in that letter too Marcia sent an affidavit of nonsupport for the Hills to sign so that she could get financial aid at her college and strike out on her own.[65]

From Nellie this elicited the discussion of the Mayo women (Marcia's middle name was Mayo) already described. Her dad's reaction was one of "mixed emotions of irritation, pity and amusement. It reflects extreme self-consciousness egotism and immaturity. Several friends have said 'She's just going through that 'stage' perhaps a little later than usual.' Well I certainly hope so and that you will get through it and lead a normal happy life." There would be no shirking of parental responsibility, he wrote, one of which is "to inculcate into their children a sense of responsibility and respect towards their parents and other members of the family. In this detail we have apparently, so far, failed in your case, notwithstanding your utterly egotistical and unintentionally humorous remark: 'let me say that I haven't yet come across anyone who has done a better and more praiseworthy job of bringing up their children.'" Hill never criticized without advising, and his advice was often homey common sense. She should make more friends, he told Marcia at this pass, quit brooding about her inner thoughts, and get out of her isolation. "I don't like being disowned by a daughter. I would like to help you." He asked her to come home and talk thinks over, but he signed her affidavit with the proviso that he was willing and able to support her college education at any institution other than the one she was then attending.[66]

Marcia was appalled, but she kept writing and did not break the connection. Hill's reaction, she said, showed she had not expressed herself well. "It is incredible to me that you could actually believe I could be so egotistical as to set myself up as the perfectly brought up child. Even if I did think this, would it not be stupid of me to proclaim this fact to you, who obviously think I am the worst raised of all? . . . Perhaps I can give you some idea of the immense distance between our worlds and attitudes if I say, in contrast to your statement, that I most ardently hope that I will not 'lead a normal happy life.' If I do I will regard my life as wasted. I would a thousand times rather live a tragic but full life than a normal happy one. . . . Maybe it's just the generations. . . . It makes me feel very sad (but not guilty), Daddy, when I realize how impossible it is for us to ever communicate." As was his habit, Hill wrote pencil notes in the margins of this letter before he filed it away: "silly," "how sad."[67]

Despite all this, Marcia remained at Berkeley and graduated from there, at the height of controversy on campus and turmoil in the nation, in June 1968. "Of my six daughters," Hill commented to Leonard Read, "she is the only one that I have trouble communicating with. I do not know what is in her mind. . . . She may be an 'Intellectual.'"[68]

As with Nellie, Marcia's husband, a professor of economics at Ohio State University named David Lindsey, whom she married just after her college graduation, was attractive to Hill and in communication with him long after the divorce in 1971. And as with Marcia, there was no extra sympathy with his daughter's side of things in marital troubles merely by reason of blood. Marcia became a simultaneous translator in Russian and in French for a company in Rockford, for Jaeger Instruments in German, and, in 1977, for the United Nations.[69] "She got the job over a lot of competition, " Ellen wrote, "but you can imagine what her father thinks of it!"[70] Ideology was strong, moral determination was ultra-strong, and it was always there for good or ill in the personality of Leroy Hill.

Holly Hill was a little more than a year younger than Marcia and at first did not get much written credit from her father except for her looks. He wrote in 1961 that Holly, then fourteen and a sophomore in high school, had "no talents as yet but seems to have some sex appeal." A slumber party of that year was mentioned as producing a "terrific" noise where 11 girls sounded like 111. Holly followed her older sisters through Keith School and Downer Seminary in Milwaukee and attended Hillsdale College in Michigan. In 1967 her father again commented on her looks: "Holly is becoming very beautiful but I don't think she realizes it—which makes it all the more so."[71]

Holly continued to please, perhaps by being lovely and stable, outdoorsy like her mother, and perhaps savvy enough to keep her mouth shut on certain topics. She married Bruce MacAdam in 1970, a boatbuilder and Outward Bound supervisor in the wilds of Maine, and the two seemed well suited and happy. She was the only daughter who remained married during Hill's lifetime and the only one who presented him with a grandchild, Ethan Hill MacAdam, born in 1974 and, as Leroy put it, "the first male in the Hill line in nearly 80 years." Two years later Holly had a second boy, whom Ellen thought looked like Leroy.[72]

Perhaps there were not so many ideological fireworks with Holly as with some of the others, and there is no question that Hill liked the stimulation of fireworks, but she was a joy in another sense. It was time by daughter number four for a more traditional personality. Her sister Lizzie remembered that Holly was Hill's favorite daughter.[73]

Elizabeth (Lizzie) was born in 1949. In 1961 Hill called her "the brat" and said she made trouble for everyone. In 1967 he noticed that she was taller than her mother, going through the pimple stage calmly, and had been accepted at Boston University.[74] That same year she wrote a poem, quoted earlier, about her dad. "Cal. contributed in eighteen ninety four / One great American more. / He grew to be like no other / A pride to community and mother. / At Berkeley he was tops in all. / Academics, leadership and just having a ball. / Whatever business he ventured —gained, / And soon all that he touched was famed. / Air Associates put him at the top / By making him President of the shop."[75]

When Lizzie left home that year (she and Isabella left the same year, leaving her parents alone for the first time since 1942), her dad advised her to guard against "experimental adventures with L.S.D. and Marijuana. I have always been scared of this and similar drugs. You have only one body and mind and they are too valuable to take chances with." He wrote to her about Vietnam also. He was not sure how he felt about the war, he said, except that "I am revolted by the killing and wounding of Americans for a cause which does not seem to be clear to anyone." Communists, he said, were socialists in a hurry, and she would have to realize that her dad was an American first and last. "So don't get me mixed up with the Vietniks, peaceniks, beatniks, hippies, kooks and hop-heads that are getting a lot of publicity on some of the college campuses. . . . I didn't approve of the U.S. entering WWI but I enlisted the day after war was declared. . . . We hope you will keep your very good mind open and not get indoctrinated with some blind emotional belief."[76]

Smooth, but not too smooth! There was an exchange with Lizzie in 1968, for instance, about her travel plans. Hill was for travel within limits, "but I don't want anything to happen to you during your silly age that would interfere with subsequent enjoyment of that 'short life' that you seem so anxious not to let slip by."[77] Elizabeth Puryear Hill's reply was very much in the mode of other Hill girls responding to the dominant personality of their father. "I was very disappointed by your letter and the general attitude it conveyed. You seem to think of me as no more than a child whose only aim is irresponsible, immoral fun. You do not respect or trust me. . . . I'm not only your daughter—I'm a person."[78] Once more libertarian philosophy and parenting met in the field at the Hill household, and the proper mix of independence and dependence, gratitude and growth in children was the issue.

Hill kidded Lizzie a little in 1969 when she talked about going into a career in oceanography, comparing that dream to Nellie's of becoming an engineer. Her actual course was more modest. She was in San

Francisco in 1970 hoping to take a yoga course to restore self-discipline which she said she had lost. It did not concern her greatly, however, as she noted that "I'll probably live to about 80 or 90 and I have lots of time to do whatever I want." "I received your nutty letters," her father wrote her. "You sound as though you were leading a pretty random existence. Marijuana has a very strange effect on the mentality of many people according to some authorities. It can't be proved but the effect seems to be permanent so it is difficult to prove that a person's mentality is due to its use. . . . You sound as though you consider the risk only that of being caught." Little sister Isabella had just gotten caught with marijuana at school, and Lizzie's response had been lackadaisical.[79]

Lizzie attended the University of New Hampshire, pursuing her oceanography idea and working on a fishing boat in Vancouver in the summer of 1973, and then the University of Illinois, where she intended to get a medical degree but did not. In 1975 she became a cook in a small restaurant in Rockford, where she worked while living at home.[80]

While her father observed that Lizzie seemed to be living a full life and enjoying not only working at her cook's job but constructing wooden rocking giraffes, her mother wondered "why she took all that expensive education." In 1976 Lizzie had taken up with a country singer—"Leroy disapproves of *him*—long hair, etc." Still, Hill himself was resigned after he had given it his best effort and admitted of his daughters in the mid-1970s that "they are all beyond any family control or influence so I guess Ellen and I will be free to live where and how we want to."[81]

Lizzie, literary and observant, recalled in the 1990s "Life with Father" in detail. The house on Main Street in Rockford, she remembered, had thick walls and many bedrooms—"which gave every member of the family the space and privacy and quiet that my parents expected for themselves." But there were moments. When Lizzie was four or five, she was in the nursery dancing and skipping in a circle around the room to music from a record player, calling her imaginary friends to join in. "I was shocked to see my father leaning against the wall near the door, his arms crossed and a smile on his face. I had no idea how long he'd been there but I was mortified. I had hoped . . . that my father would see me as a more dignified person than I had just demonstrated myself to be, but I was relieved to see that he was pleased. He said: 'Go on, dance some more.'" He was similarly encouraging when Elizabeth tried to learn the guitar, and told her of his banjo playing as a boy. He added, however, that he had never had the fingers for it, and it looked like she didn't either.[82]

There was the spanking story, almost archetypal and maybe partly legendary—like the one about Hill's having won the New Hampshire camp from Dome Harwood in a poker game. Ellen felt one day at the lake that Lizzie needed a spanking and assigned the task to Leroy. He found a big stick and got a footstool and put it by the screen door that overlooked the lake, waiting for Lizzie to finish her breakfast, which she did slowly. Then she walked over to him. He said: "Are you ready for your spanking?" Lizzie said "No" and walked past her dad down to the lake. When she returned he was there. "Are you ready for your spanking?" "No, not yet." She sat in the living room reading picture books. At last Leroy got up, looked over at her, smiled, and said: "I guess there isn't time for a spanking today." Her feeling, she remembered, was that "he left me free to skip back down to the lake feeling forgiven."[83]

She remembered Hill as an "impressive organizer." The basement of the house was filled with parts for plumbing and electrical repair, arranged in specially shaped shelves that he had made and labeled. And there was a roomfull of "thingamajigs and whatchyamacallits" that "looked too complicated to understand." These were arranged and labeled "in a way that impressed the observer with the importance of their mysterious purposes." Upstairs was a closet full of slides and photographs and movie reels, dated, labeled, and arranged chronologically. And of course there were his equally carefully preserved and arranged personal archives.

Leroy Hill was an "imposing man," Lizzie noted, 6 feet 3 inches in his prime—not fat but with a paunch. "My mother said that when she married him, Leroy, then in his forties, looked like Clark Gable. We all have a picture of him taken on the beach that shows this is so." His "imposing" look included "thick eyebrows" that "bristled accusingly above a pair of piercingly straightforward eyes, which could become twinkly and convivial in the turn of a breath. A strong jaw indicated a will that could probably move mountains, but was softened by an often mischievous smile." When Lizzie was a teenager, her friends had to pass by his office "where he sat like a lion in his den." They would say "Hello, Mr. Hill" and hope that would be enough. He was hard of hearing by that time, though he accused all his children of muttering and said teenagers talked as though they had marbles in their mouths. So he would respond to this greeting with "What did you say?" in a growling bass voice. Then he would ask who they were, but never remembered their names no matter how many times he had met them. Once a boyfriend of Lizzie's had the courage to engage Hill in conversation, which endeared that boy to him. "He's got a good character," he told his daughter. "He's shorter than you but that doesn't matter. Why don't you keep him around?"[84]

The Hill machine shop was a wondrous playground for all the girls. Her dad's attitude toward it, Lizzie wrote, "was like a concerned and troubled parent toward a dear but wayward child." Once Lizzie's friends asked if they were rich and she conveyed the question at the dinner table, to which the answer was that they would be going to the poorhouse if the machine shop did not improve. But for the kids, visits to the shop were great, particularly when they were invited to the company Christmas party where cartoons were shown for the kids. Often the girls would make the trek to the shop with their dad on Saturdays, just as Hill had with his own dad so many years ago in Wisconsin. They looked forward to being lifted on the crane or walking on the iron walkways surrounding the room full of machines. What's more, these were machines that made machines. "We would watch, fascinated, as a newly made machine punched holes in a piano keyboard, or put together typewriter platen rolls, or performed other, more esoteric tasks, such as putting together needle bearing gears, or variable resistors in six steps." When Lizzie would ask about these things, Leroy would try to explain and then get irritated when she did not get it. Meanwhile, she imagined bringing a doll to the shop and having it be Ulysses escaping crashing dangers as it rotated on a plate in the shop.[85]

Lizzie was right too when she noted that in addition to an imposing appearance, her dad had a voluble personality and did nothing by halves. He used a lot of salt, pouring it onto his food and explaining that he needed to do it because he had low blood pressure. He consumed huge amounts of cream at breakfast, and Ellen took to putting a pitcher of cream in front of his place. "His hand would reach out from one side of the *Chicago Daily Tribune* and reach for the pitcher and pour most of it on his oatmeal or strawberries. Had God not wanted people to eat cream, he said, He would not have made it taste so good. Dome Harwood used to say that Leroy had to go to four doctors before he found one who told him it was fine to have three or four cocktails a night. Whether it was fine or not, that was the way it was going to be.[86]

Isabella Britain Hill, the youngest daughter, was born in July of 1952. Her early nickname was "Squeaky," and Hill noticed in her at age eight an interest in fish and insects and engineering and math qualities. In 1967 she left home for the Northfield School at East Northfield, Massachusetts, leaving the elder Hills alone in the commodious Rockford house just at the time of Leroy's fiftieth class reunion at the University of California.[87]

Izzy did not turn out to be an engineer, but she had a creative and somewhat technical bent. She failed modern history at the Northfield School, but did well in theater and dance at the Perry Mansfield School and camp in Steamboat Springs, Colorado, where she went in the summer of 1970. That same year, she was caught smoking marijuana, occasioning a considerable family exchange. The next summer she attended a photography school in Boston and continued the study of photography in San Francisco that fall and later at the Art Center College of Design in Pasadena. She sent her dad creative notes hand-written on the back of large photographic prints she had made until he complained that such nonstandard items would not fit into his filing system. Like the other girls, Isabella got her share of gentle chiding, particularly about finances. In 1975 Leroy wrote to wish her a happy birthday (she was twenty-three years old) and to inform her at the same time that she would hereafter be excluded from the family health insurance policy. She should recognize, he said, that "I do not have a free pass on the airlines—the travel card simply means that the bill comes to me." But, still, he missed her. "I am sorry that you live so far away. It does seem as though all of my children want to live as far away from home as possible—at least until it suits their convenience."[88]

In another letter he took her to task for wanting to quit school at Pasadena, as she had earlier in San Francisco. "I have reread your pitiful letters of July 1st and 2nd," he wrote and said he was sorry she was having such a hard time. The answer, however, was not quitting. He sent her money to get her camera repaired and suggested she "cheer up and stop worrying so much." He wrote Marcia, however, that the sad letters continued and that Isabella "holds LD tearful phone calls with mother and me."[89]

Isabella did drop out of school in 1976 due to the effects of stress. Ellen's comment was curt: "Don't know what stress she can be under—everything paid for—maybe too much is done for these kids so that they worry about getting out in the world."[90] No doubt Leroy felt the same way. But there is a note in his files for 1976, when he was suffering from the effects of a stroke, that he would guarantee Isabella's Bank of America credit card for sums up to $10,000 a month.[91] From an eighty-one-year-old "Daddy," frustrated as he might be with the troubles of a daughter in her early twenties, still came the patient talk and the hard-boiled warmth with which he had always dealt with his children.

One Single Imperative

In the spring of 1968 Leonard Read sent Hill an essay called "Life Begins at Seventy," which fit his friend as well as it did himself. "I propose," Read commented, "to ride my bicycle until I fall off."[1]

But Hill's health became, if not fragile for his years, at least more of a concern in the 1960s and 1970s. In 1958 he could record cheerily in his diary that "Dr. Paynter to peer up my asshole & blood count—nothing wrong."[2] But his friends and relatives (Uncle Fred, Walter Chalaire, his old school chum Scotchie Campbell) were dying with some regularity in the 1960s, and Hill got more of a sense of his own mortality. He and Ellen really did quit smoking for keeps (1963), he got trifocals (1966), and the drinking calmed down some (to two drinks a day for a time). "My back felt like hell," he wrote in 1967 on a visit Antigua to see Bev. "Tried dancing, no good." His arthritic knees caused him considerable pain, though it did not stop him from dancing with all his invited "girlfriends" at his eightieth birthday party in 1974. From Europe, where he and Ellen were attending the Mt. Pelerin meetings, he wrote Alice Blue in 1972: "I am slipping I guess. But people can't last forever and neither can you and me."[3]

Still, giving up was no solution. Hill drove and fixed the D4 cat at Pleasant pond and built a hydraulic lift with Dome Harwood when well into his eighties. His advice to Blue, who had moved to Tonga, taken up with a Tonganese man (who bilked her of a good deal of her limited money), and become terribly depressed, was to "stop thinking about dying and your physical ailments. You are a lot younger than I am and I'm not going to die for a hell of a long time. . . . I can still dance better than anybody half my age."[4]

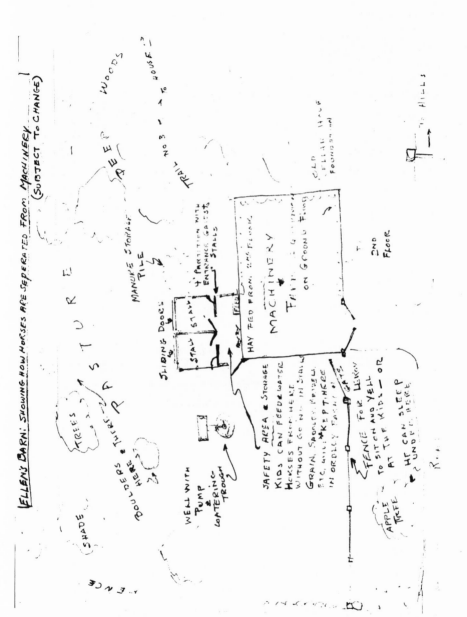

Ellen's Barn, one of many drawings by Dome Harwood of the Pleasant Pond construction in New Hampshire.

Ellen and Leroy at Pleasant Pond.

Whatever his energy to pursue it, increasingly the single imperative in Hill's life was the defense of liberty as he defined it. John Stuart Mill's famous definition in his essay "On Liberty" has been criticized some, but it would suit Hill fine. Mill's "simple principle" was that "the sole end for which mankind are warranted individually or collectively, in interfering with the liberty of action of any of their number, is self-protection. . . . He cannot rightfully be compelled to do or forbear because it will be better for him to do so, because it will make him happier, because in the opinions of others to do so would be wise or even right." These would be good reasons to try to persuade, but not to compel. In granting

267

liberty, there should not be too much worry about passion, Mill thought. "The danger which threatens human nature is not the excess, but the deficiency of personal impulses and preferences." Trade was a "social act," and freedom of individual action was as important a right as freedom of speech. There was no excuse in the mind of either Mill or Hill for homogenizing human potential in the narrow mold of government, either in economic or moral matters.[5]

Unlike most economic conservatives, Hill did not look to religion as support for his outlook. Ellen, as Leroy put it, "went in a little for religion," and in that he was tolerant of her. It was "OK," he wrote, when Nellie and Marcia were confirmed at church in 1956. "There are a lot of people who get a lot of satisfaction out of religion and I never do or say anything to spoil their fun."[6] But it was not for him. Daughter Nellie remembered: "Once I asked my father if he believed in Jesus Christ. He was sitting at his desk, studying something. He looked up at me with that slanty green glint in his eyes. 'No I don't,' he said. 'Why not Daddy?' 'If someone told you the moon were made of green cheese would you believe it?'"[7] In 1962 he asked a funeral home to quote him the lowest possible price on the disposition of his remains or those of members of his family. "I am not affiliated with any church," he said, "and any religious expenses should not be included."[8]

He did not need religion to persevere, however. Alice Blue wrote him in 1956 that he was her model of the perfect individualist. "Believe me, the sheep are the ones who do OK in this world—unless they're equipped to be real leaders with what it takes of brains and $$." She put Hill in that leader category. "I've always been proud of you and probably have an entirely incorrect idea of your business activities—but you've stood like a rock against the oppression that has insidiously snared this big USA until it can hardly move—and you've done all right bludgeoning your way thru without compromise."[9]

Hill could get discouraged, however, and did so more as the years passed. "We have lost the Republic," he wrote in 1965, misdating the letter 1945. "We are ruled by a gigantic bureaucracy in which decisions are made at the whims of the leaders." In 1963 he had nothing nice to say about a certain IRS agent: "The S.O.B. doing my review is waiting for a chance to bother me. He doesn't have the foggiest idea of what he is doing, but he knows that I made more money than he did and he is sure there is something wrong about it, and besides he sincerely believes that the government should own all the means of production and we should all work for the government so he is doing his part to bring about a workers' paradise." Perhaps he was dying and he was of a dying breed, he thought sometimes. But his advice to his co-workers in the field was similar to his health advice to his friend Alice Blue: "Don't give up. One of the great satisfactions is the realization that you recognize the truth. It gives you a feeling of superiority."[10]

In the summer of 1975, however, came the first of a series of strokes that were easily the most debilitating health problem Leroy Hill had ever had. He had snorkeled in Grand Cayman that January, but the stroke put those things forever behind him. "My age caught up with me," he wrote Alice by dictating to Ellen, "and my right hand is paralyzed." There were mental effects, too. "I don't know whether you have answered my letters or not," he told Beverly in 1976, "because my memory is not very clear." His speech was affected, so he saw a speech therapist, and he had trouble sleeping.[11]

These handicaps did not affect his determination. His grizzled mien and grim determination suggested, more than anything, the Lion in Winter. He would not call his strokes by name, but referred to them as heart attacks (and in fact they were probably caused by heart fibrillation). He continued to drive to work, but his depth perception was bad. "I drive when we're together," Ellen wrote, "and it infuriates him."[12] He and Ellen continued to travel (to Brussels and the Greek islands in the fall of 1975; to Antigua, where Hill went swimming, in 1976; to Finland and Bermuda in 1977), and he continued to tinker and fish at Pleasant Pond. But their life did change.[13] "He is very busy trying to learn to be an executive," Ellen noted in 1977, "—delegate things to other people— which he has never done." As always, she tried to get his mind off business. "I hope that after tomorrow," she wrote on April 14, 1977, "he can take an interest in something besides his taxes, etc." "There are lots of things Leroy can't do," she said, "though he is a wonder at most things."[14]

Helplessness had zero appeal. After a time of Ellen's making his diary entries, he began making them again himself, though in a shaky hand and with some compromise in the sense. He typed a letter to Nellie in the summer of 1976 himself: "Your birtday days packages arrived just in time for my departure. The hand griggen hand balls and patts were put wark work away. The sarble egges will just be for future amusement. I am read the little description of the doctor's wife, Mrs. Helen Hillyer Brown. I am only 12 than. Then close friend Cliff Crosby and his older brother and his dad and mother who burned out. Here gifts are perfect. I thanks you them."[15] The effects of the strokes were communicated verbatim, but it was also clear that Leroy Hill himself was still in there, and his whole life with him.

His humor now appeared only on rare occasions, but it was there too. Nellie remembered him "sitting glumly at the breakfast table facing another day of limited activity. Mother began rushing around, getting her tennis things together and a smile crawled over Daddy's face as he watched her hurrying from room to room. 'Why is he smiling?' I asked her, although she appeared to be oblivious to his expression. 'He thinks it's funny that I drive all the way across town just to get exercise,' she said."[16]

His take-charge attitude remained as he tried to do something about his disabilities. In 1978 he read in the *Wall Street Journal* about a physician in Chicago who could bypass a blood clot. Hill spent a week there, but the doctor said he could not help reverse the destroyed cells in the brain, though he did do a coronary bypass. In 1979 Hill attended a special school at the University of Michigan. The average age was forty-two, and Hill was the oldest in the class. It helped him psychologically, as he exchanged letters with the nurses and students, but not physically.[17]

The frustration of reduced energy and diminished capacity was relatively brief, though it must have seemed long indeed. He had aphraxia, not aphasia, and therefore knew what he wanted to say or write, but was increasingly unable to do so. This incapacity went on for six years before the strong heart, aided by a pacemaker, finally ceased in 1981. Leroy Hill was eighty-seven years old. His last diary entry was in December of 1977—sixty-seven years after his first one—and it reflected his boyhood habit of recording what time he went to bed. "Me + Ellen went to bed at 10:17."[18] After that entry, life but relative silence.

No better brief summary of Hill's approach to things could be given than a comment of Ellen Hill's in 1992, as this biography was getting underway. She wrote that her husband was a "happy man, secure in what he believed to be right."

Certainly that was true of, and not unrelated to, his later life with her. He kept meticulous records, not so much for others as for himself—as a check on his wisdom and development and as a record of the adventure life was to him. He loved responsibility and the ability to help other people, and he had "broad shoulders," taking those depending on him in his family as seriously as he did his employees at Air Associates. "Sometimes I think it may have been good for Leroy that he didn't kill himself with all those Air Associates headaches—wonder what would have happened??," Alice once wrote him, "But you didn't have to start at the bottom—and you knew what you wanted—and what it takes to get it—brains—judgment—everything—even the human things—home and family—smart guy."[19]

One of Hill's daughters was with her dad at a restaurant during the period of his final illness when an old friend came up to a pensive and quiet Leroy and said to him, "Isn't it great being retired?"

Hill answered: "No, I wish I could do it all over again."[20]

Notes

Leroy Hill: Boy Engineer

1. C. Joseph Pusateri, *A History of American Business*, p. 8.

2. Pencil notes for an autobiography, box 47, FF8, F. Leroy Hill Collection, Ablah Library Special Collections, Wichita State University. Abbreviated hereafter as FLHC.

3. The photo, taken in 1908, is in Childhood Diaries, Feb. 9, 1908, FLHC.

4. "Recollections—FLH, 5/28/72" [with later additions], box 48 FF2, FLHC, pp. 1–6.

5. Dominic Pacyga and Ellen Skerrett, *Chicago: City of Neighborhoods*, pp. 127–33; Harold Mayer and Richard Wade, *Chicago: Growth of a Metropolis*, p. 66.

6. "Recollections," pp. 1–6.

7. Harvey J. Graff, *Conflicting Paths: Growing Up in America*, pp. 11–15, 304. For an insightful study of recollections of childhood in that era, see Richard Coe, *When the Grass Was Taller: Autobiography and the Experience of Childhood*.

8. Childhood Diaries, Feb. 5, 1906.

9. Ibid., Feb. 17, 1906; April 2, 1907.

10. "Recollections," pp. 2, 8.

11. Irvin J. Wyllie, *The Self-Made Man in America: The Myth of Rags to Riches*, p. 29.

12. Seymour Lipset and Earl Raab, *The Politics of Unreason: Right-Wing Extremism in America 1790–1970*, p. 10.

13. Richard Sennett, *Families against the City: Middle Class Homes of Industrial Chicago, 1872–1890*, p. 47.

14. Henry F. May, *Coming to Terms: A Study in Memory and History*, p. 25.

15. Sennett, *Families against the City*, pp. 13, 19, 22, 49, 64. For the sentimental value of children, see Viviana Zelizer, *Pricing the Priceless Child: The Changing Social Value of Children*.

16. Childhood Diaries, Feb. 4, 5, 1906; "Recollections," p. 5.

17. Childhood Diaries, Feb. 14, 1906.

18. Ibid., Feb. 20, 1906.

19. "Recollections," pp. 3–4.

20. Childhood Diaries, April 3, 12, 14, 1912.

21. Ibid., Aug. 10, 1910.

22. "Recollections," p. 5.

23. Childhood Diaries, Feb. 8, 1906.

24. Ibid., May 29, 1907.

25. "Recollections," p. 7.

26. Childhood Diaries, June 2, 4, 6, 1907.

27. "Recollections," p. 6.

28. Childhood Diaries, April 6, 1908. One of the California groups had a ritual that consisted of tramping in front of an open fire and yelling things like "Behold! the brave Ivanhoe is at hand. . . . Give the countersign or ye shall die," or "I challenge ye to mortal combat."

29. Pencil notes for an autobiography.

30. Interview with Ellen Hill by Craig Miner, June 22, 1992.

31. "Recollections," p. 7.

32. Childhood Diaries, Mar. 11, 1906.

33. "Recollections," pp. 7–8.

34. Peter Egan, "The Kindness of Druids," *Road and Track,* Feb. 1989, p. 20.

35. See Siegfried Giedion, *Mechanization Takes Command: A Contribution to Anonymous History.*

36. Childhood Diaries, Feb. 8, 1906.

37. Ibid., Feb. 8, 22, 24, Mar. 3, 26, 1906.

38. Ibid., June 8, 1907.

39. Ibid., June 7, 1907.

40. Ibid., Feb. 11, Mar. 13, 26, 1906.

41. Cinthia Gannett, *Gender and the Journal: Diaries and Academic Discourse,* pp. 100–105, 108.

42. Childhood Diaries, note at end of vol. 1 (1906).

43. Ibid., preface to vol. 1.

44. Ibid., Jan. 7, 1908.

45. Ibid., June 16, 1908.

46. Despite his maturity in so many ways, Leroy did not get long pants, the early-twentieth-century mark of passage from boyhood, until graduation from the eighth grade in 1908. Childhood Diaries, Dec. 20, 1908.

47. Gannett, *Gender and the Journal,* p. 112.

48. Ibid., p. 107. See also Thomas Mallon, *A Book of One's Own: People and Their Diaries.*

49. Mallon, *A Book of One's Own,* p. xiii.

50. Ibid., p. xiv.

51. Graff, *Conflicting Paths,* pp. 13–15, 24, 317.

52. Karen Burke LeFevre, *Invention as a Social Act,* pp. 10, 17, 19, 34.

53. Gayle R. Davis, "The Diary as Historical Puzzle: Seeking the Author behind the Words," *Kansas History* 16 (1993): 168.

54. See Thomas Cochran, *Business in American Life: A History; Cochran, 200 Years of American Business.*

55. Joseph Schumpeter, *Theory of Economic Development.* Also see Peter Kilby, *Entrepreneurship and Economic Development;* Peter Drucker, *Innovation and Entrepreneurship: Practice and Principles;* and David McClelland, *The Achieving Society.* Much of this analysis is conveniently summarized in Pusateri, *History,* pp. 3–14.

56. Tom Peters, *Thriving on Chaos: Handbook for a Management Revolution.*

California

1. Gordon Thomas and Max Witts, *The San Francisco Earthquake*, pp. 267–71.

2. Joseph Jackson, ed., *The Western Gate: A San Francisco Reader*, p. 441.

3. Gunther Barth, *Instant Cities: Urbanization and the Rise of San Francisco and Denver*, pp. viii, 116, 130–32, 138, 160, 182, 191.

4. Roger Lochtin, *San Francisco 1846–1856: From Hamlet to City*, p. 2.

5. Robert Cherny and William Issel, *San Francisco 1865–1932: Power and Urban Development*, pp. 5, 24, 26, 42, 53–54.

6. "Recollections," pp. 8–9.

7. Cherney and Issel, *San Francisco*, p. 71.

8. Childhood Diaries, Feb. 4, 1910.

9. Works Progress Administration, *A Guide to the Golden State*, pp. 180–81; Dorothy Riber Joralmon, "Growing Up in Berkeley, 1900–1917," *American West* 20 (1983): 46.

10. WPA, *Guide to the Golden State*, pp. 180–81; Verne A. Stadtman, *The University of California*, pp. 185, 188.

11. Cherney and Issel, *San Francisco*, p. 49.

12. "Recollections," pp. 9–10.

13. Kevin Starr, *Americans and the California Dream 1850–1915*, pp. 288, 302–3, 401, 407.

14. May, *Coming to Terms*, pp. 16, 20.

15. Joralmon, "Growing Up in Berkeley," pp. 43–48.

16. Childhood Diaries, Jan. 19, 23, 1908.

17. Ibid., Mar. 24, July 2, 4, 7, 12, 1908.

18. Ibid., July 19, 26, 1908; Mar. 18, Apr. 21, 24, 1909.

19. Ibid., May 21, 1909.

20. Ibid., Sept. 26, 28, 1909.

21. Ibid., Mar. 25, May 7, 1910.

22. Ibid., Dec. 14, 1911, Oct. 13, Nov. 24, Dec. 10, 1912.

23. Ibid., Feb. 3, 4, 12, 1912.

24. Ibid., Dec. 13, 1911, mentions the beginnings of this project; see also Apr. 17, 1912.

25. "Recollections," pp. 10–11.

26. Childhood Diaries, Dec. 17, 1911, Sept. 29, 1912.

27. Ibid., May 1, 1908.

28. Ibid., June 15, 1912.

29. Ibid., Mar. 14, 1909, June 19, 1909.

30. Ibid., Aug. 1, Sept. 18, 1909; "Recollections," p. 10.

31. Childhood Diaries, Mar. 12, 1911.

32. "Recollections," p. 10.

33. Childhood Diaries, Feb. 8–11, Mar. 8–13, July 4, 1908.

34. Ibid., Dec. 30, 1908.

35. Ibid., Oct. 10, 1909.

36. "Recollections," pp. 12–13.

37. Childhood Diaries, July 8, 1908.

38. This expression is taken from Childhood Diaries, Oct. 17, 1908.

39. Childhood Diaries, Nov. 26, 1908.

40. All her letters to Leroy in the 1930s and 1940s have been preserved in the Correspondence series, FLHC.

41. Childhood Diaries, June 1, 1912.

42. Ibid., May 27, 1908.

43. Ibid., Mar. 23, 1912.

44. May, *Coming to Terms*, p. 17.

45. Childhood Diaries, Aug. 10, 14, 1910.

46. "Recollections," pp. 16–21.

47. Childhood Diaries, Sept. 29, 1912, Dec. 20, 1908, Apr. 30, 1912.

48. "Recollections," p. 21.

49. Childhood Diaries, Jan. 8, 1912; "Recollections," p. 11.

50. Ibid., p. 21.

51. Childhood Diaries, Mar. 4, 1909, May 5, 15, 1909.

52. Childhood Diaries, Feb. 18, 1912, May 15, 1912. The author is not certain of the meaning of these terms, nor certain he wants to find out.

53. Beth L. Bailey, *From Front Porch to Back Seat: Courtship in Twentieth-Century America*, p. 13.

54. John Modell, *Into One's Own: From Youth to Adulthood in the United States 1920–1975*, pp. 69–75.

55. Ibid., p. 99.

56. Robert Griswold, "Ties That Bind and Bonds That Break: Children's Attitudes toward Fathers, 1900–1930," in *Small Worlds: Children and Adolescents in America, 1850–1950*, ed. Eliott West and Paula Petrick, p. 268.

57. Joseph F. Kett, *Rites of Passage: Adolescence in America, 1790 to the Present*, pp. 217, 225.

58. Modell, *Into One's Own*, pp. 69–73.

59. "Recollections," pp. 21–22; Childhood Diaries, May 24, 1912.

60. Ibid., Aug. 8, Sept. 12, 1912.

61. Ibid., Mar. 9, 1913.

62. Ibid., May 28, 1908.

63. Ibid., June 9, 10, 1909.

64. "Recollections," pp. 11–12; Childhood Diaries, Dec. 20, 1908.

65. "Recollections," p. 22.

66. Ibid., p. 15.

67. Childhood Diaries, Feb. 2, 1906, May 10, 1909, Apr. 21, 29, 1912.

68. Ibid., June 30, 1908.

69. Ibid., Nov. 8, 1908.

70. Ibid., Apr. 24, 1912.

71. Ibid., Dec. 20, 1912.

Work and War

1. Childhood Diaries, Dec. 25, 27, 1912.

2. Ibid., Dec. 21, 1912, Jan. 3, 1913.

3. Ibid., Jan. 13, 1913.

4. Albin K. Longren of Topeka, Kansas, for example, used this type of engine in his 1911 biplane design.

5. Childhood Diaries, Jan. 8, 1913.

6. Ibid., Jan. 10, 1913.

7. "Recollections," pp. 24–25; Childhood Diaries, Jan. 28, 29, 1913.

8. Childhood Diaries, Feb. 3, 1913; "Recollections," p. 24.

9. Childhood Diaries, Feb. 7, 12, 1913.

10. Ibid., Feb. 20, 28, Mar. 1, 3, May 23, 1913; "Recollections," p. 24.

11. "Recollections," p. 24; Childhood Diaries, Mar. 10, 17, 27, 1913.

12. "Recollections," p. 25.

13. Childhood Diaries, June 17, 1913.

14. Stadtman, *University of California*, pp. 163–64, 181–84.

15. Childhood Diaries, June 24, 1913.

16. Ibid., June 25, 26, 27, 30, July 3, 1913.

17. "Recollections," pp. 28, 29.

18. Ibid., pp. 28–29.

19. Ibid., pp. 29–30.

20. F. L. Hill to F. A. Potter, Sept. 14, 1917, Correspondence series, FLHC. Unless otherwise indicated, all letters cited in the notes are from the Correspondence series, which is arranged chronologically and alphabetically.

21. Agreement, J. L. Hicks and F. L. Hill, Jr., Sept. 1917; J. L. Hicks Gas Engine Company Prospectus, Sept. 8, 1917, box 4, FF1, FLHC; Hill to Andrew Moore, n.d. [Nov. 18, 1918, or later].

22. F. L. Hill to F. A. Potter, Oct. 3, 1917.

23. Hill to B. M. Woods, Oct. 23, 1917.

24. F. A. Potter to Hill, Oct. 24, 1917.

25. F. A. Potter to Hill, Nov. 15, 1917.

26. Hill to F. A. Potter, Nov. 17, 1917.

27. D. C. Demarest to Leroy Hill, May 29, Dec. 3, 1918; Hill to Frank Hicks, July 11, Oct. 1, 1918; Hill to D. C. Demarest, Nov. 13, 1918.

28. Chief Engineer, Hall-Scott Motor Car Company, to Navy Department, Dec. 11, 1917.

29. Hill to Frank Hicks, Oct. 1, 1918.

30. John Rae, *Climb to Greatness: The American Aircraft Industry, 1920–1960*, pp. 2, 12–13.

31. Major E. J. Hall to Hill, Feb. 25, 1918.

32. Daylogue Diary (1918–22), Jan. 1, 8, Feb. 5, 25, 28, Mar. 7, 9, 11, 12, 14, 1918. Hill's "Recollections" are confused here. He has Harold Crow coming to work with him in Dayton in Dec. 1917, when it is clear from the diary that he came in Apr. 1918, and there are

inconsistencies about how long he worked where. Given that these memoirs were written in 1975 and that contemporary daily diaries and letters are available, where there is a conflict I am relying on the chronology first recorded by Hill.

33. Peter Young, ed., *The Marshall Cavendish Illustrated Encyclopedia of World War I*, 10:2988–95; Quentin Reynolds, *They Fought for the Sky*, p. 287.

34. James Hudson, *Hostile Skies: A Combat History of the American Air Service in World War I*, pp. 15–16.

35. Hill to D. C. Demararest, Nov. 13, 1918; "Recollections," p. 30.

36. Reynolds, *They Fought for the Sky*, p. 287.

37. "Recollections," p. 30.

38. Daylogue Diary, Mar. 15, 31, Apr. 1, 2, 4, 1918.

39. Ibid., Apr. 10, 1918.

40. Ibid., Apr. 11, 1918; "Recollections," p. 30.

41. Daylogue Diary, Apr. 6, Apr. 12–14, 1918; "Recollections," p. 31. Hill's statement in "Recollections" that he told Hall he did not want to return to work for him, but to stay in the navy and become an aviator, is probably mistaken since Hill had already been turned down for air officers' training and had already tried to obtain a discharge from the navy altogether.

42. "Recollections," p. 31; Daylogue Diary, Apr. 15, 1918.

43. Daylogue Diary, Apr. 16, 25, 1918.

44. Ibid., Apr. 16–19, 1918; "Recollections," p. 32.

45. A. A. Hoehling, *The Great Epidemic*, pp. 23–33; Alfred Crosby, Jr., *Epidemic and Peace 1918*, pp. 4–8, 311, 319.

46. Daylogue Diaries, Apr. 28, 1918; "Recollections," p. 32.

47. The Brissette incident comes from "Recollections," p. 32; and Daylogue Diaries, Apr. 30–May 4, 1918.

48. "Recollections," pp. 32–33.

49. C. R. Roseberry, *Glen Curtiss: Pioneer of Flight*, pp. 394–403.

50. "Recollections," pp. 32–33.

51. Daylogue Diaries, May 9, 1918.

52. Ibid., May 12, 13, 16, 19, 20, 1918; Hill to W. J. Campbell, Apr. 29, 1919.

53. "Recollections," p. 33.

54. Daylogue Diaries, June 10, 18, July 16, Aug. 1, Oct. 8, 1918.

55. Ibid., Oct. 12, 14, 1918.

The Salesman

1. Daylogue Diary, Nov. 17, Dec. 6, 12, 14, 30–31, 1918.

2. Ibid., Jan. 6, 1919; "Recollections," pp. 35–36.

3. Daylogue Diary, Jan. 24, Feb. 5, 20, Mar. 17, 19, 22, 25, 1919; "Recollections," p. 36.

4. Daylogue Diary, Feb. 13, 1919.

5. Hill to J. M. Henderson, Sacramento Bank, Feb. 14, 1919; Daylogue Diary, Jan. 19, 1919.

6. "Recollections," p. 36.

7. Daylogue Diary, Mar. 27, 28, Apr. 2, 3, 19, 1919.

8. "Recollections," p. 37.

9. Daylogue Diary, Apr. 30, May 6, 8, 9, 1919.

10. Daylogue Diary, Mar. 15, 16, 1919.

11. "Recollections," pp. 37, 38.

12. Ibid., p. 37; Daylogue Diary, June 25, 1919.

13. "Recollections," p. 38; Daylogue Diary, Aug. 7, 16, 23, 25, Sept. 2, 1919.

14. Daylogue Diary, Sept. 5, 8, 9, 11, 1919.

15. Ibid., Oct. 4, 1919.

16. "Recollections," p. 40.

17. Daylogue Diary, Nov. 15, 1919, Jan. 3, Apr. 17, 1920.

18. Ibid., Apr. 30, 1920.

19. Daylogue Diary, June 1, July 15, 1920.

20. "Recollections," p. 47; Daylogue Diary, Aug. 6, 1920.

21. Victor was the eldest of the Loughead brothers and began early spelling the Scottish family name Lougheed. Allan and Malcolm eventually changed it to Lockheed. See Richard Sanders Allen, *Revolution in the Sky: The Lockheeds of Aviation's Golden Age*, p. 4.

22. "Recollections," pp. 45, 47.

23. Victor Lougheed, *Vehicles of the Air: A Popular Exposition of Modern Aeronautics with Working Drawings*, p. 21.

24. Robert Wohl, *A Passion for Wings: Aviation and the Western Imagination, 1908–1918*, pp. 1–2.

25. Lougheed, *Vehicles of the Air*, pp. 23–24, 40–41.

26. Hill to Harold Crow, May 5, 1920; Hill to Crow, Sept. 19, 1920.

27. "Recollections," p. 98.

28. "Recollections," p. 48.

29. Ibid., p. 51.

30. Hill to E. C. Bell, Nov. 9, 1920.

31. Hill to George Sandford, June 8, 1921.

32. Daylogue Diary, May 15, 1921.

33. "Recollections," pp. 54–55.

34. Ibid., pp. 48–58; Hill to Harold Crow, Sept. 19, 1920.

35. Crow to Hill, Nov. 21, 1920.

36. Hill to Crow, Nov. 27, 1920.

37. Hill to Crow, Dec. 27, 1920; Hill to Crow, Jan. 15, 1921. His no-smoking resolve lasted for about three months. See Daylogue Diary, July 22, 1921.

38. "F. Leroy Hill—Activities," 1974, typescript, box 48, FF3, FLHC.

39. Daylogue Diary, Feb. 17, Mar. 4, 6, 7, 24, Apr. 6, 1921.

40. Ibid., Apr. 8, 16, 19, May 7, 10, 18, Aug. 7, 1921.

41. "Recollections," pp. 58–59.

42. David L. Lewis, "Somewhere West of Jackson: Toolin' West in a T in '20," *Chronicle: The Quarterly Magazine of the Historical Society of Michigan* 20 (1984): 19–21.

43. Victor N. Page, *The Model T Ford Car*, pp. 42, 77–78, 81, 89–91, 133, 137, 166, 216, 228; Albert Stephenson, "Secrets of the Model T," *American Heritage* 40 (July/Aug. 1989): 73–77.

44. Daylogue Diary, Sept. 11, 12, 13, 14, 17, 19, Oct. 3, 7, 1921.

45. "Recollections," pp. 59–61.

46. Daylogue Diary, Oct. 14, 29, Dec. 3, 1921.

47. Ibid., Nov. 22, Dec. 4, 5, 10, 16, 20, 25, 1921.

48. Ibid., Jan. 21, Feb. 5, 1922; "Recollections," p. 63.

49. "Recollections," pp. 63–64.

50. Daylogue Diary, Feb. 12, 1922; "Recollections," p. 65.

51. Daylogue Diary, Mar. 20, 1922; "Recollections," p. 66.

52. Daylogue Diary, Apr. 13, 17, 1922; "Recollections," p. 66.

53. Daylogue Diary, Apr. 17, 23, 27, May 30, June 3, 1922.

54. "Recollections," p. 67; Daylogue Diary, June 4, 13, 1922.

55. Daylogue Diary, June 28, July 5, 11, 1922. Hill's diary writing leaves off at this point for a number of years.

56. "Recollections," p. 68.

57. Ibid., p. 71.

58. Ibid.

59. Melba Hill to Hill, July 27, 1935.

60. Melba Hill to Hill, Sept. 23, 1934.

61. Melba Hill to Hill, Mar. 22, 1934.

62. "Recollections," p. 70.

63. Ibid., pp. 71–74.

64. Howard F. Bennett, *Precision Power: The First Half Century of Bodine Electric Company,* pp. 2–3, 31–32, 68, 84–87.

65. Ibid., pp. 101–8.

66. "Recollections," pp. 71–74.

67. Hill, letter to the editor, *Chicago Tribune,* Apr. 7, 1925.

68. "Recollections," pp. 75–76.

69. Ibid., pp. 76–78.

70. Bennett, *Precision Power,* pp. 90–91.

71. "F. Leroy Hill—Activities."

72. "Recollections," pp. 85–86.

73. Bennett, *Precision Power,* pp. 104, 111.

74. Hill to Bodine Electric, May 23, 1928.

75. Investment accounts, 1927–28, box 4, FF3, FLHC.

76. Invoices, box 4, FF3, FLHC; "Recollections," p. 81.

77. "Recollections," pp. 81–82, 88.

78. Harold Crow to Hill, June 22, 1927.

79. "Recollections," p. 83.

Air Associates

1. "Recollections," pp. 79–80; Roy A. Anderson, *A Look at Lockheed*, p. 13.
2. "Recollections," p. 84; Ray Acre to Hill, Feb. 11, 1928.
3. "Recollections," p. 88.
4. Hill to Air Associates, Feb. 13, 1928.
5. "Recollections," p. 89; unknown to Lockheed Aircraft Company, Feb. 11, 1928.
6. Acre to Hill, n.d.; Anderson, *A Look at Lockheed*, p. 23.
7. "Recollections," pp. 89–90.
8. Acre to Hill, n.d.
9. Crow to Hill, Apr. 9, 12, 1928.
10. "Recollections," p. 94.
11. Ibid., p. 92.
12. Ibid., pp. 94–96, 109.
13. Haven Page to Hill, June 15, 1928; Secretary to Hill, Aug. 23, 1928; Agreement, Sept. 15, 1928, FLHC.
14. "Recollections," pp. 98, 98a.
15. Acre to Hill, Aug. 6, 1928.
16. "Recollections," p. 98a.
17. Nellie Hill's letters, received weekly for about a decade, were segregated by her son into a separate file. See "Mom," box 3, FF22–32, FLHC.
18. "Recollections," p. 104.
19. Ibid., pp. 100–105.
20. Hill to Crow, Sept. 14, 1929.
21. William Lear to Hill, Mar. 6, 1928.
22. "Recollections," p. 103.
23. Ibid., pp. 103, 106.
24. Hill to Crow, July 5, 1929.
25. Air Associates, Executive Committee Minutes, Mar. 31, 1930, FLHC.
26. Gilbert Colgate, Jr., to Hill, Aug. 8, 1929.
27. "Recollections," pp. 112–13. Hill's "Recollections" leave off at the year 1930.
28. Hill to Roland Palmedo, Oct. 26, 1929.
29. Hill to Haven Page, Nov. 3, 1929.
30. Hill to Page, Nov. 30, 1929.
31. Ibid.
32. Crow to Hill, Nov. 25, 1929; Crow to Hill, Nov. 1929.
33. Page to Hill, Dec. 27, 1929.
34. "Recollections," pp. 114–15.
35. Melba Hill to Hill, Nov. 14, 1930, Oct. 27, 1932, June 22, 1933, Feb. 16, 1935.
36. Air Associates, Executive Committee Minutes, Jan. 8, 1930, FLHC; Page to Hill, Jan. 22, 1930; Hill to Crow, June 30, 1930.
37. Hill to Acre, Jan. 26, 1931; Page to Hill, Nov. 24, 1931.

38. Alexander Klemin to P. T. Wetter, Feb. 18, 1931.

39. Chart of sales, n.d., FLHC; Hill to Stockholders, Oct. 1933, FLHC.

40. Crow to Howard Mingos, Dec. 20, 1934.

41. Report to Number One Shareholder, Alice Blue, Inc., Mar. 1, 1938; Alice Clemo to Hill, Sept. 20, 1937, Oct. 13, 1938. The clipping is attached to the Mar. 1 letter.

42. Hill to Isabella Hill Perkins, May 24, 1933.

43. Mary Lougheed to Hill, May 6, 1935.

44. Allan Lockheed to Hill, June 12, 1934, June 17, 1935, Sept. 4, 1938; Hill to Allan Lockheed, June 25, Aug. 8, 1934.

45. Roland Palmedo to James Taylor, Jan. 24, 1935.

46. Alice Clemo to Hill, Jan. 1, May 4, Oct. 29, 1935, July 6, 1940. Most of the ellipses are in the original: it was her style.

47. Hill to Ray Acre, June 12, 1937.

48. Acre to Hill, Mar. 7, 1936.

49. Hill to Acre, Dec. 1, 1936.

50. Page to Hill, Feb 21, 1934, Nov. 10, 1935.

51. Nellie Hill to Hill, Dec. 20, 1932.

52. Nellie Hill to Hill, Oct. 16, Dec. 28, 29, 1932.

53. Nellie Hill to Hill, July 12, 1933.

54. Nellie Hill to Hill, Nov. 9, 1934.

55. Nellie Hill to Hill, Apr. 12, 1939, Mar. 3, 1940. The Mar. 3 letter, among others, mentions Al, the black helper.

56. Hill to Lynn, Aug. 14, Oct. 13, 1935.

57. Hill to Lynn, Aug. 27, 1936.

58. Hill to Acre, Sept. 11, 15, 1936.

59. Page to Hill, Oct. 12, 1936.

60. Page to Hill, Oct. 26, 1936.

61. Hill to Page, Nov. 6, 1936.

62. Page to Hill, Nov. 9, 1936.

63. Hill to Page, Mar. 3, 1937; Hill to Acre, Mar. 31, 1937.

64. Page to Hill, Mar. 25, 1937, Nov. 23, 1938.

65. Apartment lease, Aug. 24, 1937, FLHC.

66. Hill to Acre, Mar. 31, 1937; Hill to William H. Stewart, Dec. 13, 1939. Hill sold his plane for $2,500 at the end of 1939.

67. Hill to Factory Mutual Liability Insurance Company of America, Mar. 15, 1938; Hill to Graham Motors, Feb. 2, 1939.

68. Hill to Victor Lougheed, Sept. 27, 1937.

69. Hill to Acre, July 3, 1937.

70. Hill to Acre, May 5, 8, 1937.

71. Patent drawings, Dec. 14, 1937, Correspondence series, FLHC.

72. Hill to James Perkins, June 27, 1937; Hill to Page, Aug. 19, 1937; Hill to James Perkins, Mar. 24, 1938.

73. Clipping, *New York Times*, May 19, 1938, FLHC.

74. Jack Kennedy, "The Nicholas-Breazy Airplane Company: The Garage That Grew Wings," *American Aviation Historical Society Journal* 27 (Spring 1982): 35, 43; 27 (Summer 1982): 101, 110; 27 (Fall 1982): 163, 169, 179.

75. Hill to Acre, Nov. 28, 1939.

76. Hill to Acre, Dec. 26, 1939.

77. Clipping, 1939, Strike Scrapbook, box 54, FLHC.

78. Nellie Hill to Hill, Feb. 18, 1936, June 20, July 15, 1940.

79. Isabella Perkins to Hill, Feb. 19, 1938, July 12, 1937.

80. Nellie Hill to Hill, Nov. 7, 1938, Jan. 6, 1939, Sept. 5, 1940. The Sept. 5 letter on the lipstick controversy is a classic.

81. Hill to U.S. Department of State, Apr. 27, 1940; Isabella Perkins to Hill, Sept. 28, 1939; Hill to Nellie Hill, July 9, 1940; Beverly Hill to Hill, June 13, 1940.

82. Beverly Hill to Hill, Aug. 26, Dec. 8, 1940; Ellen Hill to Craig Miner, July 22, 1993. Jimmy Perkins was captured and sent to a Japanese prison camp. He was traded in 1944 and returned home completely emaciated.

83. Isabella Perkins to Hill, Oct. 15, 1934, Sept. 11, 1936.

84. Nellie Hill to Hill, May 16, June 12, 1939. The discount card remains in the archives.

85. Isabella Perkins to Hill, Sept. 23, 1936.

86. Interview with Ellen Hill, June 22, 1992; Ellen Hill to Craig Miner, July 22, 1993.

The Picket Line

1. Milton Derber, *The American Idea of Industrial Democracy, 1865–1965,* pp. 392–93.

2. John Blackman, *Presidential Seizure in Labor Disputes,* p. vii.

3. Ibid., pp. xv–xvi, 1–4.

4. Philip Taft, *Organized Labor in American History,* pp. 416, 420, 451–57.

5. Ibid., pp. 463, 493; Irving Howe and B. J. Widick, *The UAW and Walter Reuther,* pp. 47–51.

6. John Rae, *Climb to Greatness: The American Aircraft Industry, 1920–1960,* pp. 39–57.

7. Ibid., pp. 81–84.

8. Howe and Widick, *UAW,* pp. 62–63.

9. Ibid., pp. 79–80; Roger Keeran, *The Communist Party and the Auto Workers Union,* pp. 212–13.

10. Keeran, *Communist Party,* p. 185; Martin Halperin, "The 1939 UAW Convention: Turning Point for Communist Power in the Auto Union?" *Labor History* 33 (1992): 190–216.

11. Nelson Lichtenstein, *Labor's War at Home: The CIO in World War II,* p. 51.

12. Rae, *Climb to Greatness,* pp. 84–99.

13. "Diary of Events," 1941, box 19, FF1, FLHC.

14. Hill to Acre, Feb. 13, 1938.

15. Hill to Acre, Mar. 28, 1938.

16. Hill to Acre, Mar. 28, 1938.

17. Acre to Hill, Apr. 6, 1938.

18. Ellen Hill to Craig Miner, October 19, 1993.

19. Hill to Haven Page, Mar. 28, 1938.

20. C.I.O. complaint to NLRB, Case No. II-C-1577, Aug. 29, 1938, box 20, FF1, FLHC. Most of the Air Associates labor documents cited in this chapter are filed in boxes 19–20.

21. Mimeographed transcripts of meetings in March and April 1938 at law offices of Scandrett, Tuttle & Chalaire, pp. 4–9, FLHC; National Labor Relations Board, "Aviation Equipment Company Ordered to Cease Unfair Labor Practices" (press release), Feb. 12, 1940, Doc. R-2625.

22. [Hill], "Memorandum of Events Relative to Air Associates Employee Negotiations," [1938].

23. Ibid.

24. F. Leroy Hill, "Statement before the Senate Committee on Education and Labor," June 7, 1939, p. 3.

25. Hill to Edward Burke, Mar. 7, 1939; Hill, "Statement before the Senate Committee," p. 6.

26. Hill to R. C. Ingersoll, Oct. 24, 1938.

27. U.S. Court of Appeals (2d Cir., Oct. 1940), Transcript of Record, *National Labor Relations Board, Petitioner, vs. Air Associates, Incorporated, Respondent*. Also see *Brief for Respondent* from the same case.

28. Transcript of Meetings, Mar. 21, 1938, p. 17.

29. Ibid., pp. 2–3.

30. Ibid., pp. 4–6.

31. Ibid., pp. 8–11.

32. Ibid., p. 12.

33. Ibid., Mar. 25, 1938, p. 8.

34. Walter Chalaire, ibid., Apr. 21, 1938, p. 4.

35. Ibid., p. 8.

36. Hill to Acre, Aug. 7, 1939.

37. Transcript of Meetings, Mar. 21, 1938, pp. 20–21; Mar. 25, 1938, p. 14; Apr. 21, 1938, p. 10.

38. U.S. Court of Appeals, Transcript of Record, pp. 107, 216, 218–19, 231. See also Memo on Discharge of William Berger, Aug. 20, 1938, Labor Relations folder, FLHC. As was typical of him, Hill dismissed Berger personally and withstood a hail of abuse. "The trouble with you fellows," Berger said, "is that you sit upstairs and find fault with the time I spend on jobs and count your profits. If you'd spend more time down here you'd understand better what I'm up against."

39. Hill to Employees, Dec. 6, 1938; Record of Negotiations, Air Associates, Incorporated and United Automobiles, C.I.O., for a Collective Bargaining Agreement, Session of June 18, 1941, pp. 8–9.

40. Hill to Burke, May 31, 1938.

41. Ibid.

42. Hill to Burke, Mar. 7, 1939.

43. Hill, "Statement before the Senate Committee," June 7, 1939. See Hill to Burke, Mar. 4, 1939, for the agreement leading to this testimony.

44. Hill, letter to editor, *New York Herald Tribune*, Oct. 28, 1939 (clipping). For another example, see letter to editor, *New York Herald Tribune*, May 15, 1939.

45. Hill to Rush Holt, Sept. 8, 1940.

46. Ibid.

47. U.S. Circuit Court of Appeals, Brief for Respondent, p. 37.

48. Unidentified clipping, Jan. 20, 1940, FLHC.

49. CIO poster, 1938, box 19, FF2, FLHC.

50. Gilbert Tucker to Hill, Aug. 1, 1939.

51. Hill testimony, Sept. 22, 1938, U.S. Court of Appeals, Transcript of Record, 1:39–46.

52. E Systems, ECI Division, *When We Were Air Associates*, pp. 12–13, box 19, FF8, FLHC.

53. Air Associates, Annual Report, Year Ended Sept. 30, 1938, FLHC.

54. Air Associates, Annual Report, Year Ended Sept. 30, 1939.

55. Air Associates, Annual Report, Fiscal Year Ended Sept. 30, 1940.

56. On stock prices, see Hill to Isabella Perkins, July 6, 1940.

57. Air Associates, Annual Report, Fiscal Year Ended Sept. 30, 1941; Air Associates, Annual Reports, 1947–49.

58. E-Systems, *When We Were Air Associates*, p. 30.

59. For an extensive account by Hill of his contributions, see Hill to Haven Page, Jan. 21, 1940.

60. Hill to Acre, July 11, 1938.

61. Hill to Acre, Dec. 16, 1940.

62. Hill to Acre, Feb. 20, 1939. There are numerous letters on this theme.

63. Hill to Acre, Apr. 19, Apr. 26, 1941.

64. Hill to Acre, Apr. 26, 1941.

65. Hill to Acre, July 26, 1940.

66. Hill to Acre, May 31, 1941.

67. Hill to Acre, Jan. 3, 1940.

68. Hill to Acre, July 8, July 24, 1940.

Explosion

1. Hill to Isabella Perkins, July 6, 1940.

2. Joel Seidman, *American Labor from Defense to Reconversion*, p. 3.

3. Nelson Lichtenstein, *Labor's War at Home: The CIO in World War II*, p. 56.

4. Seidman, *American Labor*, pp. 18, 41.

5. Ibid., pp. 42–44.

6. Ibid., pp. 44–48.

7. Howard Kaltenborn, *Governmental Adjustment of Labor Disputes*, pp. 2, 92–93.

8. Walter Galenson, *The CIO Challenge to the AFL: A History of the American Labor Movement 1935–41*, pp. 185–88; Lichtenstein, *Labor's War at Home*, pp. 55–65; Seidman, *American Labor*, pp. 49–51.

9. Lichtenstein, *Labor's War at Home*, p. 65; James Prickett, "Communist Conspiracy or Wage Dispute? The 1941 Strike at North American Aviation," *Pacific Historical Review* 50 (1981): 215–33; Kaltenborn, *Governmental Adjustment*, p. 94.

10. Taft, *Organized Labor in American History*, p. 542.

11. This is well demonstrated by an account of contemporary events at Brewster Aeronautical on Long Island by a union organizer there. See Al Nash, "A Unionist Remembers: Militant Unionism and Political Factions," *Dissent* 42 (Spring 1977): 181–89.

12. E Systems, *When We Were Air Associates,* pp. 17–18.

13. Hill to Acre, Apr. 24, 1941.

14. Andy Charles to Hill, Aug. 29, 1940.

15. "Diary of Events."

16. Charles Baird, "A Tale of Infamy: The Air Associates Strike of 1941," *The Freeman,* Apr. 1992, pp. 152–53.

17. "So That the Facts Are Clear," July 27, 1941, box 19, FF1, FLHC; Baird, "Tale of Infamy," p. 154.

18. "So That the Facts Are Clear."

19. "Diary of Events."

20. Acre to Hill, Aug. 2, 1941.

21. Hill to Isabella Perkins, June 20, 1941.

22. Hill to Automobile Mutual Insurance Co. of America, June 30, 1941.

23. Record of Negotiations, Air Associates, Incorporated, and United Automobile Workers, C.I.O., for a Collective Bargaining Agreement, 1941, mimeographed, pt. 4, pp. 25–26, box 20, FF10, FLHC.

24. "So That the Facts Are Clear"; Baird, "Tale of Infamy," p. 154.

25. Hill, "Diary of Labor Relations—1941," box 19, FF1, FLHC; *New York World Telegram,* July 17, 1941; *New York Sun,* July 17, 1941; *Jersey Observer,* July 17, 1941, Strike Scrapbook, box 54, FLHC. Newspaper clippings cited in this chapter are from this scrapbook.

26. Baird, "Tale of Infamy," pp. 154–55.

27. Craig Miner, *Grede of Milwaukee,* pp. 70, 96.

28. Interview with Ellen Hill by Craig Miner, June 22, 1992.

29. *Bergen Evening Record,* July 17, 18, 1941; "So That the Facts Are Clear"; "Diary of Labor Relations—1941," FLHC.

30. Baird, "Tale of Infamy," p. 155.

31. *Bergen Evening Record,* July 19, 1941.

32. *New York Herald Tribune,* July 21, 1941.

33. Baird, "Tale of Infamy," p. 155.

34. Ibid., p. 155.

35. *Newark Evening News,* July 24, 1941; *Jersey Observer,* July 25, 1941.

36. Joseph Wisenwski to Franklin Roosevelt, July 15, 1941; Fred Kulka to Parnell Thomas, n.d., box 20, FF11, FLHC. There are stacks of these messages in the Hill papers.

37. *Bergen Evening Record,* July 30, 1941.

38. Ibid., Aug. 12, 1941.

39. Record of Negotiations, pt. 1, p. 17, FLHC.

40. Baird, "Tale of Infamy," p. 155.

41. Record of Negotiations, pt. 3, Aug. 1, 1941, pp. 14–15.

42. Ibid., pp. 27–30.

43. Baird, "Tale of Infamy," p. 155.

44. Record of Negotiations, preliminary session, June 17, 1941; pt. 4, Aug. 4, 1941, pp. 24–25.

45. Record of Negotiations, preliminary session, June 17, 1941, p. 6; pt. 3, Aug. 1, 1941, p. 31.

46. "So That the Facts Are Clear."

47. Baird, "Tale of Infamy," p. 155; "Diary of Events."

48. *New York Herald*, Oct. 1, 1941; advertisement, Oct. 3, 1941, Strike Scrapbook, box 54, FLHC.

49. Baird, "Tale of Infamy," p. 155.

50. Ibid., p. 156; "Diary of Events."

51. *Wall Street Journal*, Oct. 10, 1941.

52. "Diary of Events."

53. Hill to Gurden Wattles, Oct. 21, 1941; *New York Times*, Oct. 20, 1941; *Bergen Evening Record*, Oct. 23, 1941.

54. "Diary of Events"; *New York Times*, Oct. 24, 1941; Baird, "Tale of Infamy," p. 157.

55. Baird, "Tale of Infamy," p. 157.

56. "Diary of Events."

57. Ibid.

58. Hill to Isabella Perkins, Oct. 39, 1941.

59. Warren Lightfoot to Hill, Oct. 21, 1941.

60. Hill to Acre, Nov. 10, 1941.

61. *New York Times*, Oct. 31, 1941. The executive order was NR8928, Oct. 30, 1941. Baird, "Tale of Infamy," p. 159.

62. *New York Herald Tribune*, Nov. 5, 1941; "Diary of Events"; Baird, "Tale of Infamy," p. 159; E Systems, *When We Were Air Associates*, pp. 19–20.

63. *Air Facts* 4 (Dec. 1, 1941).

64. Hill to Acre, Nov. 4, 10, 19, 1941.

65. *New York Times*, Nov. 2, 1941; *New York World Telegram*, Nov. 21, 1941; *Philadelphia Inquirer*, n.d.; *New York Times*, Nov. 21, 1941; *New York Sun*, Nov. 24, 1941; *Trenton Times*, n.d.

66. Hill, letter to editor, *Trenton Times*, Dec. 6, 1941.

67. Edward Anderson to Hill, Nov. 29, 1941.

68. Hill to Walter Fruend, Nov. 4, 1941.

69. Leland Ford to Robert Patterson, Dec. 15, 1941.

70. *Congressional Record*, Nov. 3, 1941.

71. *Chicago Tribune*, n.d.

72. Blackman, *Presidential Seizure*, pp. 91–92, 139, 143, 211.

73. Hill to Nellie Hill, Nov. 19, 1941.

74. Nellie Hill to Hill, Aug. 6, 1941, Jan. 26, 1942.

75. Isabella Perkins to Hill, Aug. 19, 1941.

76. Beverly Hill to Hill, Sept. 4, Nov. 8, 1941.

77. Interview with Ellen Hill by Craig Miner, June 22, 1992.

78. Hill to Lois Hardy, Dec. 8, 1941; Hill to Sydney Nesbitt, Nov. 7, 1941.

Rockford

1. Interview with Ellen Hill by Craig Miner, June 22, 1992.

2. Walter Chalaire to Hill, Apr. 22, 1942.

3. Mary Lougheed to Hill, Mar. 20, 1944.

4. Diary, Jan. 7, 1942, Nov. 6, 1949.

5. Ibid., Jan. 16, 24, Feb. 26, Apr. 7, 1942, Sept. 29, 1943, Aug. 15, 1944; Hill to Ray Acre, [c. Oct. 1945].

6. Elizabeth Hill, "Reminiscences," 1992, typescript, box 48, FF1, FLHC; Hill to Alice Blue, June 15, 1975.

7. The girls' birthdays are recorded along the way, but a complete list is at the back of the 1973–77 diary.

8. Elizabeth Hill, "Reminiscences," 1992.

9. Ellen Hill to Craig Miner, Oct. 19, 1993.

10. Diary, Mar. 5, May 23, 30, 1942; Hill to Maxwell Balfour, Jan. 17, 1952.

11. Hill to Leland Ford, Jan. 9, 1942.

12. Hill to Haven Page, Feb. 21, 1942; Hill to Francis Bonner, Feb. 28, 1942.

13. Acre to Hill, Mar. 5, Apr. 7, 1942; Hill to Acre, July 23, 1942.

14. Acre to Hill, July 28, 1942. Hill collected his claim of $15,070 from Air Associates in Aug. 1942, just before the birth of his daughter Nellie. Hill to Acre, Aug. 14, 1942.

15. Hill to Acre, July 20, 1942; Diary, July 18, 1942.

16. Hill to Russell Carter, Oct. 28, 1942; Acre to Hill, Aug. 12, 1942.

17. Hill to Acre, Aug. 15, 1942.

18. Hill to V. Thomas Sake, Aug. 12, 1942.

19. Hill to Acre, Aug. 15, 1942.

20. Inteview with Ellen Hill by Craig Miner, June 22, 1992. For examples of these letters, see Hill to Leon Clausen of Case, Sept. 8, 1942; Hill to Walter Fry, Aug. 28, 1942. Hill was going to publish the Harding piece, but Pearl Harbor intervened, and the attention of the reading public turned elsewhere.

21. "F. Leroy Hill—Activities," June 1974, box 48, FF1, FLHC.

22. Ibid.; "Renegotiation," Aero Screw Co. file, FLHC. See also Hill to Chalaire, Apr. 12, 1942. For liquidation of Aircraft Standard Parts, see Hill to Isabella Perkins, Feb. 25, 1942.

23. Ellen Hill to Craig Miner, Oct. 19, 1993.

24. Hill to Acre, Nov. 7, Dec. 15, 1942, June 12, July 24, Nov. 8, 1943. On competition see Mar. 16, 28, 1944.

25. Acre to Hill, July 31, 1943; Hill to Acre, Mar. 15, 1944; Hill to O. P. Harwood, Feb. 17, 1945; Diary, Nov. 20, 1943.

26. Hill to Glenn Rearick, Nov. 26, 1943; Hill to War Department, June 10, 1943; Hill to Army Air Forces, Midcentral Procurement District, May 2, 1944; Renegotiation Agreement with Aero Screw Company, Sept. 25, 1943, Renegotiation file, FLHC.

27. Diary, Jan. 29, July 27, 1943, Feb. 7, 1944; Hill to Acre, Feb. 20, 1945.

28. Hill to Robert Collins, Dec. 5, 1944.

29. "History of the Cotta Transmission Company from 1942 to November 1979."

30. Diary, Feb. 16, 1944.

31. Hill to Hank Jungar, May 18, 1943.

32. Hill to Acre, July 20, 1942; Hill to Walter Chalaire, Feb. 5, 1945.

33. Partnership Tax Returns, Aero Screw Tax file.

34. Hill to Walter Chalaire, Feb. 5, 1945.

35. Hill to F. A. Potter, Nov. 20, 1945; Hill to Acre, Dec. 27, 1945; Hill to Charlie Gaver, Feb. 2, 1946; "F. Leroy Hill—Activities (68)."

36. Hill to Peter Smith, Aug. 31, 1945.

37. Hill to Walter Chalaire, Sept. 24, 1945; Hill to Earl Harding, Dec. 8, 1945.

38. "F. Leroy Hill—Activities (68)." The partnership agreement for Hill Machine was signed in May 1945. See Hill to Acre, May 24, 1945.

39. Hill to Peter Smith, Aug. 31, 1945; Hill to Acre, Aug. 27, Sept. 16, Oct. 13, 1946; Hill to Howard Hansell, Sept. 16, 1946; Hill to Clifford Bradbury, Dec. 16, 1946.

40. Siegfried Giedion, *Mechanization Takes Command*, pp. 574–80.

41. Acre to Hill, Feb. 3, 12, 1943.

42. Hill to Acre, Feb. 5, Mar. 17, May 4, Dec. 9, 1943; Acre to Hill, Feb. 11, Apr. 23, Aug. 9, 1943.

43. Acre to Hill, Apr. 8, 1943.

44. Hill to Acre, Apr. 10, 12, 1943.

45. Hill to Walter Chalaire, Oct. 30, 1944; Hill to Julius Devine, Mar. 2, 1945; Hill to Clifford Thompson, Nov. 5, 1946; Hill to F. A. Volk, Nov. 2, 1945.

46. Hill to Walter Chalaire, Apr. 9, 1945.

47. Victor Lougheed to Hill, Mar. 6, 1943.

48. Hill to O. P. Harwood, Jan. 25, 1945, with Harwood's original undated letter and map attached.

49. Hill to O. P. Harwood, Mar. 23, 1945; Hill to Acre, n.d.; Ellen Hill to Craig Miner, Oct. 19, 1993.

50. Hill to Haven Page, Apr. 3, 1945; Diary, Mar. 25, Aug. 14, 1945; S. P. Beers to Hill, May 2, 1945.

51. Hill to Acre, Dec. 3, 1946; Russell [last name unknown] to Hill, Apr. 23, 1945; Hill to Harwood, Nov. 26, 1946.

52. H. J. Allemang to Charles Stevenson, Jan. 14, 1947; Hill to Howard Hansell, Jan. 15, 1947; Diary, Apr. 23, 1947.

53. "List of Activities"; Hill to Harwood, Mar. 6, 1947.

54. Hill to Harold Snyder, Apr. 9, 1947.

55. Hill to O. P. and Leona Harwood, Sept. 13, 1947; Hill to Acre, June 15, 20, 1947.

56. Hill to J. T. Mascuch, Sept. 19, 1947, Nov. 4, 1947, Dec. 9, 1947; Hill to O. P. and Leona Harwood, Sept. 13, 1947; Hill to Automotive Mutual Insurance Co. of America, Feb. 22, 1947.

57. Diary, Jan. 6, 13, May 21, 1948, Aug. 17, 1949; Hill to Harwood, May 22, 1949.

58. Hill to Howard Hansell, Feb. 28, 1948.

59. Hill to Harwood, May 22, 1949.

60. Hill to Richard S. Boutelle, Aug. 21, 1949.

61. Hill to Boutelle, Sept. 5, 1949.
62. Hill to Haven Page, Dec. 28, 1952.
63. Hill to Isabella and Jim Perkins, Sept. 25, 1949.
64. Hill to Harwood, Mar. 18, 1950; Diary, May 16, June 3, Oct. 11, 1950.
65. Hill to Art Carrington, June 25, 1950; Hill to Ernest (Dyke) Dichman, Apr. 9, 1950.

A Voice in the Wilderness

1. Diary, July 6, 1946; Hill to George Bourne, Sept. 23, 1951; Hill to James Perkins, July 25, 1954.

2. Interview with Ellen Hill by Craig Miner, June 22, 1993.

3. Hill to P. D. Cornwell, Oct. 11, 1951; unknown to William O'Keefe, July 17, 1945.

4. Fred A. Potter to Hill, Nov. 5, 1951; Potter to Hill, July 30, 1950.

5. Diary, Feb. 9, 1948; Hill to Isabella Perkins, Mar. 24, 1962; Alice Blue to Hill, Apr. 30, 1956.

6. For Grede, see Craig Miner, *Grede of Milwaukee.*

7. Sara Diamond, *Roads to Dominion: Right-Wing Political Movements and Political Power in the United States,* pp. 20–39, 52–53, 124.

8. Lipset and Raab, *The Politics of Unreason;* Richard Hoftstadter, *The Paranoid Style in American Politics and Other Essays,* pp. ix, xii, 4, 23, 24, 31.

9. William B. Hixson, Jr., *Search for the American Right Wing,* pp. 53, 55, 58–59, 62, 65, 88, 97.

10. Lipset and Raab, *Politics of Unreason,* p. 12.

11. Hill to James Perkins, Feb. 29, 1948.

12. Hill to Dan Smoots, Aug. 1, 1958.

13. Hill, letter to the editor, *Wall Street Journal,* Dec. 29, 1957.

14. Earl Harding to Hill, Jan. 15, 1958; Hill to Earl Harding, Jan. 28, 1958.

15. Hill, letter to the editor, *Wall Street Journal,* Apr. 25, 1958 [perhaps unpublished].

16. Hill to Everett Dirkson, May 30, 1958.

17. Hill to Board of Police and Fire Commissioners, Belvidere, Illinois, with copy to Chicago Motor Club, Sept. 18, 1948.

18. Hill to Cadillac Motor Car Company, Sept. 17, 1951; Cadillac Motor Car Company to Hill, Sept. 28, 1951.

19. Earl Harding to Hill, June 23, 1949.

20. Hill to Robert Thurston, July 17, 1949.

21. Hill to C. E. Reid, Mar. 4, 1958.

22. Hill, letter to editor, *Wall Street Journal,* Apr. 16, 1969; Hill to Everett Dirksen, Feb. 15, 1957.

23. Hill to Earl Harding, Jan. 29, 1951.

24. Diary, Nov. 2, 1948, Apr. 8, 1952; Hill to O. P. Harwood, Nov. 17, 1950.

25. Hill to Thaddeus Ashby, Oct. 11, 1953; Hill to Leo Allen, Jan. 9, 1957.

26. Ellen Hill to Henry Taylor, Oct. 24, 1948.

27. Ellen Hill, "Development of Higher Regard for Cultural and Moral Values," speech delivered at Keith School, Mar. 14, 1951, FLHC.

28. Hill to George Bourne, Sept. 23, 1951.

29. Hill to Harwood, Dec. 21, 1962; Hill to Holly Hill, Oct. 14, 1963.

30. Hill to Dichman, Sept. 12, 1954.

31. Hill to unknown, Feb. 16, 1970.

32. Hill to Walter Selck, Jan. 30, 1958; Hill to R. S. Rimanoczy, Oct. 22, 1959.

33. Hill, letter to the editor, *Dan Smoot Report*, Nov. 7, 1960.

34. Hill to Marcia Hill, Nov. 12, 1960.

35. Hill to Peter Miller, June 10, 1961.

36. Ibid.

37. Beverly Hill to Hill, Feb. 13, 1962.

38. Hill to Alice Blue, Nov. 10, 1963; Robert Welch to Hill, Sept. 18, 1962, with cartoon attached; Hill to Alice Blue, July 17, 1960.

39. Hill to John Anderson, Aug. 17, 1962.

40. Hill to John Anderson, Apr. 14, 1963.

41. Hill to John Anderson, Feb. 23, 1966.

42. Hill to John Anderson, May 6, 26, 1966.

43. Hill to O. P. Harwood, Dec. 19, 1966.

44. F. Leroy Hill, "The Surplus Problem—Everybody's Problem," *National Economic Council Papers* 15, no. 3 (June 15, 1960), FLHC.

45. Hill to Felix Spittler, July 13, 1960.

A Harem of Curls

1. Hill to William Lear, Oct. 9, 1949; Hill to Alice Blue, Jan. 8, 1952; A. M. Andrews to Hill, Jan. 15, 1952; Audio Film Center to Hill, Sept. 25, 1953; Diary, Apr. 9, 1953, Feb. 26, Mar. 7, 1954, Jan. 1, Mar. 23, 1957.

2. Hill to Alice Blue, Jan. 8, 1952.

3. Hill to Jim [Perkins], Oct. 2, 1961.

4. Ibid.

5. Hill to Andy Charles, Feb. 12, 1966.

6. See "F. Leroy Hill—Activities (68)."

7. Hill to Howard Hansell, Dec. 3, 1957.

8. Diary, May 31, 1954, Apr. 17, 1957.

9. Hill to Charles Garver, May 12, 1959; Hill to William Bohn, June 4, 1961; Diary, Oct. 29, 1963, May 14, 1964; Hill to O. P. Harwood, May 30, 1964.

10. Hill to Leonard Read, Dec. 31, 1965.

11. Hill to Thurston Twigg-Smith, Mar. 11, 1962; Hill to James Perkins, Sept. 14, 1962.

12. Hill to William O'Conner, Aug. 9, 1970.

13. Hill to Haven Page, Apr. 21, 1963.

14. Hill to Dichman, Sept. 12, 1954; Diary, Apr. 7, 1967.

15. Hill to Alice Blue, Mar. 17, 1968.

16. Hill to O. P. Harwood, May 22, 1949, Feb. 28, 1964.

17. Ellen Hill to Marcia Hill, Apr. 22, 1965.

18. Alice Blue to Hill, Apr. 30, 1974; Hill to Alice Blue, Aug. 17, 1975.

19. Poem by Elizabeth Hill, July 16, [1967], FLHC.

20. Hill to O. P. Harwood, Sept. 25, 1956.

21. Hill to Alice Blue, Jan. 11, 1953.

22. Hill to Mark Coomer, Apr. 8, 1962.

23. Nellie Hill, "Recollections," 1992, FLHC.

24. Alexander Klein, ed., *Natural Enemies: Youth and the Clash of Generations*, pp. xxiii–iv.

25. Marvin Rintala, *The Constitution of Silence: Essays on Generational Themes*, pp. 3–17.

26. Klein, *Natural Enemies*, pp. 2, 4.

27. Henry Malcolm, *Generation of Narcissus*, pp. 3, 8, 12, 34, 44–45, 61.

28. Ibid., p. 117.

29. Philip Slater, *The Pursuit of Loneliness: American Culture at the Breaking Point*, pp. 22, 24–25, 60, 69.

30. Ibid, p. 3–4, 59, 61, 67.

31. Leslie Fiedler, "The New Mutants," in *Natural Enemies*, ed. Klein, pp. 206, 208.

32. Anne Kriegel, "Generational Differences: The History of an Idea," in *Generations*, ed. Stephen Graubaud, p. 25.

33. Fiedler, "The New Mutants," p. 214.

34. Beverly Hill to Hill, Jan. 1943; Beverly Hill to Nellie Hill, July 30, 1943; Hill to Nellie Hill, Nov. 19, 1944.

35. Ellen Hill to Craig Miner, Oct. 19, 1993.

36. Beverly Hill to Leroy and Ellen Hill, Oct. 15, 1947; Ellen Hill to Craig Miner, Oct. 19, 1993.

37. Hill to Nellie Hill, Oct. 5, 1947.

38. Beverly Hill to Hill, Nov. 24, 1942.

39. Beverly Hill to Hill, Jan. 1943, June 29, Aug. 1, 1943.

40. Hill to Alice Blue, Jan. 11, 1953.

41. Ellen Hill to Craig Miner, Oct. 19, 1993.

42. Hill to Beverly Hill, Jan. 22, Apr. 27, 1952; Hill to O. P. Harwood, Apr. 27, 1952.

43. Hill to Beverly Hill, Dec. 8, 1952.

44. Hill to Beverly Hill, Feb. 3, 1954.

45. Hill to Beverly Hill, June 16, July 5, 1957; Hill to Leonard Read, Sept. 9, 1958; Hill to Margie Nise, Feb. 26, 1961.

46. Hill to Marcia Hill, Jan. 20, 1967.

47. Beverly Hill to Hill, Jan. 16, 1969; Hill to Alice Blue, Oct. 14, 1972; Hill to Alice Blue, June 15, 1975.

48. Ellen Hill to Craig Miner, Oct. 19, 1993.

49. Interview with Ellen Hill by Craig Miner, June 22, 1992.

50. Nellie Hill to Leroy Hill, Feb. 27, 1957; Hill to Acre, Oct 1945; Nellie Hill, "Recollections"; interview with Ellen Hill by Craig Miner, June 22, 1992.

51. Hill to O. P. Harwood, Sept. 25, 1956.

52. Hill to Nellie Hill, May 10, 1959, May 23, July 4, 1960.

53. Hill to Earl Harding, Aug. 13, 1960.

54. Hill to Nellie Hill, Sept. 24, 1960.

55. Hill to Thurston Twigg-Smith, Mar. 11, 1962; Hill to Alice Blue, Feb. 23, 1966; Nellie Hill to Leroy and Ellen Hill, Mar. 3, 1969; Hill to Beverly Hill, Nov. 23, 1969; Nellie Hill to Leroy and Ellen Hill, Oct. 28, 1970.

56. Nellie Hill to Leroy and Ellen Hill, Aug. 3, Oct. 2, 1971, Feb. 18, 1975.

57. Nellie Hill to Leroy and Ellen Hill, Apr. 30, 1971; Hill to Alice Blue, Aug. 30, 1971, June 15, 1975; Hill to Nellie Hill, Oct. 24, 1971.

58. Bill Sildar to Hill, Oct. 31, 1971; Hill to Sildar, Nov. 7, 1971; Sildar to Hill, Dec. 12, 1971.

59. Diary, Mar. 20, 1956; Nellie Hill to Ellen Hill, Nov. 19, 1971.

60. Hill to Marcia Hill, Nov. 12, 1960.

61. Hill to Marcia Hill, Feb. 4, May 8, 1961.

62. Hill to Marcia Hill, May 8, 1961; Marcia Hill to Hill, Sept. 20, 1962; Hill to Marcia Hill, Sept. 24, 1963.

63. W. J. Rorabaugh, *Berkeley at War*, pp. 5, 12, 17–18, 44, 127, 130, 134, 136, 138.

64. Hill to Brodie Smith, Feb. 16, 1964; Hill to Nellie Hill, Feb. 4, 1965.

65. Marcia Hill to Leroy and Ellen Hill, Apr. 17, 1965.

66. Hill to Marcia Hill, Apr. 22, 1965.

67. Marcia Hill to Hill, May 4, 1965.

68. Hill to Leonard Read, June 17, 1968.

69. Hill to Marcia Hill, Jan. 10, 1969; Hill to David Linsey, Mar. 17, 1970; Hill to Alice Blue, Aug. 31, 1973; Hill to Marcia Hill, July 13, 1975.

70. Ellen Hill to Alice Blue, Nov. 18, 1976.

71. Hill to Margie Nise, Feb. 26, 1961; Hill to Marcia Hill, Mar. 5, 1961; room deposit receipt for Holly Hill, Dec. 31, 1964; Hill to Marcia Hill, Jan. 20, 1967.

72. Bruce MacAdam to Hill family, Apr. 12, 1970; Holly Hill to Leroy and Ellen Hill, July 19, 1970; Hill to William P. Lear, May 28, 1974; Ellen Hill to Alice Blue, Nov. 18, 1976.

73. Elizabeth Hill, "Reminiscences."

74. Hill to Margie Nise, Feb. 26, 1961; Hill to Marcia Hill, Jan 20, 1967.

75. Poem by Elizabeth Hill.

76. Hill to Lizzie Hill, Oct. 12, Nov. 8, 1967.

77. Hill to Lizzie Hill, Feb. 25, 1968.

78. Elizabeth Hill to Hill, Feb. 28, 1968.

79. Hill to Beverly Hill, Nov. 23, 1969; Lizzie Hill to Hill, Mar. 7, 1970; Hill to Lizzie Hill, Mar. 11, 1970.

80. Hill to Alice Blue, May 28, 1973, June 15, 1976; Hill to Isabella Hill, June 28, 1975.

81. Ellen Hill to Alice Blue, Nov. 18, 1976; Hill to Alice Blue, Aug. 30, 1971, May 28, 1973.

82. Elizabeth Hill, "Reminiscences."

83. Ibid.

84. Ibid.

85. Ibid.

86. Ibid.

87. Hill to Margie Nise, Feb. 26, 1961; Hill to Marcia Hill, Nov. 13, 1967.

88. Hill to Isabella Hill, Feb. 11, 1969; Lizzie Hill to Hill, Mar. 7, 1970; Hill to Alice Blue, Aug. 30, 1971; Hill to Isabella Hill, June 28, 1975.

89. Hill to Isabella Hill, July 13, 1975; Hill to Marcia Hill, July 13, 1973.

90. Ellen Hill to Alice Blue, Nov. 18, 1976.

91. Hill to Don Hammans, Mar. 16, 1976.

One Single Imperative

1. Leonard Read to Hill, June 17, 1968; for essay, see Foundation for Economic Education file, FLHC.

2. Diary, May 15, 1968.

3. Diary, Mar. 26, 1967; Hill to Alice Blue, May 28, 1973; Hill to Henry Manne, Sept. 1, 1974; Hill to Alice Blue, Oct. 14, 1972.

4. Hill to Alice Blue, June 15, 1975.

5. See Gertrude Himmelfarb, "Liberty: 'One Very Simple Principle?'" *American Scholar*, Autumn 1993, pp. 531–50.

6. Diary, Apr. 15, 1956; Hill to Alice Blue, Aug. 15, 1967.

7. Nellie Hill, "Recollections."

8. Hill to Fitzgerald & Son, Feb. 17, 1962.

9. Alice Blue to Hill, Nov. 24, 1956.

10. Hill to Alice Blue, Aug. 26, 1945 [1965]; Hill to O. P. Harwood, Jan. 19, 1963; Hill to Richard Higgins, May 28, 1969.

11. Diary, Jan. 10, Sept. 11, 1975; Hill to Alice Blue, Aug. 17, 1975; Hill to Beverly Hill, Jan. 23, 1976.

12. Ellen Hill to Alice Blue, Nov. 18, 1976.

13. Diary, Sept. 8, 1975, Apr. 19, 1976, June 17, July 18, 1977.

14. Ellen Hill to Alice Blue, Nov. 18, 1976, Apr. 14, 1977.

15. Hill to Nellie Hill, July 13, 1976.

16. Nellie Hill, "Recollections."

17. Ellen Hill to Craig Miner, Jan. 6, 1994.

18. Diary, Dec. 31, 1977.

19. Alice Blue to Hill, May 12, 1959.

20. Nellie Hill, "Recollections."

Bibliography

Primary Sources

F. Leroy Hill Collection, Ablah Library Special Collections, Wichita State University, Wichita, Kansas.

The Hill Collection, in the possession of Ellen Hill at the time this biography was written, was subsequently transferred to Wichita State University. It now occupies 60 linear feet of shelf space there, extends from 1907 to 1981, and contains diaries, correspondence, business documents, personal papers, scrapbooks, artifacts, photographs, and blueprints. The existence of this remarkable personal and business archive is what made this biography possible. Of course, the life of Hill himself was the thing that made it worthwhile. The documents used most extensively in this book are the Diaries (boxes 1–2), the Correspondence series (boxes 3–17), and "Recollections—FLH, 5/28/72" (box 48), a 115-page memoir in typescript covering Hill's birth to about 1930. Also used are the Business Papers series (boxes 18–46), especially material on Air Associates (boxes 19–21); the Personal Papers series (boxes 47–48); and a Strike Scrapbook (box 54). The organization within each series is chronological, and there is a detailed finding aid to the collection. In addition, several interviews were conducted with Ellen Hill, Leroy Hill's widow.

Secondary Sources

Allen, Richard Sanders. *Revolution in the Sky: The Lockheeds of Aviation's Golden Age.* Rev. ed. New York: Orion Books, 1988.

Air Facts, Nov. 1, Dec. 1, 1941.

Anderson, Roy A. *A Look at Lockheed.* Princeton: Newcomen Society, 1983.

Bailey, Beth L. *From Front Porch to Back Seat: Courtship in Twentieth-Century America.* Baltimore: Johns Hopkins University Press, 1988.

Baird, Charles. "A Tale of Infamy: The Air Associates Strike of 1941." *The Freeman,* April 1992, pp. 152–59.

Barth, Gunther. *Instant Cities: Urbanization and the Rise of San Francisco and Denver.* New York: Oxford University Press, 1975.

Bennett, Howard. *Precision Power: The First Half Century of Bodine Electric Company.* New York: Appleton-Century-Crofts, 1959.

Blackman, John. *Presidential Seizure in Labor Disputes.* Cambridge, Mass.: Harvard University Press, 1967.

Bibliography

Cherny, Robert, and William Issel. *San Francisco 1865–1932: Power and Urban Development*. Berkeley: University of California Press, 1986.

Cochran, Thomas. *Business in American Life: A History*. New York: McGraw-Hill, 1972.

———. *200 Years of American Business*. New York: Basic Books, 1977.

Coe, Richard. *When the Grass Was Taller: Autobiography and the Experience of Childhood*. New Haven: Yale University Press, 1984.

Crosby, Alfred, Jr. *Epidemic and Peace 1918*. Westport, Conn.: Greenwood Press, 1976.

Davis, Gayle R. "The Diary as Historical Puzzle: Seeking the Author behind the Words." *Kansas History* 16 (1993): 166–79.

Derber, Milton. *The American Idea of Industrial Democracy, 1865–1965*. Urbana: University of Illinois Press, 1970.

Diamond, Sara. *Roads to Dominion: Right-Wing Movements and Political Power in the United States*. New York: Guilford Press, 1995.

Drucker, Peter. *Innovation and Entrepreneurship: Practice and Principles*. New York: Harper & Row, 1985.

Elder, Glen, John Modell, and Ross Parke, eds. *Children in Time and Place: Developmental and Historical Insights*. Cambridge: Cambridge University Press, 1993.

Egan, Peter. "The Kindness of Druids." *Road and Track*, Feb. 1989, pp. 20ff.

E Systems, ECI Division. *When We Were Air Associates, Inc., 1927–1957*. St. Petersburg, Fla.: E Systems, 1977.

Galenson, Walter. *The CIO Challenge to the AFL: A History of the American Labor Movement 1935–41*. Cambridge: Harvard University Press, 1960.

Gannett, Cinthia. *Gender and the Journal: Diaries and Academic Discourse*. Albany: State University of New York Press, 1992.

Giedion, Siegfried. *Mechanization Takes Command: A Contribution to Anonymous History*. New York: Oxford University Press, 1948.

Graff, Harvey J. *Conflicting Paths: Growing Up in America*. Cambridge: Harvard University Press, 1995.

Graubaud, Stephen, ed. *Generations*. New York: W. W. Norton & Co., 1979.

Himmelfarb, Gertrude. "Liberty: 'One Very Simple Principle?'" *American Scholar*, Autumn 1993.

Hixon, William B., Jr. *Search for the American Right Wing: An Analysis of the Social Science Record, 1955–1987*. Princeton: Princeton University Press, 1992.

Hoehling, A. A. *The Great Epidemic*. Boston: Little Brown, 1961.

Hofstadter, Richard. *The Paranoid Style in American Politics and Other Essays*. New York: Alfred A. Knopf, 1965.

Howe, Irving, and B. J. Widick. *The UAW and Walter Reuther*. New York: De Capo Press, 1973.

Hudson, James. *Hostile Skies: A Combat History of the American Air Service in World War I*. Syracuse: Syracuse University Press, 1968.

Jackson, Joseph, ed. *The Western Gate: A San Francisco Reader*. New York: Farrar, Strauss & Young, 1952.

Joralmon, Dorothy Riber. "Growing Up in Berkeley, 1900–1917." *American West* 20 (1983): 42–48.

Kaltenborn, Howard. *Governmental Adjustment of Labor Disputes*. Chicago: Foundation Press, 1943.

Keeran, Roger. *The Communist Party and the Auto Workers Union*. Bloomington: Indiana University Press, 1980.

Kennedy, Jack. "The Nicholas-Breazy Airplane Company: The Garage That Grew Wings." *American Aviation Historical Society Journal* 27, nos. 1–3 (Spring–Fall 1982): 34–54, 97–119, 162–84.

Kett, Joseph. *Rites of Passage: Adolescence in America, 1790 to the Present*. New York: Basic Books, 1977.

Kilby, Peter. *Entrepreneurship and Economic Development*. Englewood, N.J.: Free Press, 1971.

Kinnard, Lawrence. *The History of the Greater San Francisco Bay Region*. 3 vols. New York: Lewis Historical Publishing, 1966.

Klein, Alexander, ed. *Natural Enemies: Youth and the Clash of Generations*. Philadelphia: J. B. Lippincott, 1969.

LeFevre, Karen Burke. *Invention as a Social Act*. Carbondale: Southern Illinois University Press, 1987.

Levine, David, et al. *Essays on the Family and Historical Change*. College Station: Texas A&M University Press, 1983.

Lewis, David L. "Somewhere West of Jackson: Toolin' West in a T in '20." *Chronicle: The Quarterly Magazine of the Historical Society of Michigan* 20 (1984): 19–21.

Lichtenstein, Nelson. *Labor's War at Home: The CIO in World War II*. Cambridge: Cambridge University Press, 1982.

Lipset, Seymor, and Earl Raab. *The Politics of Unreason: Right-Wing Extremism in America 1790–1970*. New York: Harper & Row, 1970.

Lochtin, Roger. *San Francisco 1846–1856: From Hamlet to City*. New York: Oxford University Press, 1974.

Lougheed, Victor. *Vehicles of the Air: A Popular Exposition of Modern Aeronautics with Working Drawings*. Chicago: Reilly and Britton, 1909.

McClelland, David. *The Achieving Society*. Princeton, N.J.: D. Van Nostrand, 1961.

Malcolm, Henry. *Generation of Narcissus*. Boston: Little Brown, 1971.

Mallon, Thomas. *A Book of One's Own: People and Their Diaries*. New York: Ticknor & Fields, 1984.

May, Henry F. *Coming to Terms: A Study in Memory and History*. Berkeley: University of California Press, 1987.

Mayer, Harold, and Richard Wade. *Chicago: Growth of a Metropolis*. Chicago: University of Chicago Press, 1969.

Miner, Craig. *Grede of Milwaukee*. Wichita, Kans.: Watermark Press, 1989.

Modell, John. *Into One's Own: From Youth to Adulthood in the United States 1920–1975*. Berkeley: University of California Press, 1989.

Nash, Al. "A Unionist Remembers: Militant Unionism and Political Factions." *Dissent* 24 (1977): 181–89.

Nelson, Daniel. "How the UAW Grew." *Labor History* 35 (1994): 5–20.

Page, Victor W. *The Model T Ford Car*. New York: Norman Henley Publishing, 1926.

Pacyga, Dominic, and Ellen Skerrett. *Chicago: City of Neighborhoods*. Chicago: Loyola University Press, 1986.

Bibliography

Peters, Tom. *Thriving on Chaos: Handbook for a Management Revolution.* 1978. Reprint, New York: Harper & Row, 1988.

Prickett, James R. "Communist Conspiracy or Wage Dispute? The 1941 Strike at North American Aviation." *Pacific Historical Review* 50 (1981): 215–33.

Pusateri, C. Joseph. *A History of American Business.* Arlington Heights, Ill.: Harlan Davidson, 1988.

Rae, John. *Climb to Greatness: The American Aircraft Industry, 1920–1960.* Cambridge, Mass.: MIT Press, 1968.

Reynolds, Quentin. *They Fought for the Sky.* New York: Rinehart & Co., 1957.

Rintala, Marvin. *The Constitution of Silence: Essays on Generational Themes.* Westport, Conn.: Greenwood Press, 1979.

Rorabaugh, W. J. *Berkeley at War.* New York: Oxford University Press, 1989.

Roseberry, C. R. Glenn *Curtiss: Pioneer of Flight.* Syracuse: Syracuse University Press, 1991.

Schumpeter, Joseph. *Theory of Economic Development.* Cambridge, Mass.: Harvard University Press, 1934.

Sennett, Richard. *Families against the City: Middle-Class Homes in Industrial Chicago, 1872–1890.* 1970. Reprint, New York: Vintage Books, 1974.

Seidman, Joel. *American Labor from Defense to Reconversion.* Chicago: University of Chicago Press, 1953.

Slater, Philip. *The Pursuit of Loneliness: American Culture at the Breaking Point.* Boston: Beacon Press, 1970.

Stadtman, Verne A. *The University of California 1868–1968.* New York: McGraw-Hill, 1970.

Starr, Kevin. *Americans and the California Dream 1850–1915.* New York: Oxford University Press, 1973.

Stephenson, Albert. "Secrets of the Model T." *American Heritage* 40 (July/Aug. 1989): 73–77.

Stewart, Susan. *On Longing: Narratives of the Miniature, the Gigantic, the Souvenir, the Collection.* Baltimore: Johns Hopkins University Press, 1984.

Strauss, Leo. *Natural Right and History.* Chicago: University of Chicago Press, 1953.

Taft, Philip. *Organized Labor in American History.* New York: Harper & Row, 1964.

Thomas, Gordon. *The San Francisco Earthquake.* New York: Stein & Day, 1971.

West, Eliott, and Paula Petrick, eds. *Small Worlds: Children and Adolescents in America, 1850–1950.* Lawrence: University Press of Kansas, 1992.

Wohl, Robert. *A Passion for Wings: Aviation and the Western Imagination, 1908–1918.* New Haven: Yale University Press, 1994.

Works Progress Administration (WPA). *A Guide to the Golden State.* 1939. Reprint, New York: Hastings House, 1954.

Wyllie, Irvin. *The Self-Made Man in America: The Myth of Rags to Riches.* 1954. Reprint, New York: Free Press, 1966.

Young, Peter, ed. *The Marshall Cavendish Illustrated Encyclopedia of World War I.* 11 vols. New York: Marshall Cavendish, 1984.

Zelizer, Viviana. *Pricing the Priceless Child: The Changing Social Value of Children.* New York: Basic Books, 1985.

Index

A

Index

Index

Index

Index